Cyber Warfare
Problems and Controversies

Cyber Warfare

Problems and Controversies

Ajoy Banerjee

HOW
ACADEMICS
an imprint of Highlyy Publishing LLP

ISBN: 978-93-95522-11-3 (Hardbound)
First Published : 2023

Published by :

HOW ACADEMICS

an imprint of Highlyy Publishing LLP
4/30 A II Floor, Double Storey Buildings
Vijay Nagar, Delhi-110009
Editorial: +91 9811026449
Sales : +91 9999953412
Email: info@howacademics.com
Website: www.howacademics.com

Printed in India

Contents

Preface

In the ever-evolving landscape of modern conflict, where bits and bytes can be as potent as bullets and bombs, the concept of warfare has transcended the boundaries of the physical realm and has found a new battleground in the vast and intricate terrain of cyberspace. "Cyber Warfare" seeks to be your compass in this uncharted territory, a comprehensive exploration of the multifaceted world of cyber warfare. As the world becomes increasingly interconnected and reliant on technology, the realm of cyber warfare has emerged as a critical domain of conflict. This book is a journey into the heart of this domain, offering both newcomers and seasoned professionals a deep dive into the history, tactics, threats, and ethical dilemmas surrounding cyber warfare. It is a testament to the profound impact that technology has had on the nature of modern warfare and the urgent need for a thorough understanding of this ever-shifting battlefield.

The chapters within this book have been meticulously curated to provide readers with a holistic perspective on the subject. From delving into the historical roots of cyber warfare and its evolution over time to dissecting the offensive tactics and procedures employed by state actors and malicious hackers, we traverse the spectrum of cyber conflict.

We explore the complex interplay between technology and society in the age of the internet, examining how cyberspace has become an arena for not just nation-states but also cybercriminals, hacktivists, and terrorists. We scrutinize the threats that loom large in cyberspace, considering the implications of Society 4.0, fundamentalism, and terrorism in this digital age.

In the realm of warfare, boundaries are constantly shifting. Hence, we venture into the ethical and practical limits of cyber warfare, discussing the fine line that separates defense from offense and the implications of crossing it. The financial arena is not exempt from the reach of cyber warfare, as demonstrated in our exploration of currency warfare and its intersection with cyber strategies. We delve into the intriguing world of social networking and intelligence gathering strategies, with a special focus on the Middle East, where cyber warfare has assumed a unique dimension. Blockchain technology, touted for its security, is not immune to exploitation, and we unveil the latest practices in blockchain forensics, essential for tracking and countering cybercriminal activities. Finally, we look eastward to gain insights into Chinese perspectives on future warfare and what they might mean for global security, particularly in relation to the United States. As the digital age continues to shape the contours of our world, this book serves as a guiding light, illuminating the path through the complex labyrinth of cyber warfare. It is a testament to the pressing need for vigilance, preparedness, and ethical conduct in this ever-evolving realm. With each chapter, we invite you to embark on a journey that will empower you to navigate the digital battlefield with knowledge, wisdom, and foresight.

Chapter 1
History and Background of Cyber Warfare

The cyber warfare environment is made up of many parts from the past of human wars. Long before computers and being able to talk on the Internet, certain people set the rules for how to deal with conflict that are still used in the cyber realm. This chapter looks at the role of information in the history of human strife. It talks about how people have tried to find out about their enemies and how they have had to keep this information from their enemies. As cyber operations have become more common, the constant need for new and correct information has changed every part of a conflict that involves computer networks.

Using knowledge to fight a war is an idea that goes back hundreds of years. But the growth of huge cyber networks and more powerful computers has led many military strategists to think that the cyber realm should be thought of as a new domain of battle, just like the land, sea, air, and space domains were before. Over the last 20 years, people have become more and more dependent on information networks. These networks have become a part of society and affect almost everyone on the world. People who have never used a computer have both good and bad things happen to them because of these networks. Human conflict has moved into the world of machines, just like it has affected almost every person and every country on the planet. Because of this, the cyber domain is being used in new and creative ways to shape real-world battles and, sometimes, to carry out attacks that have the same real-world effects as those done with traditional weapons. Since everything in the cyber area was made by people, it doesn't follow the same rules as the real world. In fact, there are no rules in the cyber world that can't be changed, either by changing the hardware that makes up the environment or by changing the code that controls it. Because the cyber environment is always changing, it is hard to come up with a national cyber plan to protect a country from cyber attacks. So, countries are forced to take part in the cyber domain, no matter what their preferences, goals, or abilities are.

People often think of cyber attacks as acts of espionage or crime because cyber assets are often used for contact, business, and keeping track of huge amounts of information. A cyber attack, on the other hand, could hurt not only computer gear but also the people who live in a cyber-enhanced environment. This is because cyber networks are becoming more and more able to affect the real world by controlling infrastructure assets like electric grids. These more advanced computer attacks could become a form of warfare, especially if they kill people directly or indirectly. In the past, cyber attacks may have been seen as something that intelligence services or police should handle. Cyber attacks are already used to allow or improve physical attacks in the real world, but in the near future, they might replace physical violence altogether, achieving the same goals without putting the attacker in as much danger.

The cyber sphere has its own features that make it a unique place for cyber fighting. Unlike the real domains (land, sea, air, and space), the cyber domain is made up of nothing but man-made things, and it is still changing. Even though there are rules about what can and can't be done on a computer network, it's not clear if other types of government actually apply to the Internet. Many assumptions about what is and isn't okay in society have been shattered by computer networks. It is hard to predict how the Internet will change in the near future, let alone for the rest of the 21st century, because it has already surpassed all predictions for both its benefits and risks.

Even though the cyber world is mostly good, most people who use the Internet find it hard to use and understand. Most people who own computers don't know how dangerous they are or how their use of the Internet could make it easier for bad people to commit crimes, espionage, sabotage, terrorism, and acts of war. Even though this shouldn't totally scare people away from the cyber domain, the topics covered in this work should remind users that actions that seem harmless in the cyber domain often have much bigger effects. They should be aware of the different kinds of groups that use the Internet for their own purposes, like hostile nation-states looking for new ways to attack and steal information and terrorist groups trying to find new members and spread their message. Cyber criminals have also found that the Internet is a big new source of possible victims. Many people give out their information without understanding how dangerous it is.

Cyberspace

Cyberspace is best described as the virtual and changing place made by machine clones. According to the definition of Cyberspace, it is a web of computers, electronics, and information networks that connects people to the rest of the world. The word "Cyberspace" was first used in the science fiction book "Necromancer" by William Gibson. The book talked about a world that exists online and is made up of computers and other parts of society. The author of that book said that Cyberspace is a 3D virtual world made by a network of computers. Even though it looks like a real place, it is actually made by a computer and shows abstract data. After the book came out, the word "Cyberspace" was added to many English definitions. The New Oxford Dictionary of English says that Cyberspace is the imaginary place where people talk to each other over computer networks. Cyberspace is a virtual space with no mass, gravity, or limits, according to the definition. It is the space where networks of computer systems join to each other.

Bits and Bytes: Cyberspace is made up of zeros and ones. These values change all the time because it is a dynamic setting. It can also be thought of as a made-up place where two people can talk.

Cyberspace is compared to the human brain, with the network of computers standing in for the brain's neurons and the links between them.

So, it could be seen as a bridge between the world of matter and the world of the infinitely physical. Is cyberspace and the Internet the same thing? is a usual first question about what cyberspace is. Most people agree that the Internet and cyberspace are not the same thing in this situation. There are a number of reasons for this.

The Internet is made up of the logical and physical layers of cyberspace. At its core, the Internet is a digital communications transit system with a clear layout and a well-defined functional design in the logical building blocks that allow information to be sent. But are there information and user levels on the Internet like there are in cyberspace? Even though it's harder to separate from the picture of the Internet that most people have in their heads, the information layer is not directly related to how the networked world works. Before the ARPANET, information was stored in computers around the world in a similar way to how it is now. However, people who didn't have access to a certain computer couldn't see it. As a result of the digitization of information and control systems in computers, many people in the DoD community actually backed the development of network features. So, the information layer came before the Internet and existed before it, even though it was an important part of it.

In this way, the customer layer is the same. Again, it's hard to tell who is using the Internet from who else because it's made so that people can do a lot of different things with it. But the way customers use networked computer systems does not have a big effect on how the Internet works. Because of this, the user layer of online is not a core part of the Internet.

Vulnerabilty in the era of Information

Academics and professionals who work at the intersection of cyber-security challenges and national security processes usually divide cyberspace into four tiers. By doing this, they want to describe the many ways that people from a wide range of foreign threats face danger.

The first is the real layer of the networked world. The physical layer is made up of the real-world parts of the Internet and other network hardware. More specifically, this layer is made up of physical computers (like personal computers, servers, etc.), fibre optic lines, microwave receivers, and other types of connecting wire. In this tier, it's especially important to have cables that go under the ocean and send data packets from one side of the world to the other almost quickly. Even destroying a small part of these cables could have a big effect on how the Internet works and, by extension, how the economy works. Because of this, national security planners pay a lot of attention to these cables. During a fight, naval boats could attack or mine submarine lines. Even more worrying is the fact that these lines are weak where they "fall" on the coast, which makes them vulnerable. Such places where the sea meets the land are common, not well protected, and would be easy targets for a determined non-state attacker, even though it would take attacks on a large scale on several landing places to cause a lot of trouble.

The next layer of internet is called the logical layer. The logical layer is made up of the systems and practises that tell the networked world how to send files from one place to another. As was already said, this is mostly made up of the Domain Name System and other standards that are important to how people on Earth expect the web to work. The logical layer also has tools that people in the digital world use, both officially and illegally, to get into networks in a certain way. People all over the world use browsers like The Onion Router (TOR), which are partly designed to give people access to anonymous web traffic and encrypted websites, to do things safely (and, it must be said, often improperly). TOR is mostly the result of funds from the DoD. However, non-state actors and private companies from all over the world have made similar technologies. Dynaweb is a great example of a privately made thing that is an important part of the logical layer for non-state organisations around the world that are in conflict. Dynaweb is a platform made by Falun Gong practitioners who were forced to leave their home countries. It lets people in oppressive digital settings get around government restrictions and use the Internet more easily than they would be able to otherwise. Falun Gong is a spiritual training group that is against the law in China. Both TOR and Dynaweb are tools that make it easier for certain kinds of specialised socio-political action to happen. Because of this, they are both good examples of weak spots in the logical layer of cyberspace.

The information layer of cyberspace is made up of the text, images, and multimedia content of different databases. This is what makes up the real content of the digital world. The networked world has two more layers: the syntactic layer and the meaning layer. Since the syntax layer is made up of the informational design parts of an information system, it can also be said that it has parts of the logical layer. The whole semantic layer, on the other hand, is made up of the information that computers are made to store and protect. This information layer's explanation is short because security implementation was talked about in length in earlier chapters, and future chapters will focus on how to attack and defend a computer network.

The very top layer of internet is the user layer. This layer is clearly not made with technology. Any map of cyberspace must, however, include the major category of socio-political inputs to the other levels if cyber-security is described as the security of socio-technical systems that came about because of or were affected by the information revolution. This category is made up of the ways that people use computer tools.

Many of the things that security experts and practitioners worry about at this level are related to "cyber hygiene," or the steps that individual users take to keep their computer use in check (i.e., to keep up good security habits).From the attacker's point of view, the user layer is usually the best way for them to get in. Social engineering is a way for attackers to try to trick people into giving them identities (like usernames and passwords) or valuable information that could help them brute-force their way into digital systems. Some examples of this kind of information are dates, pet names, family names, and addresses, which are often used as passwords.

Even though there are many ways to use social engineering, phishing, spear phishing, and waterholing are by far the most common. Phishing is the act of sending out a lot of fake messages to try to get people to click on a link that takes them to a dangerous website or download malware. After clicking on a link, users are almost always asked for personal information or are forced to give entry rights to a virus that was downloaded without their knowledge. Spear phishing is just different from phishing in that the messages are sent to fewer, more specific targets instead of a large number of people. Waterholing, on the other hand, flips the phishing scenario on its head by hiding viruses or tricks on popular websites for users who are easy to trick. By "staking out the watering hole" in this way, attackers act like animals that hunt in the wild.

Information Warfare

People have used information tactics to their advantage in conflicts for as long as there has been anything that could be called "fighting."In the past, information campaigns were done by spying on the enemy's troop moves or using deception to set up an ambush. A good military leader might use a large network of spies to find out what the enemy can do and what they plan to do. This kind of spying can be done by spies in dress or by a spy who poses as a loyal soldier in the enemy's army. Information was only useful if it could be shared quickly and well, and there were risks to sharing information. If the messenger is caught by the enemy, the message could be lost and the information could be given to the enemy boss. So, the message might have to be sent either orally, with the assumption that the messenger will keep the information hidden, or in an encrypted script that the enemy won't be able to read. Maybe the enemy was given wrong information on purpose, which made it hard for them to make decisions and made it hard for them to find information.

Many theological and social treatises that talk about military operations but don't give advice on how they should be run, as well as almost all of the standard works on how to fight right, stress the importance of information campaigns. Joshua sent scouts into the city of Jericho, as told in the Bible, to find out more about its defences. The ancient Chinese general Sun Tzu, who wrote The Art of War, said that leaders should use spies to find out what their enemies are planning. The Indian military leader who won may have read Kautilya's Arthashastra, which said that spies should dress up as ascetics and be sent into the enemy's territory in groups. During the Second Punic War, Hannibal, the leader of the Carthaginians, hid his whole army behind Lake Trasimene by lying. Hannibal's men attacked, killing most of the Roman army, which had more people. They did this with almost no loss to themselves, while their opponent, who was not as smart, moved his troops in a long, vulnerable column. The Mongols had a lot of information that kept the enemy guessing about where they were and what they could do. They also kept a close eye on the enemy troops. As the enemy army searched the border for an enemy who had already broken through the defences, this practise made it look like the Mongol Horde came out of nowhere and attacked weak enemy towns. At the time it fell apart, the Mongol kingdom was the largest land kingdom in human history. It stretched from the Middle East to the Pacific coast of Asia.

Even though the size of their kingdom was impressive, it was hard to run because communication technology wasn't good enough. Since it took months to ride hard from one end of the Mongol Empire to the other, only the most general and strategic orders were useful.

Espionage was looked down upon in the early modern period, but it was still important. Uniformed troops on surveillance missions could ask to be taken prisoner and traded, but spies who lied to move among their enemies couldn't expect any special treatment if they were found. George Washington was known to have a big network of spies, but he never told anyone who they were because he knew that if he did, they would die. Major John André was caught before the deal could be made when Benedict Arnold tried to sell West Point to the British. He was doomed from the start because he wore regular clothes over his outfit. Even though Sir Henry Clinton asked Washington to free André or trade him for an American being held by the British, Washington had him killed as a spy. Even though André asked to be shot by a shooting squad like a soldier should, no one paid attention to him. He was left on the gallows to die.

Carl von Clausewitz, a famous Prussian theorist, used the phrase "fog of war" to describe all the pieces of knowledge that could help a commander if they were available. Since a commander couldn't see every move an enemy made and had to depend on what was already known, Clausewitz saw this kind of fog as both a real thing, like the clouds of smoke made by gunpowder weapons, and a metaphorical tool. Officials in the military knew how important it was to have a better idea of what was going on the battlefield, so they looked for ways to break through the fog. They tried everything from using hot-air balloons to improve vision for kilometres to building signal towers and observation platforms. Of course, as soon as there was a new way to observe, there was a way to stop it. This could be done by shooting at the balloons on purpose or by giving the observers a false impression, as was done by putting up "Quaker Guns," which were logs that were cut and painted to look like artillery from a distance. In the 1800s, a commander might have stopped when he saw hundreds of cannons he hadn't expected. This sometimes changed the result of a battle by stopping an offensive that might have been successful.

Dissemination of Intelligence

Little by little, communication systems changed over the course of the 1800s. Napoleon used a semaphore system that made it possible for a word to go from the French coast to his headquarters in Paris in just a few hours. Unfortunately, any enemy who could see the signal towers could also see the messages being sent through them, and because the method was so slow, only the simplest messages could be sent. With the creation of steam-powered railroads, it became much easier to send both messages and the huge armies needed for the big battles of the 1800s.But the railway was a defensive way to move because the tracks were always in the same place and an enemy with a little bit of intelligence could easily tear up sections of track or destroy a small bridge span, making it impossible to move troops. So, only lines where friendly forces had full control could be called on to move quickly. This made it harder to move into areas where the enemy was in charge.

In the 1800s, the telegraph system made it possible to run a war across an entire continent from a single command post. British and French politicians in London and Paris tried to send orders to their military peers in the Crimean Peninsula. People say that President Abraham Lincoln spent many sleepless nights in the White House telegraph office, desperately waiting for news from the faraway Civil War fronts. Cutting telegraph lines was a key part of every cavalry raid behind enemy lines. They did this because they thought it could cause the opposing armies to lose centralised control and coordination, which could leave the field leader, who was used to being in charge from the outside, paralysed or unable to make a decision. A better plan would have been to tap into the telegraph lines anywhere along their length and catch the signals being sent. Even worse, this kind of tap could have been used to send fake military orders to the enemy, which would have been even more dangerous. If an enemy tried to spread false information, a commander who depended on the telegraph for information could lose a lot. The only way to stop this from happening was to make an encryption system that would let messages be sent in a code that could be read on the other end. Most of the time, these codes were hard and took time to break, but an enemy could still do it if they had the right tools and time. Because of this, encryption was usually only used for the most secret information, and a lot of useful information was sent in clear text, where anyone could read it.

As the military became more dependent on communication and unified control, it became more likely that communication would break down. Early modern forces had to rely on foraging, which meant they had to move around a lot so they didn't run out of food or because they couldn't move very fast because of logistics. Instead of trying to coordinate large pack trains back to a central supply depot, most military leaders in the early 1800s used a system called a "magazine," which involved setting up supply depots along the route they planned to take. The railway made this method mostly unnecessary because it could move a lot of supplies quickly as long as the army was near a train line and the commander could send a list of what was needed. Even the most basic information processes can fail when a side is losing. This happened in April 1865, during the last days of the American Civil War. To make sure that Richmond, the capital of the Confederacy, would give up, Robert E. Lee's Army of Northern Virginia stopped defending Petersburg and began to move west towards a nearby rail link. General Lee gave the go-ahead to send trainloads of supplies to the Appomattox Courthouse rail station, where he would march his men, saying that his troops were in desperate need of food. When they got there, they would get on the trains, eat the food, and then run into the heart of the Confederacy, daring the Union troops to follow. When Lee's advance guard got to the train stop, they found a whole train full of supplies, which might have saved their army.Imagine their surprise when they found out that the only thing his troops had in big amounts was ammunition, which filled each stock car. His supply officers sent out the many goods they had, but they didn't realise that their mistake had killed his last hope and forced him to give up his whole army so that it wouldn't die of hunger. There was no way to get in touch with anyone.

When the telephone was invented, it opened up a whole new way for the military to talk to each other because it made it possible to talk about information.

It got rid of a lot of the possible confusion in telegraph messages and was almost instant. Even though telephone lines could also be tapped, it was harder to pretend to be a major figure's voice than it was to pretend to be a telegraph message. Of course, this criterion only worked if both people in a conversation could hear the other person's words and the connection was strong enough to allow that. Like telegraph lines, telephone wires could be cut, and it was expensive to make them. For unified control to work even better, telegraph and phone wires had to be run as close to the front lines as possible. But putting the cables where the enemy could reach them almost made it certain that the link would not be stable.

The wireless telegraph and radio were able to fix some of the problems with older ways of communicating because they didn't need a real network of wires to send and receive information. Instead, they sent out signs that could be picked up by anyone with a receiver set to the right frequency. No longer could wireless signals be sent directly; instead, they could only be broadcast, which made them easy to get for anyone with the right tools. This led to a new security hole. Encrypting these messages was just as hard as it had been for telegraphs and phones, but it was done in the end. Changes in the frequency of radio devices may also make people less likely to listen, but probably not for as long as the users want or need. If the enemy didn't have enough people who could understand the signals, speaking in code or a foreign language might work for a while. Mechanical encryption tools gave the false impression of an unbreakable code, at least until the enemy got a device that could break the code, like the famous Enigma machine that Germany used during World War II.

History of Encryption

The first writing examples of encryption were found in ancient Egypt. About 4,000 years ago, a scroll was found in Khnumhotep II's tomb. It told the story of his life. But the poem's real meaning was hard to figure out because it used some strange hieroglyphs. In ancient Egypt, only the richest people could go to school, and school was also a way to show off your writing skills, so encryption was mostly used to keep information safe. It was also used for religious things, like talking about taboos. History shows that the first time encryption was used for war purposes was around 500 BC. The scytale was a Spartan technological development that made it possible to send and receive secret messages. A small piece of paper was wrapped around the device, and writing was done all the way around it. Once the strip was unwound from the cylinder, the writing was hard to understand unless the reader had a similar cylinder. This was the first time that both encryption and decryption were done with the same key, which is still used in modern cryptography.

The first encryption was the substitution cypher, which used a very simple way of replacing units (letters or groups of letters) with other units based on a set of rules, such as A=N, B=O, etc. Before computers, encryption was safe because both the sender and the user kept the cypher keys. So, even if the messenger was caught, no one could figure out what the message was about.

Encryption during Roman Times

The above method worked very well for Julius Caesar's troops. The Caesar Cypher used the normal order of the alphabet, but shifted letters to a set number of letters further down the alphabet. For example, if A became E, then B became F. Even though shift cyphers are some of the easiest ways to secure information today, the Caesar Cypher wasn't broken until about 800 AD. Al-Kindi, an Arab scientist, looked at how often each letter was used in the coded message to figure out the shifting rule. The smallest words that show up often in a text, like and, the, as, and so, also help break these codes.

Encryption during WW2

Before and during World War 2, the creation of machine and electromechanical encryption and decoding changed encryption in a big way. The process made it possible for computers to be made today. Arthur Scherbius made the Enigma machine, which uses rotors and gears. Because of this, the Germans were able to give orders and share knowledge during the early stages of the war. It would have taken more than 17,000 tries spread out over a day to figure out the code. As breaking Enigma was important to the Allied war effort, cryptography became a recognised science, and Alan Turing was inspired to build and run the first machine that could use processing power to break encryption.

The development of mechanical ways to do math calculations happened at the same time that communication systems did. Charles Babbage made the Difference Engine, a mechanical computer, in 1822. It could automatically make complicated mathematical tables in a fraction of the time it took mathematicians to do it by hand. In 1856, he made an idea for an analytical engine. If it had been built, it might have been the first real computer. It would have been able to run simple software if it had been connected to a printer. The plan was to use punch cards to enter the details. The British government didn't like his ideas very much, so they stopped backing the project. Babbage's ideas have been used in recent tests, and a copy of his Difference Engine, which was finished in 1991, is now in the London Science Museum. John Graham-Cumming, a British computer programmer, started a public fundraising campaign in 2010 to raise money for the building of an analytical engine. He did this by using the remaining plans from Babbage's papers.

One of the best-kept secrets of the war was that the Allies had their own Enigma machine, which was copied and used to decode German messages. The Germans made a lot of strategic mistakes because they were too sure of their "unbreakable" code. This was partly because the Allies were soon able to decode German messages faster than their intended targets. If the Germans had known that their codes were being monitored and decrypted, they might have come up with a different way to talk, but their pride and false beliefs about how much better their technology was kept them from realising the truth until it was too late. The Germans had no idea that the Allies had built Colossus, a huge electronic computer whose main job was to break enemy codes by using a lot of math calculations to solve even the hardest cyphers.

Real-time Observation Techniques

Communication technology kept getting better, and so did the technology used to directly watch the enemy and get information about them. Scouts from the past may have climbed a tree or a hill to get a better look. In the 1800s, scouts used balloons to fly above the battlefield and used a variety of marking methods, like dropping weighted messages to their friends on the ground, to tell the rest of the army what they saw. Hot-air balloons were still affected by the wind, and while they could be tied to the ground, this made a clear weak spot that weapons could hit. Also, gunmen could no longer escape shooting at the balloon or its people. When observation balloons were used, people made smokescreens to make it hard to see. However, these shields caused problems for the people who made them because they couldn't see the enemy using the same tool.

When the Wright Brothers showed that it was possible to fly faster than the speed of sound, they opened up a whole new area for data mining and exploitation. In less than ten years, the military not only got its first plane to look around, but it also started using fixed-wing planes to directly attack the enemy with small bombs and guns. Planes can be used to fly over enemy lines and watch how they move, to see how well indirect artillery fire was hitting its target, or to harass enemy groups that are close together. In the early days of World War I, most observation planes were unarmed because of weight limits. Pilots had to land their planes before they could report what they saw. Soon, the engines got bigger, the lift capacity went up, and the designs became more aerodynamic. Some observers carried wireless telegraph equipment and, later, radios so they could share their views in person. Other planes dropped bombs on ground troops, who usually shot back with small arms.

To stop the enemy from gathering information, a third class of planes was made. These early interceptors were called "pursuit aircraft," and they were made to shoot down enemy observation planes by either destroying them or killing the pilots, who didn't have much protection. The development of chase aircraft made reconnaissance much more dangerous. This led to observation aircraft being accompanied by pursuit aircraft that could fight enemy interceptors, allowing the observation aircraft to do their job.

At the end of World War I, aeroplanes had gone from being made of flimsy materials and moving slowly to having better weapons, bigger bomb loads, and much higher speed and range. They might have had short-range radios or wireless telegraphs that let them send important information to handlers on the ground.

In the ten years after the war, many countries thought there would never be another one like it. However, they still worked to make new aircraft designs and did research on existing ones. This allowed war planners to imagine a future war that would be fought entirely in the air. Visionaries like Giulio Douhet from Italy, Hugh Trenchard from the UK, and Billy Mitchell from the US all thought that bomber planes would attack enemy towns with high explosives and poison gas. All of the early thinkers of airpower thought that there was no good way to defend against such attacks and that no modern society could take such punishment for a long time.

But before long, military planners came up with plans to fight the fleets of bomber planes that were thought to be coming. Most important was the creation of fast fighter planes that could shoot down slower bombs before they could reach their targets. Of course, a fighter pilot had to know where the bomber was in order to attack it, which brought up a whole new problem: how to stop attackers who were getting close. In the 1930s, when planes were fast, it was silly to try to protect against threats by flying patrols over weak spots to try to spot targets visually. A network of observation posts could be done, but it's not a very appealing idea. But because metal planes reflect radio waves, British engineers were able to come up with a completely new method. With their discovery, radar (radio detection and range), a ground station can find and follow a group of enemy planes coming in. Radio signals from a radar station can tell intercepting ships where to go to catch the attackers. This turns the tables on enemy bombers and gives the defenders a clear edge. Even though the Germans had more planes and better pilots, they lost the Battle of Britain in the air in 1940 because they didn't understand how important the radar systems were. Instead of making their own radar technology, the Germans put much more effort into making better interceptors. By 1945, they had used the Me-262, which was the world's first jet interceptor. When the German planes joined the fight, it was already too late, but the Allies were still shocked and scared when they saw them. When the war was over, they did everything they could to steal and copy the technology. They also wanted to catch the German scientists and engineers who had made the planes, as well as those who had made rocket engines and other cutting-edge technologies that would be important in the Cold War war with the Soviet Union.

Beginning of Advanced Persistent Threats

Before the early 2000s, the only things that counted as targeted cyber threats and cyber threat studies were those used by the US government and other nation-state agencies. In 2001, at a National Security Agency meeting that was open to the public , cyber threats and cybercrime were talked about for the first time outside of a government setting. The Department of Defence (DoD) wanted this study to be mostly about how hard it is to keep a network as big as theirs safe. But leaks and the fact that the study wasn't classified made it public that the risks were becoming widely known within the DoD.

The study suggested that there was a highly skilled and motivated cyber threat that was actively going after commercial companies as part of a bigger plan to launch more attacks in the future. Many DoD networks probably already knew a lot about this threat.

The word "APT," which stands for "Advanced Persistent Threat," was first used by the Air Force Intelligence Agency .A group of Lieutenant Colonels were talking about how to describe the new type of computer hackers, who were very skilled and well-trained and were almost certainly paid and taught by rival nation states or wealthy criminal groups. The word "APT" was made up to describe these very smart, very persistent, and very dangerous attacks. It quickly became the standard term for skilled cyber operators who work for threat teams and foreign countries. APT is currently used by almost every cyber warfare magazine and cyber-security organisation, from think tanks to the White House. This is despite the fact that it is used to classify and identify a very wide range of possible threats.

Some industry and cyber operations analyst groups, but not all, agree that an attack must meet a few general conditions to be called an APT-specific attack.

For these groups, both the whole operation and the way the attack was done must usually fit into one of the following three categories for the attack to even be thought of as a possible APT attack or hacking event:

Advanced : Operators behind the threat must have a full spectrum of intelligence-gathering techniques at their disposal. These may include computer intrusion technologies and techniques but also extend to conventional intelligence-gathering techniques such as telephone-interception technologies and satellite imaging.

Even though some of the attack's parts might not be very "advanced" on their own (like malware pieces made with widely available do-it-yourself malware construction kits or the use of widely available exploit materials), the people behind the attack can usually find and make more advanced tools when they need to. They often combine a number of targeting strategies, tools, and processes to get close to their target, damage it, and keep getting in. Operators may also show that they care about operating security on purpose, which makes them different from "less advanced" threats.

Persistent : Operators focus on a specific task and don't look for information for financial or other gain just because they can. This difference suggests that the attackers are being led by something outside of themselves. To reach the goals that have been set, the targeting is done through constant monitoring and interaction. It doesn't mean that there will be attacks and malware updates all the time. In fact, it usually works better to take a "low and slow" approach. If the operator loses access to their target, they usually try again and usually succeed. One of the operator's goals is to keep access to the target for a long time. This is different from threats that only need access to do a specific job, like regular hackers and people who want to make money by hacking computers.

Threat : APTs are a threat because they have both capability and intent. APT attacks are not done by mindless pieces of code, but by people who work together to do things. The people in charge are skilled, motivated, well-organized, and have a lot of money. Most of the time, this money comes from either the government of the host country or a very well-funded bad group, like the mafia or a crime syndicate. But there have been signs in some cases that funding may have come from one or more of these sources. In some cases, the source of funding seems to be a mix of criminal organisations and agents from the host country.

In most of the circles that study or classify cyber-security threats and APTs there are normally a few major players in the space that have relatively specific targets, tactics, and procedures or TTPs (Targets, Tactics, and Procedures):

- Russia – Mainly concerned with strengthening Russia's standing as a world power. They are frequently renowned for engaging in long-term threat operations, which frequently involve the deployment of spies and human resources. In addition, as shown in the attacks on Estonia and Crimea, the Russian APT is believed to be very well-funded and capable of engaging in kinetic cyber action (physical attacks on infrastructure or assets that result in devastation). The proliferation of social media and consumer contacts are seen by the Russian APT as a potential source of profit because they have significant specialised technology and competence in these areas.
- China – The Chinese APT groups are the most successful at the theft of intellectual property via cyberspace operations. This is done via a concerted focused national effort within the Chinese military and government, with strategic plans aimed at "leapfrogging" the enemy via their operations. This leapfrogging approach to gaining an advantage is a national-level area of focus for the Chinese. Chinese leaders are open in detailing their strategic plans in that they aim to enhance their capability in science and technology wherever possible. The Chinese APT is willing to engage in espionage all the way down to implanting hardware and chips within manufactured devices that are built in China, and they are known to use American and British intern-ships and education programs to embed their operatives within research and development groups at companies and government institutions.
- North Korea –Most of the time, the North Korean APT is not as persistent as they'd like. North Korean APT groups are mostly known for attacking organisations that hurt or hurt the country's image. This is because North Korea doesn't have a lot of connections and there are travel and logistics restrictions. While they do have a dedicated cyber operations group with extensive training (most often gained in China), their ability to conduct any significant operation beyond basic ransomware attacks is limited. As noted during the SONY exploit operation, attacking weaker targets of opportunity is their most common activity.

- Israel – The Israeli cyber group's top unit is called Unit 8200. This unit is made up of their most skilled and seasoned cyber operations people, and they have adequate funding and a laser-like focus on their activities to fight threats. Unit 8200 frequently interacts directly with Iranians during cyber threat operations, but it makes sense to assume that they are also under attack from the vast majority of Middle Eastern nation states in addition to the regular suspects that the US and NATO countries deal with. In one of the first kinetic responses to a cyber-attack this year, an Iranian-affiliated hacker organization's headquarters was attacked by the Israeli cyber operations division after it was determined that the group was behind an attack on an Israeli asset. This hacker group's annihilation by missile attacks was regarded by many researchers as one of the most important responses to cyber threat operations and is evidence that decisions made in cyber warfare can literally mean life or death.

APT exploitation and targeting also use a well-defined method and practise to try to keep their identities secret during and after exploitation or compromise. Again, this is likely for a number of reasons, but the main one is that the host country, which is paying for and directing the operation, does not want it to be known that they are taking part in a secret attack that could be harmful.

But the above meanings of APT and the clearer explanations of how this type of attack can be used are still not used everywhere in cyberspace. For many different agencies, companies, and governments, it is very hard to give a clear description of what an APT exploitation event is. Think about the fact that more than 28 different countries work in the joint operations centre of an organisation like NATO.

There are no reporting standards or methods in NATO that clearly and concisely explain the need for an APT designation. Each country and group that has been reporting or analysing its own exploitation event figures out APTs in its own way. Different APT groups and actors have actively gone after and separately hacked or used each of these different groups.

No one, not even people in different US government departments, can correctly describe an APT exploitation event or hack.

The CIA and FBI also have their own standards, most of which don't cross-reference each other and none of which have the same rules for defining specifics on these things. The National Security Agency (NSA) has its own special criteria for recognising an APT attack, and so do the CIA and FBI.

The fact that there is no single term for APT operations and exploitation shows how fluid and changing this field of study has always been. Also, this case shows how a lack of agreement and vague definitions are so common in cyber operations and analysis that it's hard at best to define one of the most important terms used in the field. This is because the word "APT" is used for such a wide range of threat groups that it is almost impossible to clearly identify and separate any one threat group..

Initial APT attacks

In the middle to late 2000s, a large part of the computer and internet industries paid little or no real attention to security or cyber risks. Instead, they focused on making their networks and products faster, more compatible, and easier to use. Concern about the future of computer security, and later cyber security, didn't become a big deal for developers or people in places of power until a coordinated, large-scale attack was found. When the Zeus Botnet was found in 2007, it was the first large-scale cyberattack that was a real danger. During this attack, which also went after the computers of the US Department of Transportation, a lot of information was stolen from government systems. Singh and Silakari (2009) also found passwords for master control systems, passwords for system managers, network and control mapping systems, and samples of proprietary code. Before this, there were several computer viruses and other computer threats, but the discovery of the Zeus Botnet and the threat group's strong engineering and programming skills led to the word "cyber" and made the study of cyber threats its own field of expertise.

In 2007, the first important warning shot was fired in the area of kinetic cyber warfare. Russia and Estonia had a serious but not very intense argument. Even though the fight didn't get much attention outside of basic news coverage around the world, the cyberattack that followed and the planning for it did. As the political and social threats got worse, the Russian government put its troops in place for an attack of Estonia. As the offensive ground actions began in Estonia, Distributed Denial of Service (DDoS) attacks shut down or severely damaged almost all of the country's internet infrastructure . Everything was "brought offline" by these attacks, including banking systems, government websites, state-run media, power grids, and any other connected system that was important for military or strategic reasons. As part of this operation, billions of packets were sent out at the same time from tens of thousands of machines and servers inside and outside of Russia. As Estonia's systems began to fail and contact and coordination broke down, the Russian military moved in and told the Estonian government what to do. Even though the Russian military or government didn't officially take credit for or admit to any of the cyberattacks, it seemed likely that a coordinated cyberattack was started at the same time as the military action. This was one of the first and most successful examples of how a simple but well-coordinated cyberattack could badly damage a defence system, mess up communications, and cause the people being attacked to lose command and control.

Beginning of Cyber Attacks

In 1994, two hackers, one a youngster from Britain and the other from Israel who was 22 years old, broke into one of the U.S. The Rome Laboratories network is the Air Force's most secret system. By doing this, they showed that many government and military systems were technically weak and could be broken into with relatively simple tools. They also showed that international and local laws had not yet caught up with the nature of computer attacks. After being charged with a computer crime, the teen got a small fine. The Israeli man, on the other hand, didn't break any Israeli laws, so he wasn't held responsible for anything other than a U.S. arrest warrant. In the next year, the U.S. As part of the 1996 budget for the Defence Department, Congress asked for a strategy on the information infrastructure. This definitely moved the problem forward and basically gave the armed forces the job of protecting government and even private computer systems from attacks, but it didn't do much to make the Internet even the most basic level of safe . As the Internet grew quickly and became easier for regular people to use, it quickly became a new way for businesses to do business. Some online stores mostly followed the same trends as brick-and-mortar stores. They just used the Internet to advertise and serve more people. Amazon.com, for example, started out as a website where people could buy books, but it quickly grew to offer a much bigger range of goods. Even though it took more than a decade for Amazon to make even a little bit of money, it quickly became a common name for almost any physical product that could be bought from home and quickly shipped to the customer. EBay, which was also one of the first companies to use the Internet, did something much more bold by making an online auction house where buyers and sellers could connect without ever meeting in person. The founders of the company only had to set up a site for auctions with enough computer power to handle millions of sales at once. They also had to set up a feedback system so that buyers and sellers could help keep the community safe. eBay charged a small fee for each transaction and even for each item offering to pay for the ease of use they offered.

As the private sector jumped on the network, the government didn't do much to make sure its structure was safe. Cybercrime is the type of illegal behaviour that is growing the fastest around the world, and it costs tens of billions of dollars every year. Many people had and still have a very unrealistic idea of how private the Internet would be. In 2000, the FBI started looking into hacking efforts by "Moonlight Maze" on government, business, and academic networks. The more they looked into the problem, the scarier it became. This was partly because they couldn't find the people who had broken into hundreds of private computers and stolen an unknown amount of data. The Russian government stopped any further investigations, which made it seem like the people who did it might have been working with the government. They found that the threats were coming from a server in Russia. Of course, it is also very likely that the Russian government's decision not to help was due to more threats from the US, whether it was real or not.

While the Moonlight Maze attacks were going on, which may have had help from the government, a different set of computer attacks called Solar Sunrise started. In 1998, two teens from California and one from Israel met in an online chat room. They then worked together to hack into more than 500 computer networks, including U.S. servers. Defence Department. The three of them seemed to be competing to see who could get into the most secure sites. There is no proof that they actually took any classified information with them. Even though they didn't do any harm, the fact that three high school students could use widely available computers to get into some of the most sensitive computer files in the country gave cyber security experts pause . Even though the Clinton administration did create the President's Commission on Critical Infrastructure Protection as a response, the government's main goal in cyberspace was to pass the Digital Millennium Copyright Act to stop digital theft. This showed that they didn't take cyber attacks seriously as a real threat and that they were almost only interested in the business side of the Internet revolution.

As part of a bombing campaign in 1999, the US and other NATT members drove Slobodan Milosevic, the president of Serbia, to pull his troops out of the breakaway province of Kosovo and put him under house arrest until his trial at the Human Rights Court in The Hague. During the attacks, there were two major hacking events that happened. When NATO jets started attacking Serbian ground troops, Serbian hackers broke into the NATO web and email servers. This took them offline and made it harder for the air war to be run. When a "smart bomb" with wrong GPS coordinates crashed into the Chinese embassy in Belgrade, China, Chinese hacker groups moved quickly to stop it. In the weeks after the attack, they used a technique called "distributed denial of service" (DDoS) to shut down or damage hundreds of U.S. government and military websites. Two years later, a Chinese fighter plane and a U.S. plane that was looking for signals information ran into each other off the coast of China. The American plane had to make an emergency stop on the Chinese island of Hainan, where the fighter pilot died. While the crew was locked up, Chinese techs rushed to check every part of the plane. While this was going on, about 100,000 Chinese hackers attacked American government websites in an organised way, showing once again the power of a well-informed public with even old technology.

Most of the most damaging computer attacks in terms of money and society have been random attacks made possible by viruses and worms. In the hacker scene, unfortunately, making a software virus that looks really good and could do a lot of damage is a way to get noticed and become famous. The hacker community will think that people who make viruses are more successful the more machines they attack. Warnings about these kinds of viruses have become too common in the West, and some computer experts say that this makes people less careful about security. When the Morris Worm got out of an MIT lab in 1988, it showed that the Internet didn't have enough security. Even though people have tried to stop this kind of software, it has only grown in the decades since. Antivirus software and computer security have become a multibillion-dollar business, but businesses that make antivirus software often don't find out about a possible security breach until it has already infected thousands or millions of computers. In 2000, Reonel Ramones and Onel de Guzman of the Philippines made the "I-LOVE-YOU" virus. It spread so quickly that it caused more than $10 billion in damage in just a few days. It was very hard to get rid of the virus because it could hide in different places and come back from machines that seemed to be clean. The next year, the much more advanced "Code Red" and "Nimda" worms took advantage of software flaws to give skilled hackers backdoor access. This made it possible to take over an affected computer from afar.

The power of destructive worms has only grown over time. The "SQL Slammer" worm, which first appeared in 2003, spread so quickly that it was able to shut down the entire Internet for more than 12 hours. Slammer is still one of the most common viruses in the world, even though it has been around for more than ten years. This is because so many people use pirated copies of operating systems like Microsoft Windows, which can't get security updates. In the same year, the "MS Blaster" worm came out soon after "Slammer" and was about as successful. This showed that fixing one problem doesn't protect users from the next problem that criminal hackers will find. Malware called "MyDoom" attacked computers running recent versions of Microsoft Windows in 2004, and by the time it was stopped, it had already caused $2 billion in damage. People said that Microsoft put out its products too quickly, which made them easy to attack.

In 2008, cyber security experts found a new worm that was spreading quickly through computers that were connected to the Internet. The programme used a bug in the Microsoft Windows operating system to quickly spread, copy itself, and move to other computers linked to the first victim. Different antivirus companies gave the malware its own name, but most people just called it "Conficker." The program's creators are still unknown, but it turned out to be a very clever piece of malware that used many ways to hide on an infected host and avoid being removed . When the Conficker worm got on a computer, it joined one of the biggest botnets ever. There's no doubt that millions of computers have been affected. Conficker was able to get into the computer networks of military and government forces all over the world because he was able to get past most of the usual ways to stop or find him. Because their flight plans could not be downloaded, a lot of French military planes had to stay on the ground.

In Britain and Germany, military computers said that the virus had attacked hundreds of computers that had to be taken off the network. Even though the Conficker botnet is very good at spreading, no one knows if it has ever used its power to do anything big. Some estimates put the number of machines in the network at 15 million, which is enough to take down almost any website, server, or network, and maybe even enough to take an entire country off the Internet. Instead, the fifth major version of Conficker tried to spread a programme that makes spam and download a fake antivirus software onto host computers.

Conficker went from one version to another by contacting a control server and asking for directions on how to change. Mark Bowden, a researcher, called the fight against Conficker "the first cyber world war" because of how hard people tried to keep the worm useful and fix the holes that antivirus and antimalware software could use to attack it. Because Conficker spread so quickly, Microsoft did something they don't usually do and released a patch outside of their regular update cycle. It also led to the creation of an international industry group that is trying to stop the virus from spreading and stop its creators from using cyber attacks. Representatives from Microsoft, the Internet Corporation for Assigned Names and Numbers (ICANN), several antivirus companies, the China Internet Network Information Centre, academic institutions, and some of the biggest Internet service providers all worked together to trick the Conficker programmers. Conficker's creators have not been named officially, but the "Conficker Cabal," a group formed to stop it, thinks it came from Ukraine based on some digital clues found in its code.

Many of the most dangerous viruses and worms used to hit any weak system, but in the first decade of the 21st century, tailored viruses became an important part of the cyber arsenal. Malware like this is designed to spread through an enemy's computer network without a clear link back to the original attacker. It could be used to look for private information, but it could also be used to cause trouble. The most well-known of these viruses is Stuxnet, which was made to attack the computer network of the Iranian nuclear project. In 2011, the "Georbot" worm began to spread through the computer systems of the Georgian government. This gave attackers access to secret files that they could use to spy on the government. The Georgian Computer Emergency Response Team was able to plant a fake file for the botmaster to find and open. This was a rare win for cyberdefenders. This started a programme that let the Georgian team take control of the attacker's computer's root file, turn on his camera, and find out where he was in Russia. It's not surprising that the attacker used a server owned by the Russian Business Network, a huge cybercrime ring in Russia, to do his job.

In 2012, a pretty simple brute-force cyber attack with a twist happened to the Saudi national oil company Aramco. The "Shamoon" bug didn't hurt websites or steal important business information. Instead, it spread as quickly as possible through the computer network and then destroyed the files on more than 30,000 computer systems, making them all useless (Leyden, 2012). There was no way to get the files back or fix the systems, which had become "bricks that couldn't even be turned on" . Even though Aramco had the money to quickly rebuild the whole network and get it back up and running in less than two weeks, the attack was still a big economic blow to the country with the most oil in the world. As of this writing, the attackers, who called themselves "Cutting Sword of Justice," had not been clearly identified.

About the same time that Shamoon was found, Iranian computer experts started telling antivirus and computer security companies about a new malware programme they had found in the computers of the Iranian gas industry. Depending on who was looking into it, the new virus was called "Flame" or "Wiper." At 20 megabytes, it was too big to spread through e-mail or other usual ways. Instead, it was made to look like a real security patch for Microsoft Windows, so the people in charge of the computers installed it. Flame was able to do things that no other malware could do. It could record sound from a computer's microphone, keep track of what keys were pressed, and use a computer's camera to take pictures. In short, Flame was the best tool ever made for spying on computers. It could not only take files from an infected computer and delete them, but it could also spy on users and make a map of the actual area around a network. After looking into the Flame code, researchers found that it was probably made in 2006. Before it was found, it had been running quietly for more than five years. Not surprisingly, it had some of the same code as Stuxnet, which shows that it was probably made in the same country and maybe even by the same design team. As of this writing, no one knew who was behind Flame, but a very small number of countries could have made something so complex.

Infrastructure Cyber Attacks: Preparations

Attacks on critical assets have always been an important part of war. Transportation networks and communication systems have been acceptable military goals for a long time. They can be attacked directly, such as at bridges and train connections, or they can be jammed or otherwise interfered with by electronic warfare operations. During the American Civil War, one of the main jobs of cavalry units was to sneak past opposing infantry troops and attack railroads in the backcountry. As a result of these attacks, both sides of the war had a hard time getting supplies and reinforcements to the front lines. This made it harder for the leaders of both sides to win the war. Because telegraph cables sometimes followed the path of trains, they could also be stopped. This was usually done by cutting the wires or destroying the poles that held them up. When Major General William T. Sherman led his famous march into Georgia, his men were especially on the lookout for attempts to hit the rail lines. Instead of just burning the tracks, they built huge bonfires out of the wooden ties and stacked the steel rails on top of them. This made the rails bend, so they had to be replaced completely. During World War II, before the Normandy landings, the Allied aircraft commanders began a major attack on the French and German rail systems. It stopped the Germans from being able to resupply their front-line troops, making it more likely that the amphibious attack will work. During the Persian Gulf War, Tomahawk cruise missiles loaded with a special "Kitt-2" package flew over Iraqi towns and released thousands of microfilaments that shorted out electrical grids. Without power, many of the Iraqi air defences are useless.

Power lines and transportation networks in the modern world can't work without computers. Counting the number of packages from regional distribution hubs to point-of-sale terminals is done with the help of software that keeps track of inventory.They are also used to move electrical power from one station to another and control traffic on the country's train and road networks. This is done to avoid power outages in certain areas. As long as they work, these changes make systems better, but when they don't, they can also cause problems that get worse over time. So, they are very helpful, but in the right situation, they can also turn a small problem into a disaster. Backdoors and logic bombs have been put in the American infrastructure that runs the electrical grid. This is a worrying sign that one or more potential enemies have taken steps to allow cyber sabotage if a war breaks out.

Chapter 2
Offensive Tactics and Procedures

Computer Network Exploitation

Computer Network Exploitation (CNE) is a cyber warfare term that comes from the military. It may be hard to understand for people who aren't familiar with the idea. Even though we might be drawn to think that "exploit" in CNE means exploits used against systems to gain privileges or remote shells, this is not the case. In this case, "exploit" means being able to use the data or information we've gathered about our subject for our own goals. CNE is officially defined as "Enabling operations and intelligence collection capabilities conducted through the use of computer networks to gather data from target or adversary automated information systems or networks." This is the digital version of spying in the old-fashioned way. CNE is the part of cyber warfare that is going on right now around the world. Cyber spying and surveillance happen all the time, but cyber attacks between nation-states don't happen as often as they could.

Intelligence and Counter-Intelligence

For CNE reasons, it can be a little hard to figure out who the enemy is. When we say "enemy" or "opponent" in the virtual world, we may be talking about the second or third order effects of our opponent's actions, or even things that have nothing to do with them. In other words, it's important to understand that even if a Distributed Denial of Service (DDoS) attack seems to come from a lot of computers in China, the Chinese may only be involved as an endpoint. To really figure out who the enemy is, we need to look at the activity's targets, sources, attacks, and backers.

Reconnaissance

Open Source Intelligence (OSINT), passive reconnaissance, and Advanced Persistent Threat (APT) are the three main types of cyber surveillance. Even though these three ways of gathering information are, for the most part, very different, they are all important in cyber warfare. Most of the time, we'll want to start with OSINT to get as much information as we can without making it clear that we're interested. When we need more detailed information that we couldn't get through OSINT, we'll switch to passive reconnaissance.

Open Source Intelligence

OSINT uses methods that are meant to keep the person being watched from knowing that they are being watched. Many of the tools we talked about in Chapter 4's part on reconnaissance tools fit right into this group. OSINT operations can be done well by investigating DNS information, hacking Google, getting information from websites, looking into the metadata of documents, and other similar methods, as long as we are careful not to give away our own interests in the process. In OSINT, we will probably start with public information, then move on to information about our jobs, then hacking Google, then getting DNS information, then gathering records. Most of the time, when we do research on a target, we start with OSINT and then move on to passive.

When we use OSINT to do reconnaissance, we will want to use information sources that don't leak information about our goals, or at least limit the amount of information that does leak. For example, we may use a public web-based whois query tool to do research on a target. However, the administrators of such an application may find it interesting that the IP address block of a known government contract organisation had a sudden high level of interest in the DNS information of systems related to the Chinese government. In these situations, it's often best to use a network-masking tool like The Onion Router (TOR) and spread these kinds of searches across many different sources.

Some network monitoring methods can also be used for OSINT, but only to a certain extent. When we need to be stealthy while sniffing on a wireless network, we are very restricted in what we can do. However, there are packet sniffing tools that are completely passive and very hard to find without taking special steps.

There are also network sniffing tools that use induction instead of direct connection to the network and are, in theory, impossible to find without finding the inductive tap itself. Even fibre optic cables, which most people think can't be quietly tapped, can be. There are low-cost ways to see how much light is leaking through the jacket of a fibre wire without having to cut it to put in a tap. Also, we can listen in on wireless network data without causing too much trouble as long as we don't mess with the network itself. Even encrypted wireless traffic can give information about the devices that are connecting to it, and the names and Media Access Control (MAC) addresses of these devices can often tell us a lot about the environment.

Passive Reconnaissance

OSINT uses more indirect ways to find out about our target area. Passive reconnaissance, on the other hand, is more passive when it comes to the real target. An example of a passive attack on a particular target is taking over a router used by the target and then making it harder or impossible for other channels to send packets to the hacked router, where we can more easily listen in on the traffic. In this case, we changed the environment to help us with our reconnaissance, but we didn't change the goal. As we talked about, the next step after OSINT is often passive reconnaissance, which may be based in part on the information gathered during that action. During passive reconnaissance, the defender might give our target information from the active nodes that are doing these jobs without meaning to. In this way, passive reconnaissance in cyberwarfare may be very different from passive reconnaissance in penetration testing.

Passive espionage is likely to use scanning tools, such as network sniffers for both wired and wireless networks, port scanners, vulnerability analysis tools, operating system fingerprinting tools, banner grabbing tools, and other similar utilities. We will try to make a list of the hardware devices, networks, and systems in the environment. We will also look at the ports that are open and the services that are running on those ports. We will take a fingerprint of the operating systems and look for weaknesses. This process is not set in stone, but it is meant to be a basic guide. There will be times when a line of interesting facts will lead us to one step before another. There is nothing wrong with changing the way we do things.

Surveillance

The person or thing being watched could be in our country or group, which is something else to think about. In recent years, these things have definitely happened more often. This is partly because of a number of major terrorist strikes. In the face of such acts, governments can often make a case for ongoing surveillance, sometimes without even involving the general public. People often do these kinds of things under the guise of stopping terrorism, drug crime, and other similar problems. Even though there are often rules about domestic surveillance, these rules are not always strictly followed and are sometimes even totally ignored for the greater good.

Voice Surveillance

In the past, voice surveillance had to be done by physically plugging a wiretap, which is a device that records sound, into the phone line at some time. Even though new ways of doing these things make them easier to do overall and from a distance, we still call them the same thing. In digital phone systems, this can be done by turning on a feature that controls the speech flow in a certain area. This makes what used to be a manual process possible with a few mouse clicks in an administrative tool. Most countries around the world have one or more wiretap rules that govern how surveillance can be done. Most of the time, if you do spying without following very specific rules, even on private systems, you may be breaking the law, which could lead to harsh punishments. When this kind of monitoring is needed, it is very important to talk to a lawyer first.

In recent years, Voice over Internet Protocol (VoIP) traffic has made big steps towards replacing Plain Old Telephone Service (POTs) as the standard for voice-based conversations in the business world. This is good news for people who want to listen in on these conversations because VoIP traffic is much easier to listen in on from afar and may have less security built in, based on how it's set up.

In essence, anyone with access to the network data and a sniffing device can listen in on unencrypted VoIP talks, which can be used for both business and personal purposes. This way, you can record both sides of a voice conversation, and it's easy to decode and play back the conversation using a tool like Wireshark or Cain and Abel. Both of these tools have a simple point-and-click interface that will play back an audio version of the conversation in a given packet capture file.

Data Surveillance

Monitoring infrastructure often uses devices that have been put in place permanently or semi-permanently in order to listen to the information going over the network or networks in question.

In smaller installations, like those we might find in a company that wants to do this kind of monitoring, this is often done by installing surveillance devices, like those made by NIKSUN, at key points in the network infrastructure. These devices can record traffic as it goes over the network so that attacks, programme usage, communications, and other network-related activities can be studied later. Such solutions work well for tracking small to medium-sized amounts of data, but they don't work well when we want to monitor much larger amounts of data, like traffic or traffic patterns for a whole country. Organisations that want to do this, which are usually states, usually come up with their own solutions or have solutions made just for them. As more businesses move to the cloud, you can expect to see more going on in this area.

Large Scale Surveillance Programs

The US government has given us a number of great examples of large-scale surveillance tools. Echelon was one of the first attempts to make large-scale monitoring of speech and data possible. The US-UK Security Agreement is signed by the US, Canada, the UK, Australia, and New Zealand. These countries run a network to gather and analyse signals intelligence. The name of this network is Echelon. Echelon is a large-scale programme that listens in on international talk traffic through satellites, phone networks, microwave links, and even data sources like faxes and emails. In the 1960s, Echelon's main job was to keep an eye on how the Soviet Union and its allies talked to each other. At the moment, it is thought to be used to collect general intelligence information and keep an eye on activities linked to terrorism and drug trafficking.

In the late 1990s, the US Federal Bureau of Investigation (FBI) started the Carnivore programme. Carnivore was a device that, when connected to the Internet Service Provider (ISP) of the target to be watched, could filter out and record all data going to and from the target. Carnivore didn't know anything about the context, so it could only sort traffic based on where it was going and where it was coming from. After a lot of backlash from the public, the Carnivore programme was cancelled in 2001 and replaced with private alternatives.

Magic Lantern, which was first made public in 2001, was another attempt by the FBI to keep track of large amounts of data. The way Magic Lantern worked was a bit different. The plan for this application was to use a Trojan horse or other exploit sent through email to record keystrokes on a faraway machine. Once the target opened the email attachment with Magic Lantern and it worked, the programme would install and, most likely, start sending logged data to a tracking station. In 2002, the FBI said that Magic Lantern was real, but that it had never been used.

Einstein is a data monitoring programme that is used by the government right now. It started as a programme in 2002 to watch the US government's network ports for unauthorised traffic and intrusions. Through several changes, it grew into a much bigger programme. In 2008, all federal departments had to use it, except for the Department of Defence (DoD) and some intelligence agencies. Einstein was made to protect the systems of the US government, but it also gathers a lot of information about these networks as it reverses them. Einstein's main purpose is "to find and describe malicious network traffic in order to improve cyber security analysis, situational awareness, and security response."

The NSA's Perfect Citizen project was made to find weak spots in important infrastructure systems and networks that are run by both public and private organisations. People who want to take part in the scheme but don't have to have been given big incentives in the form of government contracts. Some people don't like how the government keeps an eye on private businesses like power companies.

Uses of Surveillance Data

Surveillance data can be used right away, but if we have enough of it, we can also use it to find trends of behaviour among the people being watched. The US government and maybe some other groups have been looking for these kinds of trends in phone and data transactions for a while now. Since the terrorist attacks of September 11, 2001, the US government, and more specifically the National Security Agency (NSA), has been analysing the patterns of voice calls to look for signs of an attack. Using these methods, we can figure out that certain patterns of voice traffic, like a call from a country known to support terrorism to a place in the United States, followed by six calls from the American number to other lines, may be a sign of strange behaviour. This, of course, requires knowing the phone numbers to watch for such trends or having a very powerful computer, which is probably not possible right now.

Computer Network Attack

Computer Network Attack (CNA) is a military term that means "actions taken using computer networks to disrupt, deny, degrade, or destroy information in computers and computer networks, or the computers and networks themselves." Even though this term fits with the popular idea of hackers in basements waging cyber war on the enemy or of individual attackers doing similar things, we need to realise that there is a big difference between what nation states do and what non-nation states do.

It is undeniable that, when it comes to cyber warfare alone, small groups or lone attackers may be able to use similar weapons as well as a nation state, but that is often where the similarities stop.

A single hacker with access to the command and control system of a large botnet can definitely cause trouble, but sometimes only those with a lot more resources can carry out the attack as traditional warfare or as an addition to other strikes. When talking about CNA, it's also hard to tell the difference between CNA and the attacks we see every day from blackhat hackers, cybercriminals, and other groups that aren't being actively supported by a nation state, or even the attacks we do against ourselves as part of the penetration testing process. The main difference is in the size, purpose, who is behind the attack, and how thorough it is.

Most attacks done by random hackers or for penetration testing don't "go for the throat" like a normal attack might. Many of these attackers try to weaken the target environment so they can take control of it, but they don't do more damage than what might be needed or wanted in a real battle. In real cyber warfare, where the goal is likely to have a bigger effect on the target, these actions could lead to the complete destruction or inability to use important infrastructure. They could also be used to break down systems that protect against a conventional attack, like missile tracking systems, so that a conventional attack can happen.

Chapter 3
Warfare in the Cyber Age

Cyberwarfare is new in and of itself, and it also changes how traditional wars are fought. When we think about any of the ways war is already done, adding cyber powers makes them different in new ways. When we engage in cyberwarfare, it's important to think about not only the physical, electronic, and intellectual parts of war, but also why we're doing what we're doing and the passing of time.

Physical Warfare

Cyberwarfare has a big effect on how wars are fought in the real world.

Cyber attacks can happen to these things because even physical warfare, like boots on the ground, rests on technology a lot. Support for physical operations relies on a lot of different things, like getting supplies on time, moving soldiers quickly, getting messages across, and a lot more. If one or more of these actions aren't done, or worse, if they are changed to create a weakness, our fights that are only physical can quickly turn into chaos. On the other hand, physical interference can make cyberwarfare activities much harder than they need to be. Our computer systems and infrastructure aren't very strong, so if communication lines are cut, power goes out, environmental conditions can't be kept up, or any of a number of other things can't be met, they stop working.

In either case, physical fighting can affect cyber warfare attacks or be affected by cyber warfare attacks. When we ignore the physical part of online warfare, we might miss a big part of the bigger picture. Cyber warfare is a different type of warfare, but keeping it separate from other types of warfare only makes it weaker.

Electronic Warfare

Even though electronic warfare is often thought of as part of traditional or physical combat, it can have a big effect on cyberwarfare, and vice versa.

Cyberwarfare systems depend heavily on this part of the electromagnetic spectrum, where they are very sensitive to interference. Most attacks in electronic warfare happen in this part of the spectrum (think analogue vs. digital). By using electronic warfare, we might be able to shut down the structures and systems that our enemies use for cyberwarfare without hitting them with a single blow.

In the same way, the systems that allow electronic warfare to take place are usually very technical and could be attacked on a cyber level. One could imagine a situation where a nation-state used electronic warfare to try to take away an opponent's cyber power, only to find that its own electronic warfare had been taken away by a cyber attack.

Logical Warfare

We also have to think about attacks that only target computers, which we talked about at the beginning of this part. As we've already talked about in this chapter, these kinds of attacks can be used for spying and keeping an eye on things, but they can also be used to attack other systems and structures directly.These types of attacks make up most of CNA, and we will talk a lot about them in the Attacks part of this chapter.

Attacks that are only logical don't have a lot of chance of working in a bigger war effort. Even though it's easy for almost any party to get these weapons and use them well, not being able to make any more attacks is very limiting. Using traditional battles as an example, cyberwarfare without air support might be like traditional battles without air support; it's possible, but very limited.

Reactive vs Proactive Attacks

When thinking about cyberwarfare attacks, we can reply by defending against an attack or responding to what our opponents do. We can also act in a proactive way, which means that we can think ahead to what our opponents might do in response to threats or actions that seem to point towards a bad outcome. Because we have cyber capabilities, we can use tactics that aren't directly physical or obviously harmful, and we don't have to move troops or resources to do these things.

When we reply in a reactive way, we are likely to keep using the old ways of war. Even though we don't have to move resources into the area, we still have to do many of the things we need to do to get ready for a fight. Most likely, this will involve a lot of the reconnaissance activities we talked about when we talked about Computer Network Exploitation (CNE) earlier in this chapter. We may also be able to use any ongoing tracking that was already in place against our target. When these tasks are done to the point where we have enough information to launch strikes, we can move on to CNA. If we want to do cyberwarfare in a proactive way, we have a lot of different ways to fight, up to and including an all-out attack. Attacks that are planned ahead of time but aren't carried out until it's best and most convenient to do so could be very useful. Such "logic bomb" plans can be made years in advance and may even get into the hardware of our enemies. When this happens, carefully planned preemptive action can be used to totally disable the opponent just when they are most dependent on their tools and weapons to do their jobs.

The Attack Process

Most of the time, an attack is aimed at a specific system or set of systems. In this step, as shown in Figure 3.1, we will likely do more and more thorough reconnaissance and scanning to get even more specific information from the system. At this level, we may be able to do more in-depth research because we may not need to be as quiet and sneaky as we did when we were doing CNE. Then, we'll try to get into the system, either by directly attacking it or by using credentials that we've found somewhere in the surroundings, through social engineering or some other method. Once we have a system account, we may need to raise the amount of access we have in order to reach our goals. Most of the time, the goal is root or administrator level access, which gives us a lot of freedom on the machine. If we have the right amount of access to the system, we can take out any information we want, damage the environment in any way that helps us, and put in any security measures we need to make sure we can get in again.

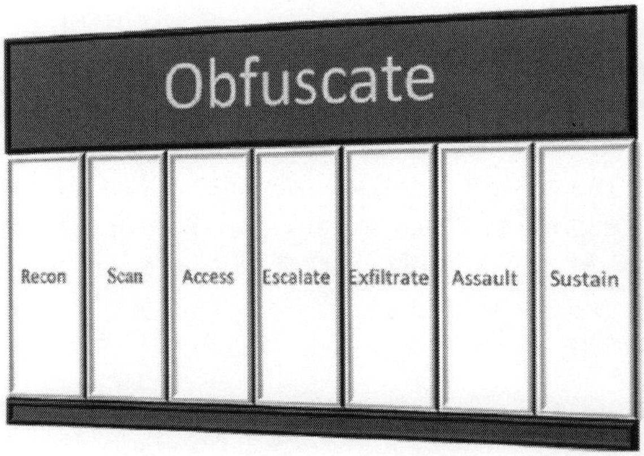

Fig3.1 : The Attack Process

During the whole attack, the attacker will also try to hide or hide away what they are doing. They might want to make it look like they are hitting from somewhere other than where they are, or they might take other steps to make sure their attacks can't be linked back to them. When the attacker leaves the system, they will probably also want to get rid of any evidence of what they did there. This kind of destruction of logs or forensic proof can use what hackers and cybercriminals have learned so far.

Recon

We talked about reconnaissance and surveillance for a long time in the setting of CNE. In that case, we would do a wide range of reconnaissance to make a map of our target area and find out more about it. Given that we might be able to get more information and need to be less sneaky, we will probably already have this kind of general information from the CNE phase when we do spying as part of the CNA and attack process. Instead, we'll be looking for much more specific information.

With a little bit of social engineering, we might be able to get specific information that will let us get into the systems in question without having to use the full range of threats we might need otherwise. Through social engineering, we might be able to find shared passwords for other services or apps. We might also be able to find account names by looking around the workplaces of people who work there or by going trash diving, among other things. Given that we need to do long-term reconnaissance at a more specific level, we might also want to put tools on a system that would let us keep an eye on it. Even at this level, software like a keystroke logger can produce a lot of information, but only a small amount of it is likely to be very useful. It may still be worth the work, though. In places where good password hygiene isn't tightly enforced with technical controls, we can often find passwords that are manually synchronised between multiple systems. This is a great help when trying to get in. If less secure protocols like telnet, File Transfer Protocol (FTP), or Post Office Protocol (POP) are allowed in the environment, we may also be able to get passwords from network data. Reconnaissance as a whole can be done with a wide range of tools and methods, which will likely change a lot based on the environment.

Scan

During the scanning part of CNA, we probably won't do the same wide-ranging port scans, fingerprinting, service versioning, and other jobs that we did during our general reconnaissance. Instead, we will probably look much more closely at the system for possible vulnerabilities. In general, we will be looking for more detailed details from both the operating system and the applications.

When we want to find out more about an application than just what it is and what version it is, we often start by looking for an exposed application that might be especially talkative, like a web access to a database, and then we dig deeper from there. This is often done by hand and takes time, but it can be very helpful. We can find out a lot of specific information this way, like the version of the database from error messages, possible user names from SQL injection attacks through the web interface, and a lot of other bits of information.

Applications can not only give us the chance to keep an eye on a faraway system, but they can also give us a way into the operating system itself. One of the main reasons why these attacks can happen is because web applications aren't safe enough.

We might also want to find out more about the operating system, such as how each patch was installed, how long it was up, and any other information that could help us figure out what's going on. When we get to the attack and escalation steps of our process, these other small facts could help us with our strikes. Carefully writing down this information can be very helpful throughout the process, as we talked about in the first half of this chapter when we talked about getting basic information.

Access

There are a number of tools and methods that can be used to get into a system. If we have been successful at social engineering, skip diving, stealing or cloning access cards like Common Access Cards (CACs), or finding accounts with synced passwords on other systems, we may have real credentials that let us quickly get in. It's a little more complicated than that, but it's more likely that we'll be able to find usernames on the system and either guess or crack passwords to get in.

We could also use client-side hacks against systems that belong to people who use our target system. This could be an easy way to get in. As a way to get in, these hacks use flaws in software running on the client, like a web browser. We are much more likely to be able to get into individual workstations to get access to credentials than we are to be able to get into a carefully kept and patched server. Client-side threats can come from the web, through email, on a USB drive, or through any of a number of other ways. These kinds of attacks work well, especially in non-technical work settings, but they might not work as well in environments with a lot of security.

We can also try to get into a system by using common flaws in an operating system or a programme. We may have already used one or more of a number of vulnerability scanning tools at some point in the process, either during the more general process of investigation or during the more specific process of attack.

Escalate

Privilege escalation, or getting more or higher level rights than we already have, may be needed once we have a certain amount of access to a system. Vertical privilege escalation means trying to get access to accounts with more privileges than the ones we already have. Horizontal privilege escalation means trying to get into accounts that we don't currently have access to but are on the same level as the accounts we do have access to.

Either type of privilege increase can be done in a number of different ways. Since we can now use the system as a user, we may be able to use a different set of bugs than we did before. We might also be able to take advantage of wrong settings or settings that are not safe. On some systems, the standard user account that we were able to access may be able to act as an administrator directly or may be able to raise their privilege level as part of the operating system's normal features.

We might also be able to use the rights of apps that are running with more freedom. Applications that run backups, different services or daemons, or other processes that need more permissions than a normal user often leave themselves open to attack. Different bugs in an application, like a buffer overflow or a race condition, can let us run any code through an application that is already working. We might also be able to access and change interpreted scripts or shell scripts that are not properly protected, allowing us to send operating system commands through them or get direct access to an operating system shell.

Exfiltrate

Once we have the necessary access to the environment, one of our main goals is to find any data that would be important to us and move it to a place where we can access it from somewhere else or straight to our own systems. The secrecy, Integrity, and Availability (CIA) framework says that exfiltration is a threat to both availability and secrecy.

We have a wide range of tools we can use to get data out of a system, from tools and protocols made just for moving data around to more general tools that can be used for this purpose. We can also use methods that aren't part of the system to get around security measures that are meant to stop us from doing this.

In simple situations, we may be able to quickly move our files or data by using common programmes and protocols. File transfers can be done with FTP, Secure Copy Protocol (SCP), Extensible Messaging and Presence Protocol (XMPP), or any of a number of other popular protocols. In many situations, these transfer protocols may be banned as outgoing traffic, but Hypertext Transfer Protocol (HTTP) traffic is often still allowed, which is fine for our needs. It is very rare and very safe that we won't be able to find some kind of outgoing procedure that we can use to send information.

Assault

The assault phase is often what makes it a military operation, since it's not usually part of penetration testing, which, in general, looks a lot like our attack process. In real cyber warfare, it's likely that once we get into a machine, gain the privileges we need, and get any interesting information out, we'll want to use the system to cause chaos in the environment. Figure 3.2 shows how the military talks about the results of these kinds of actions: deception, disruption, denial, degradation, and death. From a CIA point of view, most of these threats will be aimed at availability and integrity.

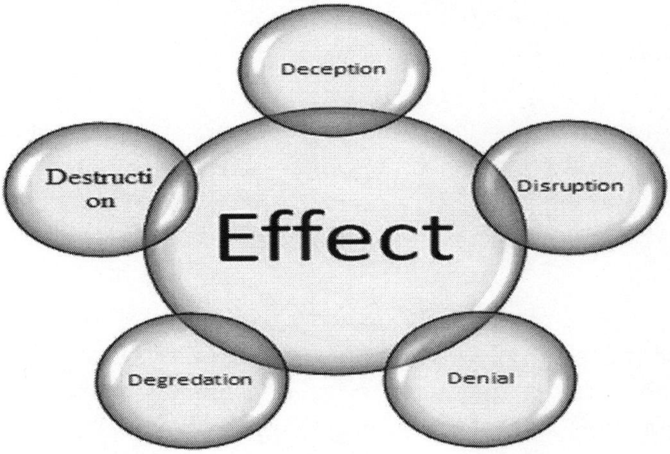

Fig 3.2

Sustain

Once we have full access to a system, we might want to change its settings to make sure we can use it in the future. When we first had the ability to do so, we may have used a specific exploit to get into the system and raise our rights, but we can't always count on those ways in being open in the future. To protect against this chance, we may need to set up new accounts, open services on more ports, install command and control software, add backdoors to apps, and take other steps.

Most likely, the most successful efforts will be the ones that are less obvious and less likely to be found by accident by a system user. Some of the more obvious ways, like making a new listening port on a computer that is connected to the internet, may be found quickly. Also, we might want to be careful about leaving these safety measures in places where another attacker could find them. Many ready-made backdoors use standard ports by default, so if we don't change it, our backdoor could be easy to find.

Obfuscate

Obfuscating is likely to be the first and last thing we do on a system we have broken or plan to break. "To obfuscate" means to "confuse, bewilder, or stupefy." We use this term to describe both the ways we might try to hide or get rid of proof of our intrusion and the ways we might try to lead investigators to a different source. Obfuscation is really a layer that runs under all of the things we will do in the attack process. Some of these acts are done before our first recon, some are done during our different attacks, and some are done as the very last thing we do before leaving a system for good.

The easiest and first things we might do to hide our tracks are things that make it hard to figure out where our strikes are coming from. These tools could be different proxies, like Tor, or devices that we use to connect to the target before hacking, IP spoofing, or any of a number of other ways we can hide where we're coming from. Even though some of these technologies might not be perfect, they do give us more protection in case our actions in the target area are found out.

We'll probably also take steps to make sure we don't leave any digital forensic evidence on the target machine. In these situations, we might change the timestamps so that they show the original time before we changed any files, clean up any tools we moved to the system, remove or change log entries, and generally make sure we haven't left any signs behind by accident. On the other side of this same process, we may want to leave these tracks behind on purpose, but change them so they lead to a different source. If we can make it look like an attack came from someone else, we may not only be able to hide our tracks, but also cause a lot of confusion and worry.

Conclusion

We talked about all the different parts of cyber warfare, such as the real, logical, and electronic parts. We also talked about reactive and aggressive actions in war and how they lead to different kinds of actions in cyberwar. We've talked about some of the most important CNE and CNA plans and tactics in terms of these processes and tools. Many of these tools are not hard to find or use, and the process can be easy. However, for a nation-state to carry out cyber operations at the level of battle, they need a lot more money, time, and knowledge.

Chapter 4
The Cyberspace Threats

Introduction

Threats to cyber security can be put into many different groups. This is clear when you look at cyber security from a world point of view. One of the most common ways to divide things is into three groups based on what drives them. When it comes to their own cyber security issues, most governments use this paradigm as the basis for their strategy. In this article, we will use a model with five stages: cyber activism, cyber crime, cyber espionage, cyber terrorism, and cyber warfare. The National Cyber Security Strategy lays out the strategic priorities that the national government will follow to reach the general goal and objectives of the country's cyber security policy. The Cyber Security Strategy also lists the key goals that will be pursued through a lot of work all over the country in order to reach these strategic goals. Cyberspace helps with almost all government activities that are important to society. It also helps a lot in areas like key infrastructure, the economy, public safety, and national security. In the cyber ecosystem, national governments focus on many different things and try to make a big difference in the protection of cyberspace. In this case, the level of cyber security is the sum of all the national and international steps that have been taken to protect every action in the cyber ecosystem. In this paper, we will look at the goals of the cyber security plans of Australia, Canada, the Czech Republic, Estonia, Finland, Germany, the Netherlands, the United Kingdom, and the United States, as well as the threats, weaknesses, and cyber weapons they face.

What does 'Cyber' mean?

The word cyber is generally believed to originate from the Greek verb κυβερεω (kybereo) to steer, to guide, to control. At the end of the 1940s, Norbert Wiener (1894–1964), an American mathematician, began to use the word cybernetics to describe computerised control systems.

Wiener said that cybernetics is the study of the fields that deal with how feedback and communication are used to control machines and live things. The cybernetic paradigm says that physical, chemical, and biological processes can be controlled by sharing and manipulating information. Cybernetics only looks at systems that work like machines and whose function and results can be mathematically modelled, determined, or at least predicted. The mechanical system is a closed system that doesn't share energy or matter with the outside world. Porter and Sthle (1969 and 2004)

Most of the time, the word cyber is used to talk about computers and robots. In his science-fiction book Neuromancer, William Gibson came up with the word "cyberspace." Gibsonian cyberspace, or the matrix, is shown in science fiction books and movies as a global digital information network where the data are coded in a three-dimensional, multicoloured way. Users join cyberspace through a computer interface. After that, they can "fly" through cyberspace as avatars or explore urban areas by entering the buildings shown by the data.

Cyber, as a concept, can be perceived through the following conceptual model :

- Cyber world: The presence of human post-modern existence on earth;
- Cyberspace: A dynamic artefactual state formed by bits (vs. static);
- Cyber domain: A precisely delineated domain controlled by somebody; and
- Cyber culture: The entirety of the mental and physical cyberspace-related achievements of a community or of all of humankind.

Several countries explain what they mean when they talk about the cyber world or cyber security in their national policy documents. All of these meanings agree that cyber security is important to keep government secrets safe, support national defence, and protect the vital infrastructures that power and support the global economy of the twenty-first century.

The Australian cyber security policy defines cyberspace based on Australia's digital economy and the importance and benefits of ICT to the whole national economy. According to the plan, "Australia's national security, economic prosperity, and social wellbeing are critically dependent on the availability, integrity, and privacy of a range of information and communications technologies (ICT). This includes desktop computers, the Internet, cell phones, and other computer networks and systems." In a nutshell, it's all about networks and computers.

At the beginning of the Canadian cyber security strategy, the following definition of cyberspace is given: "Cyberspace is the electronic universe made up of interconnected networks of information technology and the information on those networks." In this global commons, more than 1.7 billion people are linked together to share friendship, ideas, and services. Cyberspace is a universe where people share knowledge, talk to each other, and use different services. It is not limited to physical networks. The Czech Republic's plan for cyber security doesn't say what cyberspace is. "The plan is coordinated with other related strategies and ideas and focuses on unrestricted access to services, data integrity, and privacy in the cyberspace of the Czech Republic," the statement says. This description fits with the traditional meaning of data security, which puts the most importance on how easy it is to get to, how accurate it is, and how private it is.

In a strict sense, Estonia's plan for cyber security does not define cyberspace. The accounts of how cyber security is used can give you an idea of what a kind is. "The security of cyberspace is becoming a global issue, and protecting important information systems must be put on the same level as traditional defence interests in terms of national security." The strategy also says that "the security of the Internet is important for cyber security because most of cyberspace is based on the Internet." With this approach, networks, users, and information content are all brought into cyberspace. "For cyberspace to be safe, every person who uses a computer, computer network, or information system must understand that they are personally responsible for how they use data and communication tools."

Finland's cyber security plan says that a cyber domain is a place where electronic information (data) is processed and includes one or more IT systems. Also, "the use of electronics and the electromagnetic spectrum to store, process, and send data and information through telecommunications networks is a good example of how the environment is affected by these technologies."

In Germany's cyber security policy, it says, "Cyberspace is the virtual space of all IT systems that are linked globally at the data level. Cyberspace is based on the Internet, which is a connection and transport network that anyone can use and is open to the public. The Internet can be added to and increased by any number of other data networks. Cyberspace includes all information systems that can be reached through the Internet from anywhere in the world.

The Dutch cyber security plan doesn't give a lot of information about internet. In the part about cyber security, there is also a description of some kind of cyberspace. "Cyber security is the absence of danger or harm caused by ICT that is disrupted, doesn't work right, or is used in a bad way. Interruptions, breakdowns, or misuse of ICT can cause problems with its availability or dependability, leaks of private information kept on ICT media, or damage to the security of that information, among other risks or problems. This statement sticks to the usual way of thinking about data security.

The United Kingdom says that cyberspace is an interactive area made up of digital networks that are used to store, change, and send information in the following way: Also included are the other information tools that help with our operations, infrastructure, and services. The plan shows the important equipment that is needed for society to work. From an American point of view, cyberspace is the nerve centre of their [critical assets] and the country's control system. Cyberspace is made up of thousands of computers, servers, routers, switches, and fibre optic links that are all connected to each other. So, making sure cyberspace works well is important for both our business and our sense of safety. Instead of focusing on network services, information material, or the people who use the services, the definition focuses on key infrastructure.

Some terms and ideas about cyberspace are hard to describe because of the way cyberspace works and the different things that happen there. Cyberspace is an environment that people made. Land, air, sea, and space all survive without people, but cyberspace needs people there and doing things all the time. Cyberspace connects all ICT networks, databases, and information sources into a single global system. say that cyberspace structures are made up of the business, politics, armed forces, psychology, and information. Some researchers think that cyberspace also includes the social and infrastructure areas. Still, the Internet is a big and important part of this new world.

South African experts have made a model of the most important things in cyberspace. These include information, the military, the armed forces, the business, and politics. Based on this model, cyber attacks are most likely to go after economic processes. Political systems are in charge of keeping the country safe and making sure that a free society can last. The military is in charge of keeping the country safe and protecting people from cyberwarfare methods. In the cyber world, the psychological aspect is very important. Psychological tactics can change how people think and act. The North African uprisings showed how much the media can change people's minds. In every case of a computer threat, information is the most important thing. The information societies of the west rely on information that is real, reliable, and easy to find (Ibid).

The Open Systems Interconnection Reference Model (OSI) was the inspiration for a structure that Professor Martin C. Libicki made for the online world. The seven layers of the OSI model are how communication methods are put together. Each layer helps the one above it, and the layer below it helps the one above it. Figure 4.1 shows that the Libicki cyber world model has four layers: real, syntactic, semantic, and pragmatic. The network devices, switches, routers, and wired and wireless links are all part of the physical layer. The syntactic layer is made up of different system control and management programmes and features, such as network protocols, error correction, handshakes, etc., that make it easier for devices linked to the network to talk to each other. Libicki thinks that the semantic layer is the most important part of a network as a whole. It has the information and data sets in the user's computer terminals, as well as functions that the user can manage, like the printer. The pragmatic layer shows the user's information-awareness setting, which is a world where information is interpreted and where one's contextual understanding of information is made .

Cyberspace is more than just the internet. It includes not just hardware, software, data, and information systems, but also the people who use these networks and how they connect with each other. The International Telecommunication Union uses the term to refer to "systems and services connected either directly or indirectly to the internet, telecommunications, and computer networks." The International Organisation for Standardisation (ISO) defines cyber as "the complex environment created by the interaction of people, software, and services on the internet through technology devices and networks that are connected to it, but which does not exist in any physical form."

US Joint Publication 3-13 (Information Operations 2012) says that "Cyberspace is a global domain within the information environment consisting of the interdependent network of information technology infrastructures and resident data, including the Internet, telecommunications networks, computer systems, and embedded processors and controllers."

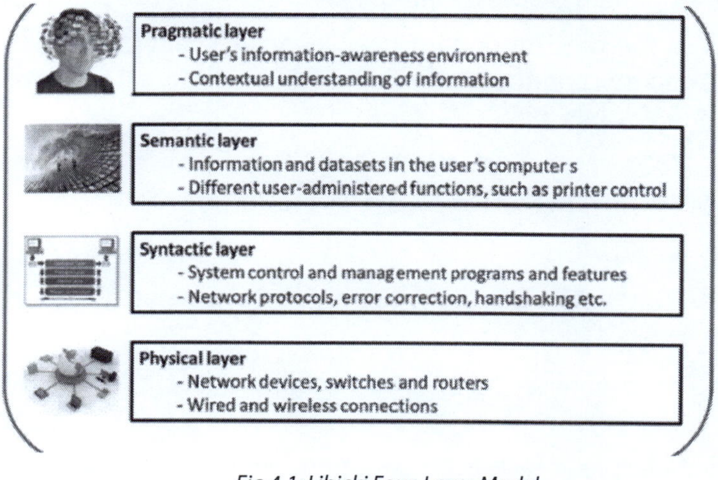

Fig 4.1: Libicki Four-Layer Model

The global cyberspace is a complex IT network with many different levels. It is made up of ICT networks run by national government agencies, businesses, and security agencies, as well as tracking and control systems for key infrastructure. Through the Internet, they connect to a world network. Users can join to this worldwide network through a variety of smart data terminals.

To sum it up, the cyber world can be thought of as a global, multidimensional ICT network that people or machines can join to through fixed or mobile data terminals and move around in virtually. In other words, the cyber world is a mix of the Internet, other physical networks, digital services, and virtual reality. It is a virtual setting where many people can be at the same time.

Classification of the Cyber Threats

Cyberattacks are getting bigger, smarter, and more powerful everywhere in the world. As the amount and worth of electronic information has grown, so have the efforts of criminals and other bad people, who have used the Internet as a more convenient, anonymous, and profitable place to run their operations. It is of the utmost concern that cyberattacks could be planned to severely damage a country's vital infrastructures or functions that are important to society, the economy, or national security.

Cyberspace threats are hard to describe because it's hard to find out where attacks come from and why they happen. It's also hard to predict how an attack will go as it happens. Cyber threats are hard to spot because it's hard to tell where national, foreign, public, and private interests end and where they begin. Because cyberspace dangers are global and involve fast changes in technology, the fight to stop them is always changing and getting more difficult.

Threats to the most important parts of society can come from inside or outside the country, and they can affect people or national systems directly or indirectly.

The risks to society's most important tasks can be broken down into three groups: physical threats, economic threats, and cyber threats.

Physical threats include:

- Natural disasters (e.g. earthquake, tsunami, volcanic eruption, flood);
- Environmental disasters (e.g. nuclear fallout, oil spill, toxic chemical discharges);
- Widespread technical disruptions (especially those in ITC systems);
- Conventional warfare with kinetic weapon systems;

- Terrorist strikes with kinetic weapon systems;
- Civil unrest (violence, sabotage).

Economic threats include:

- Deep national depression;
- Deep global depression;
- Disruption in national or global financing markets;
- Sudden global shortage of goods and services.

It's hard to describe dangers in cyberspace because it's hard to figure out where attacks come from and what drives them. It's even harder to predict how an attack will go as it happens in real time. The fact that it's hard to tell where national, foreign, public, and private interests end and private ones begin makes it even harder to find cyber risks. This makes the process even more hard to understand. Cyberspace's threats are always changing and getting harder to deal with. This is made harder by the fact that these threats affect the whole world and involve fast technological progress.

Online dangers can be put into a lot of different groups. The threat landscape is a list of possible dangers, such as threat agents and attack vectors, with information about each one. Threats can cause assets to be lost or taken over if they are able to find and use holes and weaknesses.

The European Network and Information Security Agency (ENISA) uses a cyber danger model that is made up of threats. There are many kinds of attacks and methods, as well as malware and physical threats, that could happen. In the ENISA-model, "a threat agent is any person or thing that acts (or has the ability to act) to cause, carry, transmit, or support a threat." Corporations, cybercriminals, workers, hacktivists, nation states, and terrorists are some of the biggest threats in cyberspace.

Cyber activism, cybercrime, cyber spying, cyber terrorism, and cyber warfare are five types of threats that are often grouped together based on what drives them. With a system like this, you can boil down reasons to their most basic parts: egoism, anarchy, money, destruction, and power. This fivefold model is based on the structure model shown in Figure 4.2 by Myriam Dunn Cavelty.

Level 1 is made up of cyber vandalism, hacking, and hacktivism, as well as cyber action. Their acts could cause a business or person to lose a lot of money. Anonymous, a group of hackers, has been more successful than in the past.

Level 2 crime is cybercrime. Cybercrime is described by the Commission of the European Communities as "criminal acts that are done with or against electronic communications networks and information systems."

According to the Commission, there are three types of illegal activity that fall under the heading of cybercrime:

1. Traditional forms of crime committed over electronic communication networks and information systems, such as harassment, threats or fraud;
2. The dissemination of illicit material via electronic means, such as material that encourages racial hatred or child sexual abuse;
3. Crimes specific to electronic networks, such as hacking, denial-of-service assaults, and network attacks.

Cyber spying is part of Level 3. This can be defined as doing something illegal on the Internet, in networks, programmes, or computers to get sensitive, proprietary, or classified information from competitors, groups, governments, or enemies in order to gain political, military, or economic advantage.

Cyberterrorism, which uses networks to attack vital ICT systems and their controls, is part of Level 4. The goal of the attacks is to do damage and make people afraid, as well as to get the government to give in to the terrorists' requests.

Level 5 cyber warfare is made up of three different parts: strategic cyber warfare, tactical/operational cyber warfare, and cyber warfare in low-intensity fights. Cyberwarfare doesn't have a single, agreed-upon meaning, but it is often used to describe the actions of states in cyberspace. Cyberwarfare is a state of war between two or more countries, and cyber activities are just one part of other military operations. In August 2008, when Russia and Georgia went to war, this was clear. On August 8, 2008, several Georgian and South-Ossetian websites were attacked in a way that stopped them from being used. On August 10, hackers hit the websites of Russian news services RIA Novosti and Russia Today, causing them to crash for a few hours.

In the spring of 2007, Estonia's network was attacked several times over the course of three weeks. Some of the groups that were attacked were the government, the cops, the banks, the media, and the business community. Most of the strikes on web servers, email servers, DNS servers, and routers were denial of service attacks. The Estonians said that this attack could not be called cyber warfare. Instead, they called it a cyber dispute.

Threats to society's basic tasks can come from all three of the above areas at the same time. Cyber operations and acts meant to hurt an enemy's economy are examples of conventional warfare. When it comes to terrorism, there are many things that can be done in the financial and cyberworlds that can be part of strikes that cause material damage.

Cyber warfare

Cyber terrorism

Cyber espionage

Cyber-crime

Cyber activism

Fig 4.2: The Structure of Cyber Threats

Disruptions can happen in all areas and make things worse. For example, a natural accident could cause a lot of people to lose power, which could make it hard for payment systems and the food supply chain to work. If they go on for too long, they could cause trouble in the community.

Cyber World Vulnerabilities

Threat, weakness, and risk are all tied together in the cyber world. First, there is a valuable physical thing, skill, or other right that needs to be kept safe and protected. A threat is a cyber event that could cause damage. The threat's numerical figure shows how likely it is to happen. A system's weakness is its core flaw, which makes an event more likely to happen or makes its effects worse.

There are three types of vulnerabilities: those caused by how people act, how things work, or how things work. Risk is the cost of the harm that is likely to happen. Risk is the probability of loss times the amount of loss.

It can be judged based on how much money it will cost or cause. The parts of risk management are taking on risks, reducing risks, avoiding risks, limiting risks, planning for risks, and moving risks.

Countermeasures can be put into three categories: regulation, business solutions (management, security processes, methods, and procedures, as well as the security culture), and security technology solutions.

ISO 27005 says that risks are the "possibility that a given threat will take advantage of weaknesses in an asset or group of assets and cause harm to the organisation." How bad it is depending on:

- The Asset covering its business importance, existing vulnerabilities or weaknesses and level of protection implemented through controls;
- The Threat consisting of a threat agent who – depending on their capabilities - utilizes an attack vector to compromise an asset or set of assets. The effectiveness of an attack depends on the capability of the threat agent and the sophistication of the attack;
- The Impact that takes into account the value that the asset represents for the business and the consequences when the confidentiality, integrity, availability or privacy of that asset is compromised though the threat.

Figure 4.3 shows the interaction between threats, vulnerabilities, risks and countermeasures as per the ISO 15408:2005 standard .

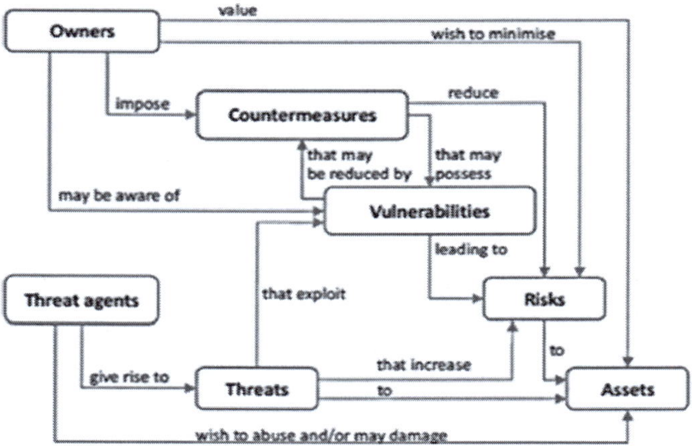

Fig 4.3: Interaction model for cyber threats, cyber vulnerabilities, cyber risks and countermeasures

Cyber Weaponry

A "cyber weapon" is a piece of software that works on computers other than the user's, much like a "virus." Malware is any hardware, software, or firmware that has been put on a device on purpose to do something bad. Even though a cyber weapon is designed to be a virus that can spread on its own, this is not a necessary condition. The most effective cyber weapons are ones that don't move at all or barely move at all in the local area network. In the second case, the cyber weapon must be put into each target in a very specific way . All of the cyberweapons that have been found, like Stuxnet and its relatives Flame, Duqu, and Gauss, are modular software. Several process objects are used to give this kind of malware the features it needs. The ones that are easy to spot are its "warhead," which is the malware payload, and its "platform," which is the delivery tool . The platform is run by a command, control, and communication module, which can run on its own or communicate with its command and control computers to get more instructions. This section finds the warhead's parts and turns them on. It can also get new warheads from its command and control servers. The part is also in charge of how the cyber weapon moves. Stuxnet was found because there was a bug in the command, control, and communication module that let it spread faster than it was supposed to . To get to its target, the weapon has one or more exploit modules that are designed to take advantage of system flaws. There are many different kinds of weak spots. For example, you could let programme code be installed into network software in such a way that it starts to run the code. A standard password in an automatic system could lead to a different kind of weakness. By taking advantage of these flaws, the cyber weapon gains partial control of the intended system and, once it has a foothold, is able to spread itself throughout the system .

With help from the attack modules, the mobility and installation modules make the malware copy itself and move around. They also install the weapon into the operating system of the target machine. The known cyber weapons can take advantage of the operating system makers' certificates. This lets them be installed as real device drivers or library code, which makes it hard for people to notice. A cyberweapon could also have a virus feature that can be installed and turned on at this point. During a system check, it affects the operating system by hiding the cyber weapon's running processes and files in the computer's file system .

If the cyber weapon is meant to spread in the LAN of the target company, it must first be put into the network, which is protected by a firewall. This can be done, for example, with corrupted USB flash drives or by sending the cyber weapon to its target via email, as was done with the Duqu Trojan. In this case, the weapon burrows into its target using a dropper package that looks like, for example, a word processing document .

Then, the delivery vehicle, which is made up of the parts listed above, will send one or more real warheads into the target. One weapon could gather information by looking for certain types of files on the target computer or network servers, stealing passwords typed on keyboards, listening in on the room through the computer's microphone, etc. Another warhead could do damage by looking for and destroying automated systems, messing up databases, and doing other things like that. Figure 4.4 shows how a basic cyber weapon is made.

In other words, cyber weapons are a group of very complex computer programmes whose targets are decided by how they work. Cyber operations use cyber weapons to get software to have the effect they want on the target. Some examples of cyber weapons are:

- Adware;
- Backdoor;
- Root-kit;
- Scareware;
- Sniffer;
- Spyware;
- Trojan Horse;
- Logic Bomb;
- Time Bomb;
- Viruses;
- Worms;
- Zombie.

ENISA (2012b) uses a cyber threat landscape model, consisting of threat scenarios. These scenarios include attack methods and techniques, malware and physical threats. The attack methods and techniques include the following:

- Abuse of Information Leakage;
- Code Injection Attacks;
- Compromising confidential information;
- Botnets;
- Denial of Service Attacks (DOS);
- Distributed denial of service attack (DDOS);
- Drive-by Exploits;
- E-mail Spoofing;
- Identity Theft;
- IP Address Spoofing;
- Keystore Logging;
- Password Cracking;
- Phishing;
- Search Engine Poisoning;

- Spamming;
- Targeted Attacks.

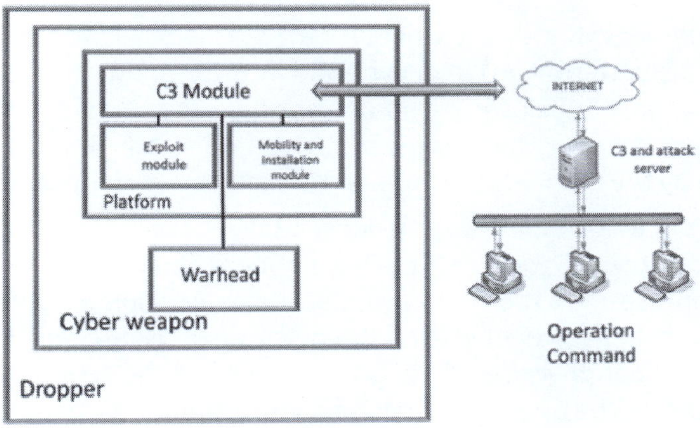

Fig 4.4 A Standard Cyber Weapon

Cyber Threats in the Cyber Security Strategies

Cybercrime is the biggest threat, according to Australia's plan for internet security. "Cybercrime is getting more common, more complex, and more successful all over the world. In the same way that ICT has helped legitimate business, we are now seeing an incredible rise in hacking. The plan also mentions the National Security Statement from 2008, which says that "as the Australian Government and society become more dependent on integrated information technologies, both commercial and state-sponsored electronic espionage will be a growing threat."

The plan divides dangers into three groups.

Cybercrime: Once an attacker has access to a computer, they can corrupt its functions, steal or alter the data it contains, and programme it to target other computers and the systems to which it is connected.

Cyber espionage: Foreign military and intelligence services are responsible for the most advanced cyber threats.

Cyber operations are another form of terrorism that terrorist networks are using as part of their plans. They use the Internet to spread lies, raise money, and find new members, among other things. In the Czech Republic's cyber security policy, cyberattacks are summed up in a short way. In the plan, it says, "Such attacks could be a new kind of war, or they could have criminal, economic, or terroristic goals and be done to make the community less stable." Characteristics and goals of the attackers change over time. So, the plan says that it is based on theft, cyberterrorism, and cyberwarfare.

The three-tier cyber threat model is part of Estonia's cyber security policy. Cybercrime, cyberterrorism, and cyberwar are all things that drive it. The plan also says that "advanced technologies and attack methods make it hard to say with certainty or clarity what motivated an attack." Threats can also be categorised by the methods they use and the amount of damage they do.

Finland's plan for cyber security doesn't say what the threat is. It only says that "threats to the cyber domain are having more and more serious effects on people, businesses, and society as a whole." The people doing it are more skilled than they used to be, and now even the government is involved. Cyberattacks can be used to put pressure on the government and the economy. In a major crisis, pressure can be used as a tool for influence along with traditional military force. Germany's cyber security policy is similar to Finland's in that it focuses on the cyber-attack as a way to define a cyber threat. "Because cyberspace is so big and open, it is possible to do strikes in secret and use weak systems as tools for attacks. With malware that is so technologically advanced, there aren't many ways to react to or track down an attack. Attacks often give no clues about who did them or where they came from." The plan also names the people who could carry out the attacks: "Criminals, terrorists, and spies do their things in cyberspace, and they don't stop at state lines. These kinds of attacks can also be caused by military actions."

The Netherlands' cyber security policy also focuses on what cyber-attacks are and how to stop them. "When cyberattacks happen, it's often hard to figure out who did it. It could be an individual, an organisation, a state, or a mix of all three. Also, it's not always clear what the cyber danger is. But many cyberattacks use the same techniques and methods, which shows how important it is for people who care about cyber security to work together more. This includes public bodies that work on specific types of threats, businesses that maintain the network and information infrastructure, and knowledge institutions that care about cyber security and the public.

In the United Kingdom's cyber security plan, criminals, spies, and terrorists are all listed as threats. "Criminals from all over the world are already using the Internet to target the UK in many different ways," the plan says. Some of the most advanced cyber threats to the UK come from other countries that want to spy on or damage our government, military, industrial, and economic assets. They also want to keep an eye on people who oppose their own governments. Terrorists already use the Internet to spread information, radicalise people who might join them, raise money, talk to each other, and plan. Terrorists are likely to keep going for high-profile physical attacks, but there is a greater chance that they will also use cyberspace to help with or carry out attacks in the UK.

The U.S. cyber security strategy, on the other hand, says this about cyberattacks: "A range of bad actors can and do attack our key information infrastructures. The biggest worry is the possibility of organised cyberattacks that could damage our country's key infrastructures, economy, or security. Cyberattacks on U.S. information networks can have very bad results, like stopping vital operations, losing money and intellectual property, or even killing people.

Different cyber security plans talk about different cyber threats, weaknesses, and types of cyber conflict in different ways. Attacks on a country's key infrastructure and information and communication technology (ICT) infrastructure are seen as the biggest threats. Since states depend more and more on networked systems, these goals are seen as essential to how society works. The key systems of society's most important tasks are the digital control systems (called Supervisory Control and Data Acquisition, or SCADA) that run the electric grid and the water supply. When they switched to modern network-based tools for their controls, they became more vulnerable. Because of this, the chance of an attack went up. Cyberwarfare is only addressed in the plans of the Czech Republic, Estonia, and the United States. It is not talked about in any of the other strategies.

Cybercrime seems to be getting worse all the time. In the Internet world, hacking in particular costs people and businesses all over the world a lot of money. Most of the important security steps in the Internet environment are meant to stop cybercrime. Cyberespionage is the third most dangerous thing that could happen. Cyber spying is done to gather information about the central government, the armed forces, the weapons industry, and business in general, as well as the academic world. Based on what has been seen, a terabyte of information is stolen every year through computer espionage. Most plans talk about cyber attacks. People don't see it as a different thing; instead, they see it as a part of terrorism. It is also not told from the usual point of view of what terrorism is. The Internet is a big part of online terrorism because terrorist groups can use it to spread information or recruit and train new members.

Key Objectives and Focus in Cyber Security Strategies

Cybersecurity tactics include a plan for how they will be used. It has specific activities that would help reach the goals of the strategy, as well as a governance system for putting the strategy into action, evaluating it, and keeping it up to date. There are also specific action plans for each activity and a master plan for putting the cyber security strategy into motion.

The goals and aims of the cyber security policy are made clear in the Australian cyber security plan from 2009. The people come first in Australia's cyber security goals: "All Australians are aware of cyber risks, secure their computers, and take steps to protect their identities, privacy, and finances online." Next, the security measures of the strategy centre on the business community, which "operates secure and resilient information and communications technologies to protect the integrity of their own operations and the identity and privacy of their customers." Third, "the Australian Government makes sure that its technologies for information and communication are safe and reliable." The plan lists seven important goals:

1. Improve the detection, analysis, mitigation and response to sophisticated cyber threats;
2. Educate and empower all Australians with the information, confidence and practical tools to protect themselves online;
3. Partner with business to promote security and resilience in infrastructure, networks, products and services;
4. Model best practice in the protection of government ICT systems;
5. Promote a secure, resilient and trusted global electronic operating environment;
6. Maintain an effective legal framework and enforcement capabilities to target and prosecute cyber-crime;
7. Promote the development of a skilled cyber security workforce with access to research and development to develop innovative solutions.

Canada's Cyber Security Strategy prioritizes the objectives and aims in the opposite manner. "The Strategy (2010) is built on three pillars: [1] Securing Government systems, [2] Partnering to secure vital cyber systems outside the federal Government, and [3] Helping Canadians to be secure online. Canada's Cyber Security Strategy will strengthen the cyber systems and critical infrastructure sectors, support economic growth and protect Canadians as they connect to each other and to the world."

1. Securing Government Systems contains the following priorities:
   a. Establishing Clear Federal Roles and Responsibilities;
   b. Strengthening the Security of Federal Cyber Systems; c. Enhancing Cyber Security Awareness throughout Government;

2. Partnering to Secure Vital Cyber Systems focuses on the following key areas:
   a. Partnering with the Provinces and Territories;

   b. Partnering with the Private Sector and Critical Infrastructure Sectors;

3. Helping Canadians to be Secure Online has two priorities:
   a. Combatting Cybercrime;

   b. Protecting Canadians Online.

The Cyber Security Strategy of the Czech Republic (2011) doesn't say what the goals are. Instead, it says, "It describes the goals and interests of the Czech Republic in the field of cyber security." This is needed to build a credible information society with strong legal foundations that is committed to secure cyber transmission and processing of information in all areas of human activity and makes sure that information can be used and shared openly and safely.

These are the strategic goals:

1. Legislative framework;
2. Strengthening of cyber security of the public administration and CI ITCs;
3. Establishment of a national CERT agency;
4. International cooperation, cooperation of the state, private sector and academia;
5. Increased cyber security awareness.

The main goal of Estonia's cyber security policy from 2008 is to make the whole country less susceptible to cyber attacks.

"Estonia's cyber security should be improved by getting the government, the private sector, and civil society to work together," The Estonian cyber security plan lists five long-term goals and the steps that will be taken to reach them. Cybersecurity is meant to:

1. Development and implementation of a system of security measures;
2. Increasing competence in information security;
3. Development of a legal framework for cyber security;
4. Development of international co-operation;
5. Raising awareness of cyber security.

The cyber security plan for Finland in 2013 is made up of three goals. The first says, "Finland can always keep cyber threats away from its most important functions." The second goal is for "citizens, the government, and businesses, both nationally and internationally, to be able to make good use of a safe cyber domain and the skills that come from cyber security measures."

The third goal in the Finnish Government Programme is that "by 2016, Finland will be a global leader in preparing for cyber threats and managing the disruptions that these threats cause."

The 10 strategic guidelines below are part of the strategy:

1. Create an efficient collaborative model between the authorities and other actors;
2. Improve comprehensive cyber security situation awareness among the key actors;
3. Maintain and improve the ability to detect and repel cyber threats and disturbances;
4. Ensure the police have sufficient capabilities to prevent, expose and solve cybercrime;
5. The Finnish Defence Forces will create a comprehensive cyber defence capability;
6. Strengthen cyber security through active and efficient participation in the activities of international organizations;
7. Improve the cyber expertise and awareness of all societal actors;
8. Provide national legislation for effective cyber security measures;
9. Assign cyber security related tasks to the authorities and actors in the business community;
10. Monitor the implementation of the Strategy and its completion.

The Cyber Security Strategy for Germany (2011) states that "the Federal Government aims at making a substantial contribution to a secure cyberspace, thus maintaining and promoting economic and social prosperity in Germany. Cyber security in Germany must be ensured at a level commensurate with the importance and protection required by interlinked information infrastructures, without hampering the opportunities and the utilization of the cyberspace." The strategy identifies the following 10 strategic areas:

1. Protection of critical information infrastructures;
2. Secure IT systems in Germany;
3. Strengthening IT security in the public administration;
4. National Cyber Response Centre;

5. National Cyber Security Council;
6. Effective crime control also in cyberspace;
7. Effective coordinated action to ensure cyber security in Europe and worldwide;
8. Use of reliable and trustworthy information technology;
9. Personnel development in federal authorities;
10. Tools to respond to cyber attacks.

According to the Netherlands' cyber security policy from 2011, the goal is to "strengthen the security of digital society so that people, businesses, and government agencies can use ICT with more confidence." To reach this goal, the state bodies in charge will work better with other groups to make sure that an open and free digital society is safe and reliable. The strategy describes the 6 most important things to do:

1. Setting up the Cyber Security Council and the National Cyber Security Centre;
2. Setting up threat and risk analyses;
3. Increasing the resilience of critical infrastructure;
4. Capacity for responding to ICT disruptions and cyber attacks;
5. Intensifying the investigation of cybercrime and the prosecution of its perpetrators;
6. Encouraging research and education.

The vision in the UK cyber security strategy is "for the UK in 2015 to derive huge economic and social value from a vibrant, resilient and secure cyberspace, where our actions, guided by our core values of liberty, fairness, transparency and the rule of law, enhance prosperity, national security and a strong society. Achieving this vision will require everybody, the private sector, individuals and government, to work together." The strategy lists the following 4 objectives for the purpose of achieving the vision:

1. The UK to tackle cyber crime and be one of the most secure places in the world to do business in cyberspace;
2. The UK to be more resilient to cyber attacks and better able to protect our interests in cyberspace;
3. The UK to have helped shape an open, stable and vibrant cyberspace, which the UK public can use safely and that supports open societies;
4. The UK to have the cross-cutting knowledge, skills and capability it needs to underpin all our cyber security objectives.

The goal of the U.S. cyber security strategy from 2003 is "to prevent or minimise disruptions to critical information infrastructures in order to protect the people, the economy, essential human and government services, and the national security of the United States." Five national objectives are listed in the Strategy. The first thing that needs to be done is to make it easier to respond to cyber attacks and limit the damage they could cause. The second, third, and fourth priorities are all about cutting down on the number of cyber threats and the general risk of cyber attacks. The fifth goal is to stop cyberattacks that could hurt national security assets and improve how these attacks are managed and dealt with internationally.

Out of all the strategies that were looked into, there were six key goals that were almost always included. These important things are:

1. Roles and responsibilities of cyber security;
2. Cyber security center / situation awareness;
3. Legislation and supervising the lawfulness of government actions;
4. Cyber security training and research;
5. Secure ICT products and services;
6. National and international cooperation.

Within the scope of these key areas, a number of different plans for action were put forward. The number of these proposals ranged from 7 to 57, and the amount of detail in each of them was very different. Most of the ideas were for different projects in the public sector. In other words, the strategies only list a number of different measures without assigning responsibilities to any body. Only the U.S. strategy has a list of who is in charge of each part of vital infrastructure.

When it comes to managing and taking care of cyber security, the strategies take very different tactics. In contrast to the German strategy, which calls for the creation of a National Cyber Security Council, the Finnish strategy says, "Each ministry is responsible for preparing cyber security-related matters and setting up administrative matters in the right way in its own sector." Many other plans only briefly talk about how cyber security is managed and who is responsible for what.

Chapter 5

Terrorism in the Website

Society 4.0 and Fundamentalism in Scrutiny

Introduction

Without a doubt, terrorism makes us feel more anxious and may make us more afraid than ever before. After 9/11, prejudiced words and phrases like "Islamophobia" and "tourist-phobia" have become more common, just to name a few. These ways of speaking come from a society of intolerance, which has its roots in the core ideas of western capitalism and got worse after 9/11. Some people say that technology needs to be used to make the world a better place. This part goes in two different ways. The writers focus on the ethical limits of technologies when they are used to try to make a society with no risks. The writers agree with Sunstein and Altheide that the precautionary principle has always led to a paradoxical situation in which "made-up fears" have become the foundation of a new stage of capitalism.

In November 2018, two young Argentinians named Kevin and Axel Avraham Salomon are arrested in Buenos Aires city. They are thought to be part of a terrorist group. Just after the G-20 Summit, the so-called terrorists were accused of sending each other pictures and letters that had to do with Islamism and radicalism. Kevin and Axel were officially charged with starting a terrorist plot to cause political chaos and instability. This event, which woke up the Muslim community from its sleep, was criticized by human rights activists, and the Muslim community, which has always been a part of society, said that Mauricio Macri's government started a witch hunt against them. Authorities say that the Police looked into a website that showed one of the suspects had direct ties to Hezbollah. This raises a very interesting question: are terrorists really fundamentalists? Is the website a good place for these extremist groups to work?

This part asks more questions about how terrorism and digital technologies are linked. Slavoj Zizek says in 2008 that terrorists or, to be more precise, jihadists are not real fundamentalists because fundamentalism supports going back to the holy texts. Fundamentalists aren't always willing to accept current (western) ways of life or western customs and traditions. Zizek thinks that fundamentalists don't use the Internet or other digital tools, but this is not true. By the way, terrorists seem to go to the best colleges in the West. They even hate the countries where they were born and raised. They know how to use technology from the West and speak their own language well. Even though the social imagination has made terrorists seem like enemies who live among us—an figure that is easy to find in movie plots, books, and video games—it is still true that terrorists are white men who live in or were born in the society they attack. They have access to the Internet and often use cheap digital tools to plan their strikes. Because of this, the government got involved with the websites. In the last few years, the most important countries have set up security offices and put money and resources into fighting cyberterrorism. Even if digital technology is a good way to stop terrorist attacks in the future and save innocent lives, and even if the precautionary principle sometimes leads to unjust arrests or a culture of illegal monitoring by the police, it doesn't change the fact that this is sometimes the case. In 2016, Robert C. Cropf and Timothy Bagwell wrote a book called Ethical Issues and Citizen Rights in the Era of Digital Government Surveillance. In it, they wrote a lot about this point that doesn't matter. After 9/11, a whole generation of people lives in a constant state of exemption. Some democratic mechanisms have been weakened in the name of security. The check and balance powers only work when the state of immunity doesn't last longer than a certain amount of time. Snowden's scandal was without a doubt one of the turning points that showed the ethical limits of government. R. Fiske writes:

> The charges -theft of government property and violating the Espionage Act -are serious indeed. But there is no doubt the Snowden's exposure of PRISM offers an exceptional look at the structure of presidential arcana. Creeping emergencies and a call for security have allowed the United States to exist within a continuous state of exemption, making the emergency coincide with normality. The threat of crisis has become justification for endless, lawless law. Constituent and constituted powers seem to have come to face to face, each threatening the other.

As we saw in the last section, liberal thinking solidified its power by putting together a complicated meta-discourse that focused on the relationship between liberalism and security. While the first one called for democracy and freedom to win as the best way to run a country, the second one protected each citizen's freedom by making sure the law and constitution were followed. Because people are free in their ideas, their "liberties" should be watched. In this way of thinking, the two forces can't be separated. This axiom has been broken by 9/11, which puts the needs of securitization above the rights of the person. Because of this complicated situation, digital technologies like digital biometric dispositifs that scan private information or simple optical readers are slowly pushing the US towards a dangerous point from which there is no turning back. The virtual world grew up around the coordination of a model of virtual government, or e-governance, which puts democracy in danger now. Today, the National Security Agency (NSA) is in the middle of a corruption scandal because Snowden suddenly revealed, after years of WikiLeaks leaks, that the US Government spied on its own people. So, Lyon and Bauman come up with the word "liquid surveillance" to talk about philosophical problems that go much deeper than the fear of terrorism. Digital technologies are used not only to improve security, as the dominant discourse says, but also to mark the position of "the selected peoples" who are safe from outside threats. Also, technology makes it easier for what some writers have called "adiaforization," which is the separation of rational planning from the harms that come from it. Drones are used to fight wars today, and they kill hundreds of innocent people. Last but not least, attackers use digital technology to spread fear and cause chaos in society. In this way, the current work looks at the limits of citizens' rights and the culture of preemption, which is based on the idea that the smaller evil is better. A ideology like this always says it wants to make people safer while taking away some of their basic rights.

Technology, Fear and Democracy

Jacques Ellul was one of the smartest people who talked about technology. His extreme view shows that modern technology is based on the idea that things can be predicted. In fact, behind the talk of productivity is the need to automate everyday life as soon as possible. The logic behind the "technique" leads to a uniform way of organizing, which assumes an autocratic way of dividing up the work. Ellul pointed out that this means that the natural world is finally ruled by a complicated set of rules that are backed by an artificial system. Here, you should do two things. On the one hand, Ellul's worries can be summed up by Weber's idea that the world has lost its magic. The ideals of efficiency, control, and standardization are what make the modern world what it is. Modern technology doesn't make the world a better place. Instead, it makes the gap between the rich and the poor bigger. On the other hand, our obsession with reason and our over-reliance on technology are slowly turning us into a techno-scientific culture that confuses the level of signs and changes the social framework in a big way. Without a doubt, Ellul starts with the idea that the search for a rational result leads to irrational responses, which, ironically, have a disorganizing effect. In line with this, Paul Virilio's polemic theory is that the interests of the big economic corporations have put science in the back seat. The capitalist system works like a big air conditioner that recycles outside stimuli but never changes the environment. The heat from outside is turned into a cool climate, but the factors that cause it never change. Science doesn't care about making our lives better right now; it only wants to reduce the risks caused by the way things are. The problem of climate change is a great example of a psychological conundrum. Scientists want to find quick and effective ways to react to climate change. They don't want to change the source of energy. In this way, digital technology is one of the most important ways that the mainstream cultural ideals of the capitalist system are kept safe. As C. Mitcham cleverly points out, in the US, digital technology is used as a strategic tool of the production and reproduction culture. The key book by Jacques Ellul, The Technological Society, came out at the same time that Marxism and the Frankfurt School began a critical conversation. Christian theorists, who have long been worried about the bad effects of technology, welcome the book with open arms. Aside from this, George Ritzer comes up with the "McDonaldization of society" theory to accurately describe the spread of a new method that, in the words of Max Weber, shows the "rationalization of the means of production." Jacques Ellul has written beautifully about the idea of "technique," which is important to understanding the idea of predictability. Even now, his work, which has both pros and cons, shines light on important texts about technology.

As the last point shows, American cultural expert Lisa Gitelman (2006) looks at the rise and growth of new media, as well as its users and platforms, at the beginning of the 21st century. She talks about the history of the phonograph, from Edison's invention to the argument over the worldwide web. From her point of view, the phonograph, which was created in the 1800s, made sounds real and stored them, creating a new kind of materiality. The web, on the other hand, does the opposite. The goal of the WWW is to turn the real world into a landscape without borders that touches on the imaginary. Changes in technology are part of a certain culture, which was shaped by the economic order before. Early capitalism slowly brought about the need to store and trade things, while a new post-modern version turned virtual information into a commodity and a new source of power. As she says:

> As different as phonograph records and the Internet certainly are, these media both emerged from and as a part of broadly shared questions about what can and should be inscribed as well as much more tacit questions of inscribability and inscriptiveness that shot -and keeping shooting- to the heart of US.

Not only was digital technology made as a continuation of other technologies (like the recorder), but it was also praised as a new way to record the world. In the 1960s, scholars said that the overproduction of science and the increase in books and information during the Cold War would always lead to chaos and fragmentation in the West. Still, this state can be changed if all the information created is framed, categorized, and redirected into a conceptual map with key terms. This system of grouping things was needed before the Personal Computer (PC) and the Internet (ARPANET) could be connected. During the Cold War, this was made worse by the fear of communism, which was replaced by the fear of "terrorism" sooner or later. So, there was a spiritual link between technology and a sense of being safe or powerful. One of the main points of this argument seems to be the use of fear, which is amplified by the media, to teach people what they should believe. Senior sociologist David Altheide argues convincingly in his 2017 book Terrorism and the Politics of Fear that terrorism is not only weakening the democratic foundations of American institutions, but it is also creating a culture of entertainment based on the consumption of news about terrorism. Altheide points out that Donald Trump would never have made it to the White House if people didn't worry about terrorists. It's important not to forget that terrorism is a threat to the way democratic systems work. In some ways, Jean Baudrillard draws attention to the connection between technology and the way people talk about the future. He talks about the story of Steven Spielberg's movie Minority Report, in which the police work together with Precogs, who are mutants who can see crimes before they happen. With the help of high technology, precogs not only created a society with no risks, but they also changed the way Roman law worked. As Baudrillard points out, this is a lot like the fear of terrorism and the "precautionary principle" that people today have to follow. Risks are not real dangers; instead, they are things that will happen in the future. Virilio, Baudrillard, and Altheide all have negative things to say about technology because they know that social change can't happen if mainstream culture values don't change in a big way.

Terrorism and the Limitations of Preemption

September 11 marks the beginning of a new time in the United States and the rest of the world, one with more fear and worry. Even though many countries, like Spain, the UK, and parts of Latin America, have to deal with terrorists on their own land, the World Trade Center killings had a big effect on how Americans felt about their safety. The way Americans lived changed a lot over time. Over the past few years, some people have said that using "digital technologies" and backing torture and other coercive methods is "the lesser evil" in the War on Terror. This brings up some very interesting issues: Is safety more important than freedom of the people? how far does the theory of the lesser evil lead to the same thing it wants to fight for? Does terrorism weaken democracy from the inside?

Vincent Casaregola says in 2016 that the way Americans have treated the War on Terror as if it were just a form of entertainment has made it okay for monitoring culture to be a part of everyday life. Films show that Americans are used to the idea that they might be watched all the time. This led to a very emotional response, which is then turned into a story by the media and entertainment companies. He does a great job of summarizing the plots of many movies with interesting endings. By asking, "Who screens security?," Casaregola argues that the culture of surveillance is based on a feeling of vulnerability and paranoia that comes from a strange conflict between "observing Other" to feel more secure and just "being observed." He says that we feel safe when the government watches us walk down the street because we think they won't mess with our private lives. At most, monitoring gives us a sense of safety. When we see a terrorist attack on TV, we then question how well our government is doing its job to protect us. But in some ways, the need for too much protection creates the right circumstances for a totalitarian control mentality to grow. After all, terrorism has changed the way things are done by making everyone a possible suspect. At least, what movies say seems to be linked to an old, deeply rooted fear in American culture: that too much security speeds up the loss of freedom. What's just as important is that Cass Sunstein's classic book, The Laws of Fear, talks about why people are afraid, or why they feel safe when they should be afraid. Sunstein first looks at the part that rationality plays in the process of fear and how that affects democracy. From his point of view, in a democracy, or at least a deliberative democracy, discussion is more important than other kinds of thinking so that people don't make mistakes by accident. This is what makes a deliberate democracy different from a populism that is based on scare tactics. In other words, a disaster that affects a community might be stopped or made less bad if the problems that affect public life are talked about, argued, and planned for ahead of time. This idea would explain why democratic societies are better prepared for disasters than authoritarian or totalitarian ones. The first country spends a lot of money on preventing and getting ready for natural disasters, while the second country doesn't give its people the tools they need to assess the risks that were already there. The problem of public fear is tied to how much the government censors information about possible dangers. Sunstein agrees that "democracies work best when they stay away from the biggest questions and try to get people who disagree or aren't sure how to solve those questions to agree on something." In the case of fear, I think it's possible to reach this kind of agreement. I think fear is based on some kind of belief that we're in danger.

Starting from the idea that people's fears are based on their past beliefs about how they see disruptive events, it seems that people tend to take serious risks in situations that are relatively safe, while in other cases they avoid real threats because they don't know about them or are too careless. His main point is that the cautious principle comes from a core belief about health, safety, and the environment that grew out of the European Enlightenment in the 18th and 19th centuries. Still, fear, like other basic feelings, works like a chain reaction or, better, like a virus that spreads to other hosts. From a social point of view, what can be seen as scary depends on how people connect with each other every day. Sunstein disagrees with the idea that Europe accepts the cautious principle while the United States does not. Since Europeans openly admit that the world should be viewed with a certain amount of risk, there will be times when capitalist states do what they need to do to protect their people' lives. On the other hand, American culture doesn't seem to care about the risks of global warming or policies that change the genes of food. This gives the wrong impression that the United States needs proof of possible risks before taking action. When scholars think about how fear affects people, they often go in the wrong way because of a false divide between the United States and Europe. In a word, he says that the precautionary principle should be thought about again in light of the following:

- The principle of precaution very well gives origin to the risks it tries to prevent;
- Over-exposure to the precautionary doctrine predisposes public opinion to panic and inaction;
- This precautionary principle is self-blinding and hides other dangers which should be faced. Societies are more interested in creating their fears for ignoring the importance of real hazards;
- The principle of precaution often initializes a set of a different set of criminal justice proceedings, subverting the normal processes.

Taking all of this into account, Sunstein thinks that the risk should be checked and tested through scientific study. Risks are often linked to what people do in their everyday lives, which can have a big impact on the lives of others. Depending on how dangerous they are for US land, practical policies or plans can be discouraged or supported. One problem with this book is that Sunstein can't explain what "contingent" really means. Also, the question of how the law can figure out penalties based only on guesswork and the somewhat vague principle of precaution comes up right away. After all, decisions should be based on what has already happened. Even though the chances of harm are high, how do you decide what to do about a crime that hasn't happened yet?

These two tricky questions show that the idea of the precautionary principle has some theory flaws. In the next part, I'll talk about the social background of how we went from a society of risk or prevention to a dark society where the death of the Other has become a way to attract and get the most pleasure out of people. Thana-Capitalism is the name given to this new stage of capitalism.

Terror and The Thanaptopic Tradition

Just after finishing my two most recent books, Tracing Spikes in Fear and Narcissism in Western Democracies Since 9/11 (Peter Lang) and The Challenges of Democracy in the War on Terror (Routledge). In the first work, I looked at the limits of psychoanalysis and how it was used to justify the growth and spread of capitalism. In the second work, I looked at how torture is used as a "lesser evil" in the dominant rhetoric of e-government. One of my arguments sounded like I was trying to make a point, as if not only is terrorism the organization of labor by other means, but so is psychoanalysis, which, by taking its ideas from old Greek philosophy, is based on the theory of scarcity, which is the basis of capitalism. Second, and most importantly, Occident carefully created a theory of security that says when the body is in danger, the part should be sacrificed (eliminated). Let me use cancer as a medical analogy. While doctors are trained to look for and get rid of the disease's pathology, cancer is caused by an abnormal growth of cells. Once some organs are affected, doctors don't think twice about removing the part. The same metaphor can be used to talk about the so-called "War on Terror" and the very real danger of ghettoization that the Muslim community faces every day. A very important point in the argument we just talked about. As was said, both works were clear criticisms of liberal democracy and the idea of a nation-state. The caustic classic The Universal Exemption, which was written by philosopher Slavoj Zizek, was not mentioned in my writings, nor did I use it in a balanced way.

In his work, Zizek criticized postmodern politics and how it relates to terrorism, torture, 9/11, and the fact that modern governments can't deal with the totalitarian spirit they have. It doesn't seem like a mistake that I didn't include this book. I'm going to save a full book review to talk more about Zizek's strong points, but most of all, I'm going to talk about how he can't understand modern society. Even though I have a background in sociology, one of the first things I had to do was avoid using too much jargon and complicated words and make Zizek's point as clear as possible. He doesn't agree with the idea that the bipolar world, in which the US fought a symbolic war with the Soviet Union, is over and has died out. Left-wing scholars have not only become some of the most conservative minds in our society today, but they also hold a cynical view that openly criticizes the effects of capitalism, but doesn't do much to move out of their comfort zone. This shows that the subject of the sentence and the subject of the sentence are not the same. In other words, postmodern politics doesn't seem too different from the terrorist's message, which says, "I want you to do what I want, but I also want you to act like you want to do it." Zizek makes a strong case that ordinary people are often subject to "extreme civility," which is meant to make people think they can move around easily but, in reality, is controlled by "the Big Other." It should go without saying that this "Big Other," which is the opposite of "little Other," is not a physical thing and has nothing to do with "the Big Brother," as many experts thought. It shows the syntactical, grammatical, implicit rules, and social conventions that shape people's and groups' behaviors every day. Whether the relationships between capital owners and workers are part of the little other or the big other, the conditions of labor abuse send a message to the big other. Zizek says, "The role of civility in modern societies is the rise of the free, independent individual. This is true not only because civility is the practice of treating others as equal, free, and independent subjects, but also because the fragile web of civility is the social substance of independent, free individuals."

As was said above, the reverse of extreme civility is the act of pretending people are free when they are not. We definitely live in a world ruled by totalitarian governments that look like liberal democracies. One thing that makes a tyrant a dictator is that he or she is likely to make laws that are so harsh that if everyone followed them literally, we would all be guilty of something. Zizek's point is meant to show that institutions are based on cultural values that not only affect how people make decisions, but also lead people even when they don't want to be led. He used examples like child molesting by the Catholic Church and torture in Supermax prisons. The priest who does these things can't be led by their instincts, but by the core beliefs of Christianity and, most of all, by the way the Catholic Church is set up. If a priest breaks these unspoken rules, he is not only metaphorically put to death (isolated), but also forced to face the institution's values. Torture does the same thing. Zizek says that there is nothing soldiers can do to keep from torturing their prisoners and getting their peers to agree with them. In what this reviewer thinks is the best part of the book (Heiner Muller Out of Joint), he talks about what liberal democracy is all about from a new perspective. He asks a very pointed question: What would happen if the party most likely to win the next election turned its back on the values that make democracy work? Is this new party being punished or forced to work in the shadows?

Zizek said that liberal democracy should be seen as formal legality, which is orchestrated to resolve the opposing positions in the game: "Democracy...

concerns above all formal legality: its minimal definition is the unconditional adherence to a certain set of formal rules which guarantee that antagonisms are fully absorbed not the agonistic game." Democracy means that no matter how the election is rigged, everyone in politics will always respect the findings. The first part of the book ends with a contrast between official "written" law and what Zizek calls "the obscene superego," which is an example of the hidden law. To show this, he uses the law in the South and the illegal actions of the KKK. Even though the law said that black people couldn't be given harsh fines, the KKK used violence as a form of discipline, which made the law legal. Any KKK member was well-known in his town, but he could be sent away if he refused a direct order from a higher-up to kill a black person. Zizek says that this is how the system keeps a light and dark side so that its members can be watched.

I've gone over the most important parts and arguments about The Universal Exemption up to this point. In the end, I think Zizek deserves a lot of credit for trying to bring together fields that were once very different from each other, like psychoanalysis and Marxism. At the same time, he plays with the idea that we live in a world where ideals have changed a lot. There is nothing like what should or ought to be done, what is good or bad. This closed system gets rid of people's personalities, dreams, and hopes to make it seem like they have more freedom than ever before. But behind these made-up feelings and stories is a system of abuse that works in the opposite direction. The clash between the two different bands doesn't lead to a third way. Instead, it validates the same cultural ideals. Leo Strauss made up a story about an elite society where some secrets should be kept hidden from the common people. Most likely, the book can be summed up by comparing it to Socrates' trial. "Because philosophy is a threat to society," the judge said, "he was guilty as charged." To put it simply, the current crisis of democracy shows that the ruling elite are still naked even after the necessary lie has been exposed. What could be wrong with Zizek's ideas? First of all, we have come up against the idea that psychoanalysis helps us understand the actual differences in capitalism better. Even psychoanalysis came from the ancient Greek idea of scarcity. Freud never thought that the concept of desire was complete or eternal, just as the Greeks didn't believe in the idea of total happiness. From Troy to Orpheus, the different Greek stories show that being happy forever only leads to bad things. Every time a person wants to have fun, the world gets in the way. This is exactly what S. Freud and psychoanalysis were based on from the beginning. Why are psychoanalysis and the tragedy of Orpheus so important to western capitalism? This is a very interesting question. A possible answer is that capitalism needs the theory of scarcity, which says that all goods in circulation are not cheap enough for everyone to buy. From this liberal point of view, each person should give up some of what they want to get the most out of their goals. The idea of shortage not only played a big part in making the modern economy what it is, but it is also the symbol of capitalism. But psychoanalysis shouldn't be thought of as something that has nothing to do with the economic world. As Zizek says in The Puppet and the Dwarf, it's important not to lose sight of the fact that Christianity offers an alternative answer to poverty and injustice in the world, which keeps the hapless workforce under control. However, Christianity is not the ideological core of capitalism. Instead, it shares the same values as psychoanalysis, which remind us that a world of total happiness is not possible. The second thing that should be talked about more is the crucifixion of Christ, which Zizek mentions and talks about in the same book. Christianity has a strange core that consists of putting all political principles on the same level, which is a revolutionary reaction. Classic cults depend on trust to stay alive, but Christianity is based on betrayal. In this way, Christianity gets rid of both the sin and the cure at once. Christianity tells us that our happiness depends on not being able to go against the way things are. So, the subject is forced to say what it wants in the plenitude. Zizek says that the Christ's army and crucifixion show that God can't save his son. Along the same lines, Job was cruelly put between the wall and the deep blue sea. Some things should be said here. On the one hand, the Greek Tragedy and psychoanalysis both share the same worries about Christianity. On the other hand, the crucifixion of Christ cannot be seen as a starting point, as Zizek did. Instead, it is part of an environment that was already there in Judaism, just like Noah's Ark. We have raised some questions about what Zizek says. We believe that modern society sets the pace for a new stage of capitalism in which the death of the Other is the main thing that is traded. People all over the world tend to look at "how the Other is suffering" in entertainment media and other places as well. This made a new society possible, which we called "thana-Capitalism." In this way, 9/11 sped up the breakdown of postmodernism into "thanaptopic-modernism," but Noah's ark is the story that backs up a Darwinist world where the winner takes all. The ark was the most cost-effective way to kill all people. When you look closer, you can see that God is upset with the world he made. Not only has the man given in to sin, but he also needs help from another person to carry out his plans. God told Noah to build an ark that could hold two of each kind of animal. The rest of the story says that the Universal Flood not only got rid of all the sin, but also gave people a chance to start over in a new place and do well. Outside of this story about the end of the world, this was thought to be the first genocide, and Noah was seen as its leader. Once God told Noah what he was going to do, Noah would tell other people or give advice to those who would be hurt by God's anger. But his quiet killed a lot of people. At that moment, God split the world into two parts: the victims, who were all people, and Noah, who was the witness. The suffering of Christ not only proved that the same thing was happening, but also showed that sacrifice (which means pain) and death are the key values of capitalism, which is based on the theory of scarcity. What should be talked about today seems to have to do with the fact that cheap (surveillance) technology has not made the world safer. Instead, it has created a split in which risk has become a commodity and a new (sad) form of entertainment. In a Thanaptopic society, where the death of the Other is a source of entertainment for people all over the world, terrorism is the air that the system needs to stay alive. This is a problem that has been going on for a long time and should be looked at again in the future.

Conclusion

Terrorism definitely makes us feel more anxious and makes us think about our fears like never before. Since 9/11, there have been more and more racist words and phrases, like "Islamophobia" and "tourist-phobia," to name a few. Terrorism has become a product that can be bought and sold as a show. At the same time, some experts say that there is a gap between old and new terrorists. L. Stampnitzky (2013) rightly points out that old definitions of terrorism referred to it as a strategy used when both sides of a fight have different amounts of power and strength. Things changed a lot right after the year 2001. Terrorists are often called "monsters" or "lunatics" who hate the West and freedom. In the days after 9/11, people in the U.S. asked themselves, "Why do they hate us?" The answer, of course, doesn't seem to be very easy to give. One possible reason was that fundamentalist groups were influenced by Islam's dogmatism and its long-standing competition with Christianity. This point of view, which was widely supported by Bush's government, always led to a wrong idea of how religion and terrorism are linked. Some voices have harshly criticized this (academic) position, pointing out that the so-called rivalry between Islam and Christianity has no basis in history. The same goes for the idea that Islam is the source of Islamist groups. It's safe to say that Islamophobia came from a culture of intolerance, which was based in the core ideas of western capitalism and got worse after 9/11. I've talked about the pros and cons of digital technology and how it can help in the War on Terror in this part. Like Zizek said, we need to change how we think about extremism and who it affects. Recently, some people have said that we need to use technology to make the world a better place. This chapter goes in another way that doesn't make sense. We pay attention to the ethical limits of technologies when they are used to make a zero-risk society a reality. We agree with Sunstein and Altheide that the precautionary principle has always led to a strange situation in which "made-up fears" have become the foundation of a new stage of capitalism. To put it another way, terrorism is the major product of a society in which the "Other's" death is a measure of entertainment. In the beginning, we talked about the brothers Avraham Salomon and how they were wrongfully jailed. This event sparked a heated discussion in Argentina, and the Muslim community was strongly criticized. The second part, which went along with the first, was a critical look at both the use of high technology to calm fears of terrorism and Jacques Ellul's original concerns, which put the conceptual limits of the technological society front and center in an elegant way. In modern capitalism, technology isn't used to make things fairer or more unequal. Instead, it's used to make the injustice worse. In the third part, there is an overview of Cass Sunstein's book The Laws of Fear, which is a harsh critique of the precautionary principle and the modern obsession with a society with no risks. Last but not least, we make up the word "Thana-capitalism" to go with Slavoj Zizek's writings about technology and terror. Even though this chapter is a first try to solve a problem that modern sociology hasn't solved yet, we're sure that our work will pay off in the not-too-distant future.

Chapter 6
The Limits of Cyberwarfare

Introduction

In this chapter, we look at how the law against war applies to cyber actions and show that most of them don't reach the level needed for jus contra bellum to apply.

For hundreds of years, the right to war (jus ad bellum) was an independent right that States could use in any way they wanted. Over time, a law came into being that regulated the use of force. This law helped lay the groundwork for a general ban on the use of force in positive international law.

The difference between "just war" (bellum justum) and "unjust war" (bellum injustum) was the first thing that stopped the government from going to war. The difference can be traced back to the time of the Romans. In fact, this idea really took off in the Middle Ages, especially because of the impact of Christianity. The just war theory says that war itself is not always bad, but the reasons for it might be. A war that is fought for a reason that is not right is illegal, but a war that is fought for a reason that is right is valid. States can still use the "just war" argument when going to war, but it no longer has any legal weight. But it's important to note that the just war theory has some effect on how international law deals with war today. When the League of Nations was created, it was a big step forward in making sure that states didn't use too much force. Article 11 of the League of countries' Covenant says that any war or threat of war is a problem for the whole League and that the League will do whatever it thinks is smart and effective to keep the peace between countries. But the Covenant didn't always say that war was bad. Instead, it said that there were wrong ways to fight. The League of Nations' Covenant did not work to stop wars, as history shows. One of the main reasons this didn't work was because they didn't go to war. Measures short of war are low-intensity uses of force that don't reach the level of war. It wasn't clear if they were legal or illegal under the Kellogg-Briand Pact or the Covenant of the League of Nations, and there was no agreement on the theory. Most experts think they are legal, though, unless they are really a cover for war. This point of view is backed up by what the state does. Between the strict categories of the Covenant, there seems to be a grey area for actions that don't involve going to war. This helps explain why Article 2, line 4, of the UN Charter says that force can't be used in most cases.

Article 2, line 4, of the United Nations Charter, which bans the use or threat of force between states, was signed in 1945. This was a turning point in how the use of force was regulated. The word "war" was changed with the more general term "use of force." Based on this change, jus ad bellum, which said that people had an endless and unrestricted right to go to war, was gradually replaced by jus contra bellum, which is the law against war and says that going to war is against international law.

Article 2, line 4, of the UN Charter sets up a system of collective security that says a state can't use force on its own. The Charter makes two exceptions to this rule: the right to self-defence (Article 51) and the use of force when approved by the UN Security Council under Chapter 7 of the UN Charter. The three limits, which are all connected, are:

1. threat or use of force;
2. armed attack; and
3. the threat to peace, breach of peace, and act of aggression.

Most people agree, though, that these words have a "cascading relationship," with "armed attack" being the more specific and a subcategory of "aggression," and "aggression" itself being a subcategory of "force." But the UN Charter doesn't say what any of these words mean.

Here's a quick rundown of the three levels: This first limit is the most general and lowest one that the UN Charter sets. Under jus contra bellum, cyber operations that achieve this level could be called cyber warfare. Article 51 of the UN Charter says that an armed attack gives the state that is attacked the right to defend itself. People disagree about what the difference is between an armed attack and the use of force. Some States and scholars think that the two ideas are the same, so that any use of force gives the State the right to defend itself. But most people say that only the most serious use of force is a military attack. In the Nicaragua case, the International Court of Justice (ICJ) took the second method and said that only the "most serious forms of force" count as an armed attack. Article 39 of the UN Charter says that the UN Security Council "shall decide if there is any threat to the peace, breach of the peace, or act of aggression." This is the third threshold. The UN Security Council's "primary responsibility" is to keep peace and security around the world. It is a government body, not a court or a group that enforces the law. Aggression has been described as "the most serious and dangerous form of the illegal use of force."

On the other hand, the words "breach of peace" and "threat to peace" have not been legally defined, so it is up to the Security Council to decide what they mean and how they should be used. Article 2, paragraph 4, of the UN Charter says how much of a threat or use of force is needed for cyberwarfare to be acceptable. Under jus contra bellum, cyber operations are only considered warfare when they hit this level or when they can be seen as a threat or use of cyber force.

Before we go into more detail about cyber activities and jus contra bellum, we need to answer a preliminary question: does jus contra bellum apply to cyber warfare? The answer is a clear "yes." The UN Charter was made almost 50 years before the first cyber operation was done, so it doesn't talk about cyber operations or have any clear rules about them. Only Article 41 has a loose connection to cyber operations because it is a measure that does not require the use of armed force: "the interruption of telegraphic, radio, and other means of communication." This behaviour is interesting for this study because it shows the only reason communication networks are used for contact right now. The people who wrote the UN Charter in 1945 did not think that communication networks could be used for armed cyber operations.

Even though cyber operations aren't specifically mentioned in the UN Charter, that doesn't mean that it doesn't relate to them. The articles of the UN Charter were written so that they can change and adapt to new trends in international security, such as changes in cyber operations. It is clear that not all cyber operations can meet or fall short of the standards of jus contra bellum for "force" and other things. The goal of this chapter is to look at each situation individually.

Cyber Operations and the Prohibition of the Use of Force

The general prohibition of the threat or use of force is enshrined in Article 2, paragraph 4 of the UN Charter:

> All Members shall refrain in their international relations from the threat or use of force against the territorial integrity or political independence of any state, or in any other manner inconsistent with the Purposes of the United Nations.

This part will only talk about the rule that you can't use force. In the next part of this chapter, we'll talk more about the second rule in this Article, which is that you can't threaten to use force.

Also, this part will only talk about the first part of Article 2, line 4. The second part, which is about how far the ban goes, won't get a long or detailed discussion.

Scholars have been arguing for a long time about whether Article 2, paragraph 4 makes a general ban or whether the second part of the paragraph limits its reach. Some critics look at the ban in a narrow way that doesn't account for the fact that there are exceptions. So, they can account for some ways of using force that aren't covered by this Article. But most scholars believe, and history backs them up, that the ban applies to all threats or uses of force between states. Article 2, paragraph 4, is taken to mean that it is against the law to threaten or use force in any way for the goals of this book. So, people no longer talk about the possible cases that would happen if the rule was taken literally.

The Prohibition of the use of Force

Article 2, paragraph 4, of the UN Charter is the most important prohibition about the use of force being forbidden. However, its importance goes beyond the UN Charter. Since the Kellog-Briand Pact in 1928, many treaties have repeated the prohibition, which doesn't come as a surprise. The following discussion analyses the characteristics of the prohibition of the use of force that are relevant.

The Prohibition of the use of Force and the International Court Of Justice

In the Armed Activities case, the International Court of Justice (ICJ) said that the ban on the use of force is "a cornerstone of the United Nations Charter."

The Corfu Channel was the first case that went to the ICJ. It had to do with using force. Since then, many cases involving the use of force have been taken to the ICJ. But the Court only decided on the use of force in four cases: the Corfu Channel, Nicaragua, Oil Platforms, and Armed Activities cases. In the nuclear weapons case and the Wall case, the Court also gave two decisions. The International Court of Justice (ICJ) has always and strictly said that using force is wrong. Most of the time, states have taken the same position as the ICJ. But some states, especially the United States, don't like how it does things. The strict way made by the International Court of Justice (ICJ) and used by most States is used in this study. The analysis won't go into great depth about each case, but it will talk about the interesting parts and conclusions of the ICJ's case law. Case law from the ICJ is often about how to use force to protect yourself.

The Prohibition of the use of Force and the Principle of Non-Intervention

The ICJ says, "The principle of non-intervention, which overlaps and is closely related to the principle of non-use of force, strengthens the principle of non-use of force, and the Court took a consistent and strict stance on this as well." In its ruling on Nicaragua, the ICJ looked at the legal opinion and state practise on this principle and agreed that it was a matter of custom. In the Nicaragua case, the International Court of Justice (ICJ) said that humanitarian intervention and "pro-democratic" or "ideological" intervention are not exceptions to the concept of non-interference. Different treaties and resolutions of the United Nations General Assembly have reaffirmed the principle of non-intervention. These include the Draught Declaration on Rights and Duties of States, the Declaration on the Inadmissibility of Intervention in the Domestic Affairs of States and the Protection of Their Independence and Sovereignty, and the Declaration on Principles of International Law Concerning Friendly Relations and Cooperation among States in Accordance with t. Article 2, paragraph 4, of the UN Charter says that any kind of intervention that uses force is not allowed. This means that military involvement is not allowed because it uses force. Article 2, line 4, says that other kinds of intervention, like subversive intervention and diplomatic intervention, are not allowed because they don't involve using force. For example, arming, training, or just giving money to armed opposition forces could be seen as an illegal action. But the ICJ says that only the first one could be thought of as using force.

The Status of The Prohibition of the Use of Force Under Customary International Law and Jus Cogens

Article 2, line 4, which says that force can't be used, has become the ban. This means that both treaty law and customary international law have the same rule. This makes me wonder if the customary rule is the same as the rule in Article 2, line 4, or if it is different. In its ban on Nicaragua, the ICJ recognised that Article 2, paragraph 4, of the UN Charter and customary international law are similar and have ties to each other. Even though the content of both rules is the same, the alternatives, such as self-defence, are different. Such written and unwritten rules can coexist and still "retain a separate existence." Even though the contract and the customary rules are the same, they could change in different ways and their content could change over time. In 1966, in the introduction to its "Draught Articles on the Law of Treaties," the International Law Commission called the rule against using force one of the first jus cogens norms.

Most people agree that it is a jus cogens that you can't use force. On the other hand, some critics have a narrow view of the general international law that says it is always wrong to use force. Some scholars have said that the rule against violence is the only thing that should be called jus cogens. But very few people understand and agree with this. So, in this part, it is said that the absolute ban on using force is an international law rule that can't be broken.

As a rule of general international law that can't be broken, the ban on the use of force is more important than treaty law and even "ordinary" customary rules. A norm of jus cogens can't be broken in the same way that a treaty or a norm of custom can. For example, the ILC's Articles on "Responsibility of States for Internationally Wrongful Acts," which name countermeasures (Article 22), distress (Article 24), and necessity (Article 25) as things that don't count as wrong, don't apply.

So, the rule that you can't use force is both a habit and a jus cogens. This makes it one of the most important rules of international law. There is no international law that says a country can't use "cyber force" right now. Because of this, the use of "cyber force" is limited by the general rule in the UN Charter and international law that says you can't use force. States and experts still disagree about whether or not there needs to be a treaty on cyberwarfare. Still, it seems that Article 2, line 4, of the UN Charter and international law as a whole are enough to stop people from threatening or using force. In fact, the rule was made so that it can be changed as security risks change. The content of the customary standard hasn't changed since the UN Charter was passed, and neither have state practises.

Cyber Operations as Prohibited Uses of Force

The UN Charter does not describe the word "force," and the word "war," which is an important part of cyber warfare, is only one kind of "force." The idea of "force" is broader and more grounded in facts. Yoram Dinstein points out that the word "force" doesn't come before the word "armed" in Article 2.4, but the full term "armed force" is used in the Preamble, Article 41 [...], and Article 46.

There are problems with not having a clear description. Before the idea can be used, it needs to be understood. The "general rule of interpretation" is found in Article 31 of the Vienna Convention on the Law of Treaties of 1969. This study follows this rule. In this case, the rule against threatening or using force must be interpreted "in good faith in accordance with the ordinary meaning to be given to the terms of the treaty in their context and in light of its object and purpose." The fact that cyber activities have become a new threat to international peace is a change in the context of this ban, but it doesn't mean that this ban is no longer important. Article 2, line 4, makes it clear that the idea of "force" is flexible enough to include cyber operations.

Below, we'll talk about what "cyber force" means, as well as the content of the idea of "force," which is still up for discussion among scholars.

The Prohibited Force is not Limited to 'Armed Force'

The UN Charter says that force can never be used. But no one can agree on what kind of force should be banned. There are still different ideas in the writings about what this idea means. Some scholars say that only armed force is against the law, while others take a wider view that goes beyond the idea of armed force. In its Advisory Opinion on nuclear weapons, the ICJ said that the ban "applies to any use of force, no matter what kinds of weapons are used." So, it looks like the Court would rather look at the use of force in a wider way than just limit it to armed force.

But it is clear that the word "force" does not mean "any kind of force." Some kinds of force were turned down at the San Francisco Conference, where the UN Charter was written. Article 2, line 4, of the UN Charter says that economic, political, and indirect force are not allowed. However, the UN Charter's travaux préparatoires show that this is not the case. So, using economic or political force does not break Article 2, line 4. However, it might break other rules of international law, such as the principles of non-intervention and economic rights. Some indirect forms of force seem to be included in the ban on the use of force, such as when a state helps another state use force or when a state helps and controls non-state players.

Does the rule against using force apply to all kinds of coercion? On this question, developed and developing states have different opinions. Developing states want a broader meaning than developed states do. Even though there is disagreement about where to draw the line between forms of pressure that are or are not part of the use of force, it is clear that Article 2, paragraph 4, does not ban all forms of coercion. For example, the ban does not cover economic and diplomatic pressure. As new tools come out, it's getting harder to explain what a "weapon" is. Because chemical, bacterial, and biological weapons don't have "explosive effects," they change the way things are usually done.

Cyber operations are hard to put in the same category as armed forces, so using them as weapons also challenges the standard way of thinking. Ian Brownlie came up with a way to figure out if using these guns is an illegal use of force:

> It would seem that use of these weapons could be assimilated to the use of force on two grounds. In the first place the agencies concerned are commonly referred to as 'weapons' and as forms of 'warfare'. More convincing is the second consideration, the fact that these weapons are employed for the destruction of life and property, and are often described as 'weapons of mass destruction'

Both parts of Ian Brownlie's description can be used to describe cyber operations. First, they are often called "cyber warfare" or "information warfare," and second, they can be used to kill people and damage property. If Ian Brownlie's definition is applied to cyber operations, it shows that the criteria for calling force "armed" or "weaponized" are not important, since many kinds of "force" today don't have the traditional traits of weapons. In the end, it doesn't seem right to only ban armed force when it comes to the use or fear of force. So, the argument about whether cyber operations are the same as armed operations seems to be pretty old, so it won't be talked about any more in this book. Cyber operations, which will be talked about in the next parts of this book, can be a use of force that is forbidden by Article 2, line 4.

Different ways to do things on 'cyber force'

There isn't a clear practise among states right now about whether cyber activities are a use of force or not. Commentators have come to very different opinions about the positions of states because they change all the time and are very different. In the next few paragraphs, we'll look at how cyber force has been talked about in the past to find the best and most true way to talk about it. Almost all commentators base their work on what the law says about the use of force, and there are three main ways to look at it: based on the goal, based on the tool, and based on the results. Few people use goal-based or tool-based methods. Instead, most people seem to use a consequence-based approach.

The Target-Based Approach

As you might expect, the target-based method focuses on the goal of cyber operations and counts them as uses of force when they break into systems that are part of "critical national infrastructure." This method has mostly been thought of in terms of self-defence, with the idea that the current laws about the use of force don't protect targeted states enough. People who like this plan say that the government could use force to defend itself if attacks were made on important assets. So, this method is too broad because it would classify cyber operations based on their targets, no matter how intense or different they are. So, you can't just use this way to decide if a cyber operation is a use of force or not. Still, it is still important because the type of equipment being attacked could be used to figure out how bad cyber operations are and what effects they will have.

The Instrument-Based Approach

The instrument-based method is based on where the attack is coming from. Most cyber operations wouldn't be considered use of force because they are hard to describe as armed or weaponized force. Even worse, this method is based on the idea that cyber operations and traditional weapons are the same. It's hard to show this similarity, which could lead to analysis that is too far-fetched. In the past, the instrument-based method was more accurate, but as new technologies and weapons that don't look like traditional weapons have come out, it has lost a lot of its value and importance. Also, it's hard to tell which programmes should be called weapons in cyber operations because they can be used for more than one thing.

The Consequence-Based Approach

The consequence-based approach looks at what happens as a result of cyber operations (virtual consequences, physical destruction, or loss of life). Cyber operations that cause physical destruction or loss of life would always be considered a use of force, but it is more controversial to include non-physical consequences. This is the way the United States and most academics do things. In fact, the best way to figure out if cyber operations meet the standards of Article 2, paragraph 4, is to look at what happens after the fact. Marco Roscini's case for combining the tool-based and outcome-based approaches is very interesting. Even though the results are obviously the most important thing, he says we shouldn't forget about the tool we used or the goal we were trying to reach. In other words, the main method is still based on results, but it is improved by adding parts of the goal-based and tool-based approaches. All of these different ways of doing things are based on the present laws that say force is not allowed. One might wonder if, instead of changing the laws that are already in place, it wouldn't be better to make a whole new set of rules for cyber activities. At first glance, this idea to make a new legal system outside of the UN Charter may seem good. There are, however, two strong arguments for sticking with the current law system: First of all, the UN Charter already gives a lot of freedom, so it would be hard to agree on those topics. So, the legal framework of the UN Charter seems fit and right. Within the framework of the UN Charter, the consequence-based method, along with some parts of the other two approaches, is the best. This book uses this approach. Each cyber action needs to be looked at on a case-by-case basis because they are all different and can have different types and levels of effects.

The Criterion of 'Gravity' or 'Severity' of the Coercive Cyber Activity

It would be very hard, if not impossible, to come up with a clear cut rule for when cyber activities count as a use of force. So, the threshold has to be looked at on a case-by-case basis using a variety of factors and facts that are specific to each situation. In the same way, this study is based on the current state of international law and cyber operation practise. This is because no cyber operation has been recognised as a use of force yet, and there hasn't been much State practise until now. Also, people all over the world don't agree on how to classify and describe the use of force online. Because cyber operations are different, it is important to know that any effort to regulate them under jus contra bellum will "be subject to great uncertainty, debate, opacity, and lack of verifiability." There is already a level of seriousness or gravity for "armed attack" and "aggression." On the one hand, the International Court of Justice (ICJ) says that armed strikes are the "most serious forms of the use of force." On the other hand, the UN General Assembly's Resolution 3314 (XXIX) calls aggression "the most serious and dangerous forms of the illegal use of force." Neither the International Court of Justice (ICJ) nor the UN Charter said how much force was too much to be illegal. But this doesn't mean that such a barrier can't exist. In the next few lines, we will try to figure out if there is a minimum level of seriousness for a state to use force and how that threshold would apply to cyber operations.

The Threshold of Gravity of the Prohibited use of Force

Several scholars who have looked at how states have used force since the UN Charter was made have come to the conclusion that Article 2, line 4 doesn't apply below a certain level of seriousness. Several examples of low-level uses of force by states that didn't count as "use of force" by the state show that there is such a threshold. The International Fact-Finding Commission on the Conflict in Georgia mentioned this point when it said that the ban on using force includes all physical force that is stronger than a certain minimum level. Other authors, on the other hand, say that there is no such limit and that "minimal uses of force" are not left out of Article 2, paragraph 4. Some low-intensity uses of force don't count as uses of force for other reasons, like trying to keep things from getting worse or trying to make things better between the states concerned.

Small-scale uses of force include targeted killings of people, operations to save nationals abroad, small counterterrorism operations abroad, police operations, "hot-pursuit" operations, and border clashes.

The ICJ has never set a clear level of seriousness for Article 2, paragraph 4. Several cases brought before the Court, however, might show that there is a minimum level of seriousness that must be met before force can be used. In its first case, the Corfu Channel case, the Court said that the involvement of British warships in Albanian waters was a violation of Albanian sovereignty, but it did not say that it was a violation of the ban on the threat or use of force. Some scholars look at this way of thinking as evidence that there is a ceiling of gravity.

Other cases brought before the ICJ could also show that there is such a bar. But, as we've already said, most cases brought before the ICJ have been about self-defence (Article 51). This makes it hard to use these cases to figure out a level of seriousness for the use of force in Article 2, paragraph 4. Other cases in maritime law enforcement seem to back up the idea that there is such a barrier. In these cases, there was only a small amount of force used against foreign ships, but the Court didn't call it force. If we look at each case on its own, it might be hard to say that there is a threshold of gravity. However, if we look at them all together, they may provide enough evidence for this view. Scholars who support the idea of a threshold point out that there are more clear examples of a threshold of gravity outside of the ICJ's case law.

Mary Ellen O'Connell, who wants there to be a minimum level of seriousness before the use of force is forbidden, brought up this point about online operations:

> Cyberspace is another area where some writers try to equate crime with armed attack for the purposes of triggering a right to resort to force under Article 51. The internet is a zone of communications and commerce where a good deal of crime occurs. Enhancing cyber security, however, should be the job of the police, not the military.

Government-backed cyber operations must be kept separate from those that are not. Article 2, line 4, actually only bans the first one. The rest should be handled by the criminal justice system. But cyber operations can only be called uses of force if they go beyond what is allowed in Article 2, paragraph 4. In the next few lines, we'll talk about this in more depth.

Cyber Operations and The Threshold of Gravity

Cyber operations are a very diverse group with a wide range of sizes and effects, such as the destruction of data, damage, and even death. Some authors use the criterion of severity to describe the threshold of gravity. This is the point at which a cyber operation started by one state against another state qualifies as a use of force. Using a severity threshold makes it possible to tell the difference between the different kinds of cyber activities and to find those who break the rule against using force. Michael N. Schmitt's important paper from 1999 suggested a "normative framework" with eight criteria. One of these factors was "severity." Schmitt was in charge of the International Group of Experts that worked on the Tallinn Manual. They used and improved these criteria in the Tallinn Manual 2.0's explanation of Rule 69 on what it means to use force. Since then, this "normative framework" has been talked about, criticised, and said again. Since this part is about Michael N. Schmitt's seriousness criterion, we won't talk about the other seven criteria any more. This "normative framework" is an interesting attempt to find a way to tell the difference between cyber operations that use force and those that use economic or political pressure. Schmitt's "normative framework" has a "severity" criterion that is mostly based on comparing the effects of cyber operations to the effects that are generally linked to armed coercion. From this perspective, the Tallinn Manual 2.0 says, "Subject to a de minimis rule, physical harm to people or property will be enough for the act to be considered use of force."

This is an interesting way to do things, and it could be used in other scenarios as well. In fact, it should be changed a little bit to include a severity level for cyber-attacks that hurt people or property physically. In the next paragraph, we'll talk more about this question, and cyber operations will be put into groups based on how serious they have to be to be called a use of force.

Differentiation of Cyber Activities

There needs to be a difference between cyber operations that cause physical damage, hurt, or death and those that only cause non-physical damage, like destroying data, messing up computer programmes, or launching a DDoS attack. Most commentators agree that cyber activities that hurt or hurt people physically are the same as using force. On the other hand, saying that cyber activities have no effect in the real world is more controversial.

Use of force is any cyber activity that causes damage, injury, or death. Cyber operations that break only one machine and have no other effects could be seen as a use of force. But the targeted state could decide not to count it as an attack. For example, a cyber operation by one state against another state with the goal of physically damaging the smartphones of government leaders could be seen as a use of force. But it doesn't seem like a state would call it that because it doesn't do much. In the case of Stuxnet, this is clear. Since the Stuxnet worm hurt the centrifuges in Iran's nuclear programme, this cyber action could be seen as a use of force. Most experts agree that Stuxnet was a use of force, but neither Iran nor any other country has ever called it that. One could say that Stuxnet didn't do much damage because it only destroyed a few centrifuges and not the whole nuclear plant. This could be why it doesn't count as a state using force, or one of the reasons why it doesn't count as a state using force. But Iran might have made this choice for some other reason. Iran might have wanted to keep things from getting worse or find another way to reply. It is important to separate the fact that Stuxnet may objectively be a use of force, which I think is the case, from a state's choice to call it that. The first question is about the law, and the second is mostly about politics and tactics.

Cyber operations that don't have real-world results are much more controversial when it comes to whether or not they count as a use of force. Some writers are very against classifying them as use of force, while others are okay with it under certain circumstances. This makes me wonder two things: first, is the fact that something has a physical effect a barrier in and of itself? Second, do people always think that physical effects are worse than non-physical ones? You can say no to both of these questions. It's true that physical impacts are easier to see and feel, which makes them more likely to be seen as a use of force. Even though cyber operations don't have any physical results, they can still have a big impact. It doesn't make sense to not count cyber operations as a use of force if they have direct or indirect affects that put the survival of the targeted State in danger.

Targeted Cyber Campaigns on Key Assets

When deciding if a cyber operation was a use of cyber force, it's important to see if the target was key infrastructure. The problem is made worse by the fact that the target is a key piece of infrastructure, which may tip the scales in favour of the use of force argument. In this part, the ideas of critical infrastructures and critical information infrastructures are explained, and then how they might affect the qualifications of cyber force are looked at.

The Perception of Critical Infrastructures

"Critical infrastructures" is an umbrella term for infrastructures, assets, or systems that a state thinks are important for keeping society running or could pose a major threat to the population. In fact, if they get broken, destroyed, or messed up, they could pose a real threat to the people or hurt the security of the State. Hackers attacking critical infrastructures is a big problem for both national and foreign security. Most definitions agree that some of the most important areas are government and public services, security, food, water, transportation, energy, health, finance, and banking. But there is no one definition of a critical area that everyone agrees on.

Most states decide on their own what a key sector and critical infrastructures are. Their goal is to figure out which buildings or assets make up vital infrastructures and how to protect them from both man-made threats like cyber threats and natural disasters. In general, states make a list of their most important sectors and then a list of the most important assets in each of those sectors.

At the international level, the UN General Assembly passed a resolution in 2003 called "Creation of a global culture of cybersecurity and the protection of critical information infrastructures." This resolution said that, in general, critical infrastructures include "the generation, transmission, and distribution of energy, air and maritime transport, banking and financial services, e-commerce, water supply, food distribution, and public health." This is not a complete list, and the resolution says that "each country will decide its own critical information infrastructures."

Based on the Directive on European Critical assets of 2008, the European Union has made the European Programme for Critical Infrastructure Protection (EPCIP) as a way to protect Europe's critical assets. The European Union makes a distinction between National Critical Infrastructures (NCI) and European Critical Infrastructures (ECI). The latter refers to "critical infrastructure located in Member States whose disruption or destruction would have a significant effect on at least two Member States." Cross-cutting factors will be used to figure out how important the effect is. This includes affects that happen when different types of infrastructure depend on each other. The directive names two ECI sectors that include a number of sub-sectors. The first is energy, which includes electricity, oil, and gas. The second is transport, which includes road, rail, air, inland waterways, ocean and short-sea shipping, and ports. This list is pretty limited because it only looks at key infrastructures that are important to Europe.

In 2004, the European Commission passed a document called "Protecting Critical Infrastructure in the Fight Against Terrorism." It had a list of important infrastructures that needed to be secured, like ECI. From this list, we can see that the following areas have important infrastructures:

1. Energy installations and networks;
2. Communications and Information Technology (e.g. telecommunications, broadcasting systems, software, hardware and networks including the Internet);
3. Finance;
4. Health Care;
5. Food;
6. Water (e.g. dams, storage, treatment and networks);
7. Transport;
8. Production, storage and transport of dangerous goods;
9. Government

The United States has over time adopted various approaches to critical infrastructures. At the moment, critical infrastructures can be connected to sixteen critical sectors which are as follows:

1. Chemical;
2. Commercial Facilities;
3. Communications;
4. Critical Manufacturing;
5. Dams;
6. Defence Industrial Base;
7. Emergency Services;
8. Energy;
9. Financial Services;
10. Food and Agriculture;
11. Government Facilities;
12. Healthcare and Public Health;
13. Information Technology;
14. Nuclear Reactors, Materials, and Waste;
15. Transportation Systems;
16. Water and Wastewater Systems.

France came up with a list of twelve types of critical infrastructures, which are put into three groups. These are:

- Government (civilian activities of the State; military activities of the State; judicial activities; space and research).
- Protection of the population (health; water supply; food supply).
- Economic and social sectors (energy; information, audio-visual and electronic communications; transport; finance; industry).

In short, the three lists of critical sectors shown above show that different states have different lists and ways of dealing with critical assets. Even though there are some differences, these lists are very close to each other.

Today's vital infrastructures rely heavily on computer systems and networks, which makes them easy targets for cyber-attacks. Stuxnet showed how a cyber operation could be used to target and hurt a nuclear plant, which is usually thought of as a piece of important infrastructure. In the same way, Germany's Federal Office for Information Security said in 2014 that a cyber operation had caused physical damage to a German steel plant. This is another example of how cyber threats can affect key infrastructures. States and organisations on the world level are very worried about this weakness. Cyber activities could hurt people in the real world in terrible ways. Cyber operations need to be kept away from important infrastructure, which is a big cyber security problem. This could be why many cyber defence exercises are built on scenarios that target critical infrastructures.

Critical Digital Infrastructure

Critical information infrastructures are a type of critical infrastructure that focus on computer networks and processes. CII are computer networks and systems that, if broken or destroyed, would have a big effect on people's health, safety, security, or economic well-being, or on how the government or economy works. In other words, CII are a sign of how much our societies, businesses, and even ourselves depend on computer networks and systems. In every way, the economies and societies of today rely on ICT technology. Since this is the case, CII can be used to describe a lot of computer systems and networks. Cyber operations against Estonia in 2007 showed how badly DDoS attacks can affect the way a state works when they shut down important computer systems and networks.

There are two parts to how vulnerable critical infrastructures are to cyber operations: the computer systems and networks that critical infrastructures depend on, and the computer systems and networks that make up critical infrastructures. From this point of view, it's important to note that the European Union passed the "Directive on security of network and information systems" , which went into effect in August 2016. The EU Member States had until May 2018 to turn this order into a law in their own countries. The directive says that digital infrastructures like IXPs, DNS service providers, and TLD name registries should be thought of as providers of vital services. It also tells the people in charge of vital services what they need to do to keep their networks and information systems safe.

Cyber Force and Critical Infrastructures

We've already talked about how the results of a cyber operation are the main thing that tells us if it's a use of force or not. Cyber actions that kill or hurt people or hurt or destroy property are probably considered uses of force. On the other hand, cyber actions that only destroy or mess up data don't seem like they would be seen as uses of force. But the type of target can also change if a cyber action is a cyber use of force or not. A cyber action that only slightly affects a public library's computer network would not be a use of force. On the other hand, a cyber operation is more likely to be seen as a use of force, even though it only had digital effects, if the network that was disrupted is a CII or is needed for a key infrastructure to work. To say it again, not all cyber operations that target and affect key infrastructures can be considered a use of force. It would be a bad idea to use such a broad meaning. Targeting a key infrastructure, on the other hand, could change a lot how cyber operations that don't have physical effects and are usually thought to be below the use of force threshold are seen. On the other hand, a cyber operation is probably not a use of force if it doesn't have any real effects and doesn't affect a key part of the targeted state's infrastructure. Critical infrastructures and cyber activities don't just have to do with using force. More will be learned about the point at which an attack becomes armed, whether cyber operations are legal, and who is responsible for fixing damage done by a cyber operation.

Recognizing a state-driven Cyberattack and its Goals

Cyber actions have different legal statuses and rules depending on where they happen. In this case, it's also important to think about what the state doing the cyber operations is trying to do and what's going on between that state and the state being hit.

In some cases, cyber actions are paid for by a state but done by people who are not part of that state. So, it makes you wonder who did these things. Even if someone makes a mistake or does something by accident, they may still be using force in a way that is against the law.

In international law, one of the most important questions is how to figure out who did something. The State is a vague concept. A State can only do something through one or more people whose actions can be linked to it. In other words, Dionisio Anzilotti said that "the activity of a State is nothing but the activity of individuals that the law imputed to the State" for the purpose of attribution.

The only people who can't use force are the government. But a state could break this rule if it told or helped non-state players use force. "War by proxies," which grew a lot during the Cold War, makes it hard to find the countries fighting and take action against them. Several cyber operations that were thought to be done by states were, at least in part, done by non-state players. For example, after Estonia was attacked online in 2007, the Estonian government said that Russia was to blame, but it admitted that it had no proof to back up this claim. But members of the Russian youth group "Nashi" admitted to being involved, and a member of the Russian parliament said that his assistant had done computer operations against Estonia. People have also thought that Anonymous or the Russian Business Network (RBN), both of which have different levels of organisation, do cyber activities for States. During the Russo-Georgian War, for instance, the RBN did cyber attacks against Georgia. Because these cyber operations seem to be done by proxies, it is hard to figure out who is behind them and how international law should be applied. These tasks can be done by State organs or other groups that are officially allowed to act on behalf of the government. Any actions taken by these groups are the responsibility of the State, even if they go beyond what they are allowed to do, unless the agent was acting in a private role. These things can also be done by groups that aren't officially allowed by domestic law, even though some of what they do could be blamed on the State.

Unauthorized Coercive Cyber Intrusions

With the purpose of a state to act against another state as a criterion, it is clear that a mistaken or unintentional act could be considered a use of force. Olivier Corten says that his views of how the government works show that this claim is more practical than legal. This factor is especially important for cyber operations that use botnets, which are networks of computers that have been infected and are being used without their owners' knowledge.

Computers from all over the world were used as part of botnets in the cyber attacks that caused trouble in Estonia in 2007. When choosing if the situation was a use of force against Estonia, it's important to know that even if States owned the infected computers, they shouldn't be held responsible for the use of cyber force as long as it wasn't done on purpose or with knowledge.

Key Situational Evidence to Assess a Coercive Cyber Activity as a Banned Use of Force

In addition to the State's intentions, two pieces of circumstantial proof or contextual factors must be taken into account: the situation in which the coercive cyber operation takes place and how well known it is.

1. The circumstances in which a cyber operation occurs may be very useful in determining whether it meets the criteria of a prohibited recourse to force. Cyber operations mainly fall into the category of low-intensity use of force, rendering it difficult to qualify them as a use of force. On this point, Rosalyn Higgins observes with regard to the 'degree of force':

> However, the degree of force used is a relevant factor in its own right, to be considered in any comprehensive analysis – for, if the Charter places the burden of the proof on that state which resorts to force to prove that it is acting justifiably, then a fortiori, any massive-scale measure raises a presumption of unlawfulness. Violence of a less intense nature may still prove a relevant factor when taken together with other circumstances.

No country or foreign organisation has ever done something in cyberspace that was a clear threat or use of force. This is because most computer attacks up to this point have been pretty small. A lot of different things affect whether or not a cyber activity is qualified.

For example, the way the countries in question get along with each other could be a decision factor. When two states get along well with each other, the bar might be higher. On the other hand, if things are getting worse between two states, it might be easy to call a cyber operation a use of force. But states might decide not to do this to keep things from getting worse.

One of the most important things about the situation is whether a cyber operation is a single act or part of a bigger situation. A single act is less likely to be considered a use of force. Olivier Corten says, "States do not usually think of a single incident as a violation of the Charter's ban on the use of force, even if it involves an act that could be seen differently in a different situation." For example, a cyber action that is done in conjunction with other operations is more likely to be considered a use of cyber force.

Most cyber operations were done on their own, which may be why none of them counted as a use of force, even though they seemed to meet the standards of Article 2, paragraph 4.

2. The publicity about the cyber operation and what it did is another piece of circumstantial evidence or a contextual factor. Publicity can be linked to the "gravity" or "severity" criterion because it can change how the public sees the operation. It is important to separate the publicity of a coercive cyber activity and its effects from the general political and strategic interests of States.

I've said this before, but there's still a lot of confusion about how cyber activities fit into the law. Given how uncertain things are right now, and to avoid the limits and complexity of international law and gain some freedom, states may choose not to make a cyber operation public and not to call a low- or medium-intensity cyber operation a use of force.

There are three main reasons for this. First, just like private players, governments never admit and show their weaknesses. If they can, they might prefer to handle a cyber operation in the privacy of their military forces. Second, because there are no clear rules and qualifications for cyber operations, States may opt to use this "grey area of law," which lets them act based on their own wants and needs.

Third, putting limits on the use of force could make both sides use more force. With this in mind, States might be more ready to call large-scale cyber operations that cause serious damage a "use of force" if they cause a lot of damage. If cyber operations hurt a State's ability to defend itself online to the point where its ability to function or even its survival is at risk, the State might be more ready to make the cyber operations public in order to get help from the rest of the world. I think this kind of support would be even more likely if the people of the state were aware of what the hacking operation did. This claim is supported by the fact that the cyberattacks on Estonia in 2007 and the Stuxnet worm that messed up Iran's nuclear project had big effects on both countries and led them to talk to each other about these cyberattacks and their effects. It is interesting to note that in both cases, the question of whether or not the cyber operations were a use of force was thought about, but no ruling was made.

Stuxnet is probably an act of violence because it hurt people and things. People have said that it has the same effect as a bomb dropped from the sky. Reese Nguyen says it did the same kind of damage to the Iranian nuclear facility that Israeli air strikes did in 1981 and 2007 when they destroyed partly built reactors in Baghdad and Syria. But Iran didn't see it as a use of force, even though it didn't seem like a small thing. Instead, it decided to respond in secret by going after a Saudi company in cyberspace. In this way, it might be hard to say that Stuxnet was an act of force, because even if it caused real damage, it might not have been bad enough to meet the definition of violence in Article 2, paragraph 4. This can also be seen as a sign that some states have higher standards for cyber operations than for physical operations when it comes to how much damage they cause and whether or not they count as a use of force. Still, this doesn't change whether or not Stuxnet is a use of force. I think so, but only if States have the political chance and desire to call it that in public.

Conclusion about Cyber Operations and the Use of Force Ban

At this time, cyber activities that damage property, kill people, or hurt people are more likely to be seen as an illegal use of force. Stuxnet is one of the few cyber attacks that caused real damage in this way. It is also the most likely one to be seen as a use of force. But this conclusion has not been publicly backed by any State, even though a lot of study says it could be a use of force.

Cyberattacks on Estonia in 2007 messed up the country's operations in a dangerous way, but they did not threaten the country's life. Some people thought this might be an example of breaking the law by using force, but this idea was quickly shot down. It should be said, though, that it's too early to know if this reluctance is something the government has always done or if it's something new. All of the other times weren't bad enough to use force. This shows very clearly that only a small number of cyber activities count as a use of force. So, it might be more useful and productive to find a better set of rules that cover the vast majority of cyber operations.

Cyber Threat and Threat of Cyber Force

Article 2, line 4, of the UN Charter was important because it made it clear that both using force and threatening to use force were against the law.

In the other part, which talks about how jus contra bellum applies to cyber operations, "cyber force" was defined in international law, and it was shown that real cyber operations done by states would have a hard time meeting the requirements of the ban on the use of force. From the point of view of States or foreign organisations, no cyber operation has ever been a threat of force, just like when force was used.

Even though Article 2, Paragraph 4 ties the "threat of force" and the "use of force" together, the goal of this part is to separate and look into the "threat of force" separately from the "use of force." Article 2, line 4, of the UN Charter is mostly talked about in the literature when it comes to cyber operations. However, the threat of using cyber force gets little attention. This part tries to close this gap by looking at cyber activities between states in light of the second rule in Article 2, Paragraph 4 of the UN Charter, which says that the threat of force is not allowed. The main point of this part is that it is better to treat most cyberoperations between states as a threat of force than to try to do so at all costs. This argument will be backed up by two main kinds of threats to use force. One choice is to openly say that you will use force if you don't get what you want.

The language of the UN Charter makes it clear that this first type of danger of force is the clearest. Simply put, Article 2, paragraph 4 of the UN Charter is broken only when a country openly promises to use force against another country to get what it wants. On the other hand, it is also possible to use force to force the threatened state to make agreements.

The Prohibition of the Threat of Force

Article 2, Paragraph 4 of the UN Charter says that the "threat or use of force" is not allowed. However, neither the UN Charter nor its travaux préparatoires say what a threat of force is. But, as this part will show, this phrase does not cover every threat between states. The first part tries to give an overview of the parts of the law that make it illegal to use or threaten to use force that are important to remember for this study.

As a first thought, it's interesting to note that the UN Charter uses the word "threat" twice. In Article 2, line 4, it says that "threats of force" are not allowed, and in Article 39, it says that "danger to the peace" is not allowed. It is important to tell the difference between these two parts of the UN Charter.

The rule against using force and the rule against threatening to use force have a lot in common. First of all, the UN Charter has two exceptions to these rules that could make the threat or use of force legal: if it is used in self-defence (Article 51) or if the Security Council gives permission (Chapter VII). Second, the wording in Article 2, paragraph 4, which has customary weight, as well as "established practise" and opinio juris, confirm that it is a rule of customary international law that you can't threaten to use force. If its position as a custom is questioned, it is less likely to be a jus cogens. It is still hard to figure out the details of the rule that says you can't threaten to use force.

"Use" in the context of military force is pretty clear, but "threat" is still not clear, as James Crawford points out correctly. At the moment, there are only three examples, and they all come from the ICJ. In all of them, the danger of force is noted only by accident. In the first case, about the Corfu Channel, the ICJ suggested that using naval force to get a country to make political concessions might be an illegal use of force. In the second case, which was about Nicaragua, the International Court of Justice (ICJ) said that the US military exercises near Nicaragua's borders and the country's growing military were not a danger of force. In response to the last point, the Court said that there is no rule in international law that limits how much a state can arm itself. The advisory opinion on the validity of the threat or use of nuclear weapons is the most important of the three cases because it limits the use of force that is not allowed by law. The Advisory Opinion also says that having nuclear weapons is not a danger of force in and of itself.

The ICJ's case law can be described as "sparse" and "scattered," and there are some big differences between the different cases. The only case that gives a clear definition is the Advisory Opinion on the Legality of the Threat or Use of Nuclear Weapons. This means that the other cases don't help much and it's still hard to come up with a clear meaning. Also, since the UN Charter was passed, experts have stopped studying the threat of force and instead focus on the use of force itself. Because of this, academics can't agree on what the fear of force means. Some commentators argue for a broader approach that includes more situations where the threat of force is illegal. Others, on the other hand, argue for a narrower approach that follows the ICJ formula and limits the threat of force to the threat of the force that is illegal.

Cyber Threat of Force

When looking at the threat of force in the cyber domain, the first question that comes to mind is whether or not a cyber threat of force can go against what Article 2, line 4, of the UN Charter says you can't do. In other words, does it matter how a state threatens another? No is the clear answer. To break Article 2, line 4, a country must tell another country, in any way, that it is ready to use force against it. The warning can be made verbally or in writing, making it clear that the State is ready to use force, or it can be a show of force that shows it is ready to use force. A cyber threat of force is a threat of force that is sent through cyberspace. So, the threat can only spread through online, but that doesn't change what the threat is or how real it is. So, it doesn't matter if the threat is legal or not according to the UN Charter. A threat of force can be made orally or in writing and sent to the threatened state in different ways, such as by phone or email. It can also get out through the press, which today includes the press on the Internet. For example, in 2013, US Secretary of State John Kerry told Israel's Prime Minister Benjamin Netanyahu, "The threat of force is real." This meant that the US was prepared to do something about Syria. This message to Syria was partly a cyber threat to use force, since it didn't directly address any member of the Syrian Government. So, the threat reached the Syrian government through news stories about the meeting and a transcript of the meeting that was put on the website of the US Department of State.

The Prohibition of The Threat to Resort to Prohibited Force

The first kind of threat of force is an open threat of force meant to get someone to give up something. The text of the UN Charter makes this clear. Since Article 2, line 4, says that "threat or use of force" is not allowed, the first step is to figure out if the threat of force is a real threat of force that is against the law. The first type of cyber force threat will be looked at in the next two parts of this subsection. In the first part, we'll talk about the first type of threat of force, and in the second, we'll look at whether cyber operations count as open threats of force.

The ICJ's Formula

In its Advisory Opinion on the Legality of the Threat or Use of Nuclear Weapons, the ICJ said that it was only illegal to promise to use force when it was against the law. In other words, an illegal threat is a promise to use force if certain conditions are met, but using force itself is against the law. In paragraph 47 of the Advisory Opinion, this response to the threat of force is explained in more detail:

> In order to lessen or eliminate the risk of unlawful attack, States sometimes signal that they possess certain weapons to use in self-defence against any State violating their territorial integrity or political independence. Whether

a signalled intention to use force if certain events occur is or is not a 'threat' within Article 2, paragraph 4, of the Charter depends upon various factors. If the envisaged use of force is itself unlawful, the stated readiness to use it would be a threat prohibited under Article 2, paragraph 4. Thus, it would be illegal for a State to threaten force to secure territory from another State, or to cause it to follow or not follow certain political or economic paths. The notions of 'threat' and 'use' of force under Article 2, paragraph 4, of the Charter stand together in the sense that if the use of force itself in a given case is illegal – for whatever reason – the threat to use such force will likewise be illegal. In short, if it is to be lawful, the declared readiness of a State to use force must be a use of force that is in conformity with the Charter. For the rest, no State – whether or not it defended the policy of deterrence – suggested to the Court that it would be lawful to threaten to use force if the use of force contemplated would be illegal.

Ian Brownlie came up with this way of thinking about the fear of force in 1963. It's important to note that neither the Advisory Opinion nor the judges' opinions explain why this formula was picked. But the way the ICJ works is clear. If there was a picture, this formula might be easy to understand.

This kind of fear of force is best shown by an ultimatum. When State A makes a demand of State B and says that if State B refuses or doesn't meet the demand within a certain amount of time, State A will use force against State B, this is an example of an ultimatum as a threat of force. President George W. Bush gave a standard example in his speech on Iraq on March 17, 2003, at 8:01 p.m.

My fellow citizens, events in Iraq have now reached the final days of decision. For more than a decade, the United States and other nations have pursued patient and honorable efforts to disarm the Iraqi regime without war. [...] Many nations, however, do have the resolve and fortitude to act against this threat to peace, and a broad coalition is now gathering to enforce the just demands of the world. The United Nations Security Council has not lived up to its responsibilities, so we will rise to ours. [...] All the decades of deceit and cruelty have now reached an end. Saddam Hussein and his sons must leave Iraq within 48 hours. Their refusal to do so will result in military conflict, commenced at a time of our choosing. For their own safety, all foreign nationals, including journalists and inspectors, should leave Iraq immediately.

After the date for the ultimatum passed, President Bush said that Operation Iraqi Freedom would begin. This statement is a good example of a verbal threat to get a concession with a clear promise to use force if the threat isn't taken seriously.

Open Threat to Resort to Cyber Force

In cyber operations, a threat of cyber force only breaks the rule in Article 2, line 4, if it is the same as an illegal use of force in the same situation. This is the most popular method among students today, and Rule 70 of the Tallinn Manual 2.0 follows this method:

> A cyber operation, or threatened cyber operation, constitutes an unlawful threat of force when the threatened action, if carried out, would be an unlawful use of force.

Is a general threat to use force enough to get around the rule in Article 2, line 4 that says you can't? The clear answer is "yes." Most threats of violence, whether they are spoken or written, are vague and don't say what kind of violence could be used. For example, the threats of force in the two cases we've talked about so far—President Bush's order to Iraq and John Kerry's warning to Syria—were broad. They didn't say how much or what kind of force would be used. Most likely, the fear of force will stay pretty general, and cyber force will be one way that the threatening state could use force.

How online force is used as a threat will depend on the specifics of each case. How the State being threatened sees the danger and how serious it is will be very important. In fact, a threat of force is only a real threat if the state being attacked sees it as such. Nikolas Stürchler has done a lot of study on the use of threats of force, and he shows how important credibility is when deciding if a threat is legal or not. A threat of force is taken seriously if the state being threatened thinks it is serious and risky enough to be taken seriously. Two made-up cases can show how important it is to have a standard of credibility. First of all, Russia probably can't threaten to use force if it tells another post-Soviet country that it will use online force. In fact, Russia has already used cyber operations against Georgia and Estonia or has been accused of doing so. This shows how real the fear is. Also, the fact that Russia and some post-Soviet states have tense relationships makes it more possible that Russia will use force, even cyber force, against these states.

Second, a threat of cyber force may not be seen as a real threat of force in other cases. A threat to use cyber force against a country with a weak Internet system might not be taken seriously. In fact, the threat to use force might not have much of an effect on the State being attacked. It is important to remember that the opposite is not true. Even a country with few cyber powers might be able to do something very bad online, so its threat of cyber force might be taken seriously. A harmful cyber action is easy and cheap to plan and carry out these days. The cases above show how important the credibility criterion is and how it can change whether or not a cyber threat of force is a prohibited threat of force under the UN Charter.

There is one more thing to say about the possibility of using cyber force as an open threat computer force threats are not likely to happen because of how the computer operation is set up. Most cyber activities are successful because they take advantage of cyber weaknesses and use the element of surprise. When a certain infrastructure is threatened, the State that is threatened will look for and fix any holes in that infrastructure that could be used to attack it. From a similar point of view, a general threat to use cyber operations against a State would give that State time to protect its infrastructure and plan some possible technical countermeasures to stop the effects of the threat to use cyber force.

Demonstration of Cyber Force as a Prohibited Threat of Force

The second way to promise to use force is to show cyber force. The first way is to say openly that you will use force to get what you want. In study on the threat of cyber force, a demonstration of force is sometimes looked at, but it is usually ignored and not studied enough. What kind of show of force goes against the rule that says you can't promise to use force? A state's demonstration of force, on the other hand, is made up of deeds, not words.

There are many ways to show force, but the most common ones are military activities like sending in troops, doing drills, building up nuclear weapons, or testing them. These acts show that one country is willing to use force against another. As we talked about in the last part, most cyber operations don't count as a real use of force. But they could be a show of force that amounts to a threat of force that is against the law. To answer this question, we'll look at two types of cyber operations with important examples: the DDoS attacks on Estonia and Georgia and the computer worm that went after an Iranian nuclear plant.

Comprehensive DDoS Strikes as an Assertion of Strength

A DDoS attack is a cyber operation that uses a lot of requests from hacked systems to try to shut down a machine or network resource. Could such a large-scale DDoS attack be seen as a show of force? It seems that the answer is yes, but only in some cases. Large-scale DDoS strikes on Estonia and Georgia will be looked at to show and prove that this claim is true.

Before the Russo-Georgian War of 2008, Georgia had to deal with a number of cyberattacks that seemed to be done or paid for by Russia. Cyber activities kept going on during the war. Most of the cyber attacks on Georgia were DDoS strikes and changes to websites. Cyberattacks that change the look and content of a website are called "website defacements." Here, the focus is on cyber actions that took place before the war began. The main goal is to figure out if these acts could be seen as a threat of force or not. The Georgian government did not see these cyber activities as a threat or a use of force.

But the tense relationship between Georgia and Russia could have made any promise to use force seem real, so the term "threat of force" makes sense. Concerning the cyber operations, it's important to know that Georgia's Internet infrastructure isn't very well developed, and the country doesn't rely greatly on the Internet. Because of this, the cyber operations didn't have too many effects, and the major one was that the Georgian government couldn't use its websites to communicate. So, it may seem hard to say that there is a threat of force in this case. It's important to keep in mind that when the war started, everyone stopped thinking about this question.

The 2007 cyber crisis in Estonia is the second case. In April 2007, Estonia started to take down a metal statue of a Soviet soldier from World War II. A small group of people with Russian roots took to the streets to protest. At the same time, there were many cyber operations going on in the country, such as large-scale DDoS attacks on the websites and servers of private and public organisations. The Estonian government said the cyberattacks were done by Russia, but Russia said it had nothing to do with them. Estonia depends a lot on its computer system, which is very different from Georgia's. A lot of Estonia's business, media, and government stopped working because of the cyber operations.

Even though Estonia and other countries didn't see these cyber activities as a use or threat of force, they could be seen as a real threat of force. In fact, their effects made it harder for the country to respond to military action because the State was partly paralysed. Also, they happened when ties between the state being threatened and the state being threatened were tense, which made any threat of force more likely. Considering how things are, these cyber operations could be seen as moves that could lead to the use of force. Based on this claim, they could be seen as a show of force, which goes against Article 2, line 4, of the UN Charter, which says that threatening to use force is not allowed. Estonia shows that a large-scale DDoS attack against a country that depends on the Internet could be a threat of force. But the situation in Georgia shows how hard this test can be to use in some scenarios.

A Computer Worm causing Non-physical Damage as a Demonstration of Force

Now I'll talk about cyber operations that don't cause physical damage to the machine they're aimed at, so they don't count as a real use of force. I say that in some limited cases, they could be seen as a threat of force.

I'll use the story of Stuxnet, a computer worm that spread to many computers around the world and damaged centrifuges in an Iranian nuclear plant, to show how this could happen. Using this example as a guide, we can imagine malware that would have done the same thing, but instead of destroying the centrifuges, it might have just changed some data, deleted the software that runs the nuclear plant, or done something else that didn't cause damage. The effects of this malware would be to show the owner of the nuclear plant and, by extension, the State that the attacker has the ability to get into the system in question. It could also be a sign that the attacker is ready and able to do more damage. To make a promise of force, the person who did it would have to show that they were ready to use cyber force. Even if this is possible in theory, doing it in real life would not be a good idea. In fact, if the attacker state did that, it would show how it could get into the system it was going after. This would give the intended state the chance to fix the system and make sure it doesn't get broken into again. The attacking state would no longer be able to do anything else on that machine. So, if the attacking state wants to keep going on the same system, this kind of action wouldn't help. It could, however, choose to do it on a certain system if it wanted to use a different flaw to get further on another system.

Malware Causing Physical Disruption as a Symbolization of Strength

A cyber attack that causes real damage could be seen as both an act of force and a threat of force. Stuxnet could be seen as both a show of force and an act of force. This shows that the country that attacked is ready and willing to fight again.

The first thing to remember is that Stuxnet caused physical damage to an Iranian nuclear plant and that it worked within the borders of the country that was being struck. But nothing stops a threat of force from being a qualification if the action crosses the line of the threatened state. In 1996, a North Korean submarine ran into trouble and ended up on a beach in South Korea. South Korea saw this as an act of war. This could be a threat of force even if it happened on the soil of the victim State. Could it be a sign that the people who made it are ready to use force against Iran? For the following reasons, the answer to this question is "yes": First, the U.S. and Israel thought it was an attempt to slow down and change Iran's nuclear project. So, it could be seen as a show of force by the US and Israel against Iran to show that they are ready to use force if Iran continues to ignore their requests. Now we need to talk about situations that look like a show of force but don't really amount to an illegal threat of force.

Military Exercises

Shows of force are not the same as military drills. Military drills, whether they happen inside or outside a country's borders, are usually announced ahead of time so that they aren't seen as a real threat of force or as a step towards using force. If a country doesn't tell other countries about a military drill, those other countries might see it as a real threat of force. In November 1983, for example, NATO held a military nuclear drill called "Able Archer." Because the military drill wasn't shared with other countries ahead of time, the Soviet Union thought it was a real plan for a nuclear attack and put its forces, including fighters with nuclear weapons, on high watch.

After the practise, things went back to how they were before. Still, a country's strength can also be shown through military drills. For example, before the 2008 Russo-Georgian War, both the US and Russia held military drills in the area that could be seen as a show of force, showing that they were ready to use force if they had to.

Cyber military drills are different from other types of training for the military. There are military drills that can be seen, like putting troops in place, doing manoeuvres, or testing weapons. These can be mistaken for threats of force. But when cyber military drills happen, other states can't see or find anything that could be misinterpreted as a threat of force. There could be strange things going on at military sites, but nothing like a fleet deployment or testing of weapons. So, there is a very small or almost non-existent chance that cyber military drills will be misunderstood as a real threat of force.

Lastly, it's important to note that general military preparation is not a threat of force as long as it's not done with the goal to use force in a specific way. We wonder if a state's use of cyber powers can be seen as a threat to use force because there is a difference between getting ready to use force and threatening to use force. To answer this question, we can look at how nuclear weapons and other nuclear warfare technologies are made.

In earlier parts of this section on the danger of force, the different ways cyber force can be used as a threat were shown and questioned. In this part, the goal is the opposite: to show that building cyber capabilities is not a forbidden use of force. Commentators and people from all over the world have given this question a lot of thought. They have tried to explain how the creation of certain weapons and the arming of states could be seen as a threat of force or a threat to peace. In this way, nuclear weapons are a very important case. Some countries think that having nuclear weapons and using them to stop other countries from getting them is a threat of force that is against the law.

The ICJ looked at this question in its Advisory Opinion on the Legality of the Threat or Use of Nuclear Weapons. Article 2, line 4, of the UN Charter says that it is against the law to make a threat just because someone has nuclear weapons or is trying to stop someone else from getting them.

Whether or not this is a "threat" in violation of Article 2, paragraph 4, depends on whether the use of force in question would be used against the territorial integrity or political independence of a state, or against the purposes of the United Nations, or whether, if it were meant as a defence, it would necessarily violate the principles of necessity and proportionality.

So, building up nuclear weapons might not be enough on its own to be considered a threat of force. 223 When it comes to Iran and North Korea, their nuclear military projects are not a threat. Instead, it comes from Iran and North Korea's real threats against other countries. In the Nicaragua case, the ICJ came up with a more general rule about how states can build their armies: there is no rule in general international law that says how many guns a state can have. So, the same conclusion can be made about building up cyber weapons, which does not always mean that force is being threatened. The US, for example, made a plan called "Olympic Games" to improve its cyber skills. This plan by itself can't be seen as a threat to use force. On the other hand, using this plan to do cyber operations against other states could be seen as a threat or use of cyber force.

This part said that for current inter-state cyber operations, the qualification as a threat of force might be better than the qualification as a real use of force. The third part of this section shows that some cyber operations can be open threats of cyber force, even though it also shows that open threats of cyber force should not be used. The best way to keep track of all the different kinds of cyber activities seems to be to qualify them as a cyber force demonstration.

Cyber operations that used to be called real uses of cyber force or open threats of cyber force are now hard to classify. On the other hand, this part showed that a few examples could be seen as illegal demonstrations of force.

Cyber Armed Attack and Cyber Aggression

Only when cyber operations reach the level of a "armed attack" does the victim State have the right to protect itself. The customary right to self-defence is protected by Article 51 of the UN Charter, and the ICJ has talked about it in a number of cases and advisory decisions. "Armed attack" is not defined in the UN Charter. In this piece, I try to explain what a "cyber armed attack" is by looking at when a cyber operation can be called an attack.

The UN Charter uses the words "force," "aggression," and "armed attack" to talk about the different ways people use force and what happens when they do. Article 2, line 4, says it is against the law to threaten or use "force." Article 39 says that it is the Security Council's job to decide if there is a threat to the peace, a breach of the peace, or a "act of aggression," which could lead to the adoption of steps that could or could not involve the use of force. Lastly, Article 51 says that the right to self-defence only applies when there is a "armed attack." What do these three ways of using force have in common? Most people agree that they have a "cascading relationship" with each other. Armed attack is a form of violence, and aggression is a form of force. Armed attack is a type of aggression that is more specific than just violence itself. But none of these words are defined in the UN Charter.

Also, the UN Charter is written in different ways in different languages, which can lead to some misunderstanding. The ratione materiae condition for the right to self-defence is an armed attack, which is called a "armed aggression" in English and a "armed attack" in French. People didn't know if the word "agression armée" meant an attack with weapons or just being mean.

In the Nicaragua case, the ICJ said that neither the UN Charter nor treaty law say what an armed attack is. In its Advisory Opinion on nuclear weapons, the Court said that the UN Charter's rules about using force "apply to any use of force, no matter what weapons are used." So, there is no reason why cyber activities couldn't be used to attack with weapons. Some cyber activities may be an illegal use of force, an act of aggression, or even an attack with weapons. This is what the states and the books on cyber operations and international law say. But it's important to remember that neither a country nor the international community has said "unambiguously and publicly" that a cyber operation has hit the level of an armed attack.

In Nicaragua v. Uganda and Uganda v. DRC, the ICJ used Article 3(g) of the "Definition of Aggression" from the UN General Assembly to decide if there had been an armed attack. 234 On December 14, 1974, the UN General Assembly passed Resolution 3314 (XXIX), which defines what it means to be hostile. 235 This decision does not have any legal force. It can only help the Security Council figure out if Article 39 of the UN Charter has been broken, which is an act of war. 236 "Aggression is the most serious and dangerous kind of illegal use of force," says the beginning of the definition of aggression. The first part of the definition of aggression says, "Aggression is the use of armed force by a State against the sovereignty, territorial integrity, or political independence of another State, or in any other way that is not in line with the Charter of the United Nations, as set out in this Definition."

Also, Article 3 says what is called an act of aggression. Article 3, paragraphs (a), (b), (d), and (g), are often seen as acts of aggression that are also armed strikes.

They are:

a. The invasion or attack by the armed forces of a State on the territory of another State, or any military occupation, no matter how short, that results from such an invasion or attack, or any annexation by the use of force of the territory of another State or a part of it;

b. The bombardment of the territory of another State by the armed forces of a State or the use of any weapons by a State against the territory of another State;

c. An attack by the armed forces of one state on the land, sea, or air forces or marine and air fleets of another state;

d. The sending by or on behalf of a State of armed bands, groups, irregulars, or mercenaries who use armed force against another State in a way that is serious enough to be considered one of the above acts, or the State's significant involvement in these actions.

We wonder if there is a gap between the ideas of force, violence, and armed attack because of how they build on each other. More specifically, are there illegal ways to use force that don't count as armed attacks? In the Nicaragua case, the ICJ recognised that there was a gap by making a difference between "the most serious forms of the use of force (those that amount to an armed attack) and other less serious forms." About whether or not this gap exists, international law is very split. Some places, like the United States, and some pieces of writing see the use of force as the same as an attack with weapons. Because of this, they say that when force is used, the right to self-defence is immediately triggered. In the same way, almost all of the experts working on the Tallinn Manual 2.0 agree that there is a gap. Both the states and the experts agree that there is a gap, but they don't agree on how big it is.

The latest book agrees with what most people think, which is that there is a gap, so only the most serious kinds of cyber force can count as a cyber-armed attack. For instance, a cyber operation that causes real damage is an example of the use of cyber force. strikes with little damage would not be considered cyber-armed strikes. For example, a hacking operation that caused one smartphone to overheat and break wouldn't count. So, since the cyber operation was against the law, the only thing the victim state could do was take steps. It was not able to use its right to defend itself. Some states and experts say that an armed attack and the use of force are the same thing. If they are, I think that in both cases, the higher bar of an armed attack should be used.

Whether or not a cyber operation is an attack rests on its "scale and effects." There are two parts to this standard: the "scale" and the "effects." The "scale" refers to how big and bad the cyber operation was (how much force was used, where it happened, and how long it went on for). The "effects" refer to the damage and deaths caused by the cyber attack. When it comes to cyber tactics, it might not always be clear if these two conditions are met. For example, DDoS strikes like the ones that hit Estonia in 2007 are likely to meet the scale criterion, since the Estonia attacks were big and powerful. But it doesn't look like they will meet the effects condition, since the attacks on Estonia didn't do much. How results are measured in cyber operations needs to be worked on more.

Cyber Operations and Their Effects

Depending on what happens, cyber operations can be put into two groups: those with physical effects (injury, loss of life, damage or destruction of property, etc.) and those with only non-physical effects (disruption, change, or destruction of data). Before getting into detail about the different effects, it's important to ask which effects should be taken into account.

Because computer networks are tied to each other, cyber operations can easily have important side effects and damage other networks. For example, on January 25, 2003, the Slammer worm246 used a weakness in Microsoft SQL Server to infect thousands of computers around the world in less than 15 minutes. The worm's goal was to attack the system memory and then look for other hosts to infect. It didn't take over the machine or change the information on the hard drive. Slammer was a big problem. For example, it slowed down and broke Internet links in a number of countries, shut down thousands of Bank of America ATMs, and stopped Continental Airlines' ticketing system, which caused the company to cancel several flights. Slammer also broke into the computer system at the Davis-Besse nuclear power plant in the United States. This stopped the Safety Parameter Display System from working as it should. Good news is that the outbreak of the system at the nuclear plant did not cause any damage. In this case, we can see how a computer worm had affects that had nothing to do with its goal of spreading over the Internet. The Tallinn Manual 2.0 says that all of the cyber operation's effects that could be expected to happen do qualify.

This good ending is also used in this book. I think this standard should be clear to everyone. For example, if someone tries to target and mess with a city's power grid, the damage, injuries, and deaths that could happen should be seen as fairly expected. In the same way, a flight crash caused by a problem with the air traffic control system should be seen as something that was likely to happen.

Cyber Operations Having Physical Consequences

Most of the time, cyber operations that hurt or kill people or damage or destroy property are seen as a use of force, and the worst ones may even be seen as hitting the level of an attack with weapons. The next question is if there is a limit to gravity or not. In other words, if a cyber operation caused damage, destruction of property, injury, or death, it would be called a cyber armed attack. This question makes you wonder how different a cyber-armed attack and the use of cyber force are. As was said above, a cyber action that kills, hurts, or causes damage is a clear example of the use of cyber force. People argue about this outside of online as well. For example, the ICJ said that armed strikes were the most serious use of force, but it thought that "the mining of a single military vessel might be enough to bring into play the "inherent right of self-defence." Cyber operations that hurt, hurt or kill people could be considered armed attacks, but only if the effects are bad enough. To meet the "effects" requirement, it seems possible that a cyber operation should have a certain level of bad physical effects. In the case of Stuxnet, you could make a case for both sides. You could say that it hit the intensity threshold, but it's more likely that it stayed below this threshold. If you only looked at how Stuxnet worked, I think it would be a use of force but not an attack. But because it was aimed at a nuclear plant, it is more dangerous and likely to be seen as an attack. The Tallinn Manual 2.0 talks about whether or not it could be called an attack with weapons because it hurt several centrifuges. It says that "some members of the International Group of Experts were of the opinion that the operations had reached the armed attack threshold (unless they could be justified on the basis of anticipatory self-defence (Rule 73)" So far, the only cyber operation that had major effects that the public knows about is Stuxnet. This shows that most cyber operations are probably not armed strikes. It does not, however, rule out the chance that a future cyber operation with serious effects could be seen as an armed attack.

Cyber Operations Having Only Non-Physical Consequences

Can disrupting, changing, or destroying data, which has no physical affects, be thought of as an armed attack? This is a tougher and more divisive question. Several countries chose to leave such options open in their cyber strategy, so they think that cyber operations that don't have any physical effects may sometimes be the same as an attack with weapons. Even if the information taken is secret military information, it is not the same as an armed attack because no one is killed or hurt right away and no property is damaged or destroyed. The theft by itself is not enough of an effect to meet the standards for the word "effects." Most critics agree with this, but some say that stealing information is likely to be an armed attack because it is important to national security.

In theory, cyber operations with serious effects that aren't physical but are still very bad could be the same as an armed attack in some very specific cases.

Accumulation of Cyber Operations short of an Armed Attack

A State may be the target of a number of cyber operations that cross the line into the use of force in some situations. But each act by itself wouldn't be enough to count as a weapon attack. The "accumulation of events" theory, also called the "pin-prick" theory or "Nadelstichtaktik," explains how to deal with these kinds of situations. This theory says that if you look at each event separately, they don't add up to an armed attack, but when you look at them all together, they do. In the Nicaragua case, the ICJ was asked if incursions "may be treated for judicial purposes as amounting, singly or collectively, to a "armed attack." This made this idea possible. And it's possible that both the Oil Platforms case and the Congo v. Uganda case took a similar method. The accumulation of events theory says that putting together small things can help you figure out if someone is trying to attack you with a weapon. This seems to be widely accepted as a way to use your right to self-defence, even though it is not without debate. Most study on cyber operations and cyber defence supports this theory because it would make it possible to handle multiple cyber operations at once.

To get the most out of cyber operations, they can sometimes be done at the same time against various targets. Several government and private groups were attacked at the same time during the cyber operations against Estonia in 2007. In these cases, the accumulation of events theory makes it possible to take into account the fact that the ongoing attack is made up of several cyber operations. This lets us figure out the best way to react based on what we now know. Also, as we've seen, most cyber operations that cross the line into the use of force may not be armed attacks. The only way to know for sure may be to look at them all at once. But the theory of the accumulation of events can only be used in certain cases because it's important to think about whether or not a single event is a use of force.

Perpetrator of the Armed Assault

When a state moves in a certain way that has a certain size and effect, that is almost always an armed attack. From a traditional point of view, an armed attack is when one state uses violence against another state and the amount of violence is high. There is no clear explanation of what an armed attack is, and no word of who might be behind it. This could be because, in 1945, it was clear that only a state could use this much force against another state. But in the past 50 years, many non-state players have come on the scene with the ability to do things that have the same effects and scale as an armed attack, especially in the context of decolonization and international terrorism. This change lead to a discussion about what makes an attack with weapons and whether the actions of a non-state actor could be considered an attack with weapons in the sense of the UN Charter.

In light of this change, it is important to find out if the non-state player works for a State or not. In other words, it is important to find out if a state can be blamed for the acts of a non-state actor. After a long time of doctrinal discussion and hesitance,267 it is now accepted that behaviour of a non-state actor that can be traced back to a state can be seen as an armed attack by the state that paid for it. When non-state actors do things that can be linked to a state and meet the conditions for an armed attack, this is an armed attack on behalf of the state that backs them. So, the State that was attacked has the right to use its right to self-defence against the State that started the attack. So, actions by a state or a non-state actor that can be linked back to a state can be seen as an armed attack by the state that did or paid for the actions. Most people think that an attack with weapons must be done by a government or on its behalf. The second question that isn't answered is whether or not an armed attack is the same as the actions of a non-state agent that can't be blamed on a state. In other words, if a non-state actor attacks with arms, does this give the state that was attacked the right to defend itself against this non-state actor? Article 2, paragraph 4, says that states can't use force. So, under the UN Charter, "use of force" means only actions taken by a state or actions that can be put on a state. Article 51, on the other hand, says nothing about who might be behind a violent attack.

One important movement in the literature is to look at armed attacks that don't just come from States but can also come from non-state actors that can't be tied to a State. So, in this broad view of what an armed attack is, a State could be the victim of an armed attack and could use its right to self-defence against another State or a non-state actor. In this case, non-state players could be attacked as a form of self-defence. Article 51 of the UN Charter could be seen as either allowing or forbidding self-defence against non-state players. The 9/11 terrorist attacks in 2001 and America's actions against terrorist groups in self-defence have given this idea some support in real life. In two cases decided after 9/11, the Wall Advisory Opinion and Congo v. Uganda, the International

Court of Justice (ICJ) has been hesitant to apply the idea of an armed attack to actions by non-state actors who are not acting on behalf of a state. But both State practise and UN Security Council practise seem to be moving in the direction of expanding the idea of an armed attack to include acts by non-state actors who are not working for a State. In 2015, France was hit by a number of terrorist strikes. Then, it was thought that France's military activities in Syria against Daesh were a way to protect itself from these attacks. The discussion isn't over, and it can't be said for sure if the right to self-defence has grown to include attacks by non-state actors who can't be linked to a state. So, according to positive international law, an armed attack must be done by or on behalf of a State. But it seems likely that international law will change over the next few decades to include armed activity by non-state actors so that it can be called an armed attack, especially since large-scale terrorist attacks are becoming more common.

In the cyber world, it might be hard to figure out how the non-state actor who did the damage is linked to the claimed sponsoring state. In the cyber world, it might seem like a good idea to include threats from non-state players in the right to self-defence. But this is a very dangerous slope that needs a lot of careful thought. The experts who worked on the Tallinn Manual 2.0 had different ideas about this, but most of them thought that non-state players also have the right to self-defence.

In the end, a cyber operation done by a state or by a non-state player on behalf of a state could be seen as an attack by the state with weapons. Under international law, cyber actions done by non-state actors without the help of a state cannot be seen as an armed attack at this time. But the law could change in the future to include armed attacks by non-state players who are not working for a state.

The Target of The Armed Attack

Armed attacks usually happen when the military of one country crosses into the land of another country. Can arms from outside a country be used to attack it? For example, does an attack on the interests of a country or on its people who live in another country count as an armed attack? The answer rests on what the target is and if it is a "external manifestation of the State" for the purpose of the right to self-defence. In other words, there needs to be a difference between State bodies and other groups and people first. Any cyberattack on a state organ that is based outside the country could be seen as an armed attack on the State.

Most people think that State organs are a way for the State to show itself to the outside world and protect itself. There is some disagreement in the writings about whether this is true for all State organs or if there needs to be a difference. Article 51 of the UN Charter makes it clear that armed units and installations outside of the country are "external manifestations of the State." Most of the time, weapons from outside a country's borders are used to attack these kinds of units and sites. So, any attack on them that is big enough and has enough effects to be called an armed attack would count as an armed attack on the intended State, giving it the right to defend itself. So, any cyber operation that goes after the computers and computer networks used by military units and sites outside of the country could also be seen as an armed attack. For example, an armed attack would be a cyberattack on the computer system on board a military plane that was going outside its country's airspace and caused it to crash. The situation with embassies and foreign envoys is more controversial, even though most people agree that hostile actions against them can sometimes be just as bad as an armed attack.

Most people think that embassies are a way for a country to show itself to the rest of the world and protect its right to defend itself. So, if we think that an attack on an embassy could be called an armed attack if it's big enough and has enough of an effect, then the same would be true of cyber-attacks on the computers and networks of an embassy. Also, it has been said that an attack on a foreign envoy while he or she is abroad could be seen as an armed attack. But this kind of attack might not be called an armed attack because it might not be very serious.

Can a cyber operation that targets a State's business interests or the interests of its citizens living abroad be called an armed attack on a State? Most people agree, but it can be argued, that an attack on civilians, ships, or planes can be seen as an armed strike, giving the flag State the right to self-defence. So, a cyberattack on the navigation system of a passenger plane that causes it to crash could be seen as an armed attack on the country where the plane is registered. As the Internet and computer networks grow, the server centre could be used as a new target. For example, if a cyber operation by State C against a server cluster owned by a company in State A or by State A itself and located in State B is serious enough, can it be called an armed attack on State A? The answer seems to be no. But since State B's computers are on its land, it may be an armed attack on State B, and the cyber operation may be a serious use of force on State B's land.

Cyber espionage against foreign military groups and sites, embassies and diplomatic envoys, and other State or private interests abroad is very common these days. When a country that wants to spy on other countries breaks into systems, it may be breaking international law. There is no doubt that cyber operations that only spy and gather information can't reach the level of intensity needed to be called an armed attack.

Cyber Operations Targeting Critical Infrastructures

"Critical infrastructures" have been talked about for a long time. It means infrastructures, assets, or systems that a state thinks are important for keeping society running or that could pose a major risk to the population. As we saw when looking at the use of force, the fact that a cyber operation is aimed at a critical infrastructure doesn't immediately make it a use of force and a fortiori an armed attack, but it may be the deciding factor. Stuxnet was an act of force because it broke and destroyed some centrifuges in an Iranian nuclear plant. But it's not clear if its size and effects were enough to count as an attack with weapons. Now, if we add that it attacked, damaged, and messed up the operation of a nuclear plant, which is generally thought of as critical infrastructure, this is likely to tip the scales in favour of Stuxnet being a cyber-armed attack. More generally, cyber operations that use force but don't amount to an armed attack because of their size and effects are more likely to be seen as armed attacks if they target key infrastructures. This is not a requirement, though, and not all cyber operations that target critical infrastructures would meet this criterion. When cyber activities only have digital effects, like stopping or destroying data, it's harder to figure out what happened. Cyber operations that have no physical results are less likely to be a use of force and even less likely to be an attack with weapons. Does the fact that they're going after important systems change this conclusion? When it comes to using force, the answer is "yes." This means that what counts as the use of force may depend on the type of target. I wouldn't call it an attack with guns so easily. But there is nothing that would stop such a licence, and the state could use it. It's important to keep in mind that cyberattacks on key infrastructures are likely to cause physical damage. For instance, a cyber operation that messes with a country's air traffic control system is likely to cause deaths, injuries, and damage.

In short, the size and effects of a cyber operation should be judged by what kind of target it is and, more specifically, whether or not it is a key infrastructure. In some cases, whether or not a cyber operation is a cyber-armed attack may depend on whether or not the target is a vital infrastructure.

Conclusion regarding Cyber Armed Attack

Most cyber activities are not likely to be an attack with weapons, let alone a use of force in the sense of the UN Charter. On the other hand, some cyber operations that are very big and have a lot of consequences may be like a military attack.

This part looked at when a cyber activity is considered an attack with weapons. It showed that the bar is very high and that most cyber activities will never be able to reach it.

Conclusion

Most of this part was about cyber operations and just war. It looked at whether cyber operations can reach and cross the three limits of jus contra bellum, which are the use of force, the fear of force, and an armed attack. No country or foreign group has ever called a cyber operation a use of force or an attack with weapons in a clear and public way. On the other hand, this chapter showed that cyber activities can sometimes be the same as using force, threatening to use force, or even attacking with arms. The result is that most of the things the government does online don't meet the rules. So, they shouldn't be looked at through the jus contra bellum rule.

Chapter 7
Currency Warfare and Cyber Warfare

As part of its military operation against the Islamic State of Iraq and Syria (ISIS), the US sent in Cyber Command to "weaken and eventually destroy" ISIS. This is the first time a government has admitted in public that it has used offensive cyber powers against an enemy while at war. At the same time, the United States was also fighting aggressively against the Islamic State's money. As part of Operation Inherent Resolve, the US is going after the Islamic State's money, both physically with air strikes and electronically with attacks on its banking infrastructure and maybe even its bitcoin holdings. Even though there isn't a lot of information, the fact that ISIS's finances are one of U.S. Cyber Command's goals is a big deal. Not only is it a big deal for military history, but it's also a big deal for currency warfare, which is an old form of war that isn't well understood. As part of a military operation, this author says that currency warfare is the use of monetary or military force against the monetary power of an enemy. The goal of this study is to look into what cyber warfare means for currency warfare at the strategic, operational, and tactical levels.

The main point of this article is that cyber capabilities, or cyber warfare, which is defined as "offensive capabilities in cyberspace to gain and keep the initiative," offer a new way to target currencies. This is because money transactions have changed from being done in person to being done online. But cyberwarfare doesn't change the main strategy goal of currency warfare, which is to subvert the enemy from the inside by using force. Cyberwarfare also doesn't change the operational goals of currency warfare, which are to stop the enemy from getting war money and government authority.

There are, of course, important ways in which cyber warfare and currency warfare "share ideas and methods." For example, both have the benefit of being anonymous, which makes it hard to tell which targets are military and which are civilian. Both also have the potential to take advantage of weaknesses caused by technology advances in more modern and wealthy countries that depend more and more on information networks. But my job here isn't to look for overlaps. Instead, I want to look at how cyber skills (also called cyber power and cyber warfare), a new technology that is being used more and more by the military, affects the cost of war from a financial point of view.

This study helps us learn more about how currency warfare is changing because money is becoming more and more digital and because cyber-warfare can now be used to target monetary power during armed battles. This investigation is being looked at from the point of view of a financial war, which has several benefits. One of these benefits is that it gives people a point of reference for figuring out how new cyber powers change or don't change the way wars are fought. Also, because this study is based on money, it is possible to talk about and evaluate currency combat, which is not very well known but has been around as long as war itself, but whose rules might be changing. This is a natural choice, since military campaigns have been aimed at enemy currencies for a long time, long before cyber power. The following questions are what led to this study: Because of online power, has the way currency wars are planned changed? Is cyberwarfare the same as currency war, or is it a completely different thing? Should we expect cyberspace to be used more to attack currencies and financial systems during armed conflicts? How does using cyber warfare to target currencies fit into combined operations at the strategic and practical levels of military strategy?

The argument here is that cyber-warfare capabilities add to and provide a new way to fight currency wars at the tactical level, but don't change the strategic or operational goals and motivations of traditional currency wars. This is clear in the 2008 Russo-Georgian War, the ongoing Russo-Ukrainian conflict (which is still going on), and the war against the Islamic State (which is also still going on).

A plan is the way in which means are used to reach certain goals. Without a plan to guide how force is used, force itself has no purpose other than to cause fear. Currency combat is hard to understand because there isn't much strategic thought about it beyond how it affects the economy. Economic warfare, which is related to currency warfare, often sees economic results as an end in and of themselves, rather than as a means to a strategic end. This is different from the strategic motivations behind economic warfare tools and methods. Strategy is different from what the goals of a fight are. Clausewitz was right when he said, "No one starts a war, or rather, no one in his sense should start a war, without first being clear in his mind what he wants to get out of the war and how he plans to fight it." Currency warfare is a unique type of war that military leaders can use to achieve the political goals of their country.

Currency warfare is based on a plan of subversion, which means to weaken the enemy from the inside. Currency warfare has the ability to do a lot of damage because it strikes at the heart of state sovereignty. It affects a state's political, military, and civilian parts by going after its money. Because of this, currency warfare has usually been used as a way to change the mood of the enemy under the cover of psychological warfare or covert operations.

The goal of currency warfare at the operational level is what I call "denial of war finance." Denial of war finance means going after an opponent's wealth, which is measured by its currency holdings, financial assets, and institutions, as well as its access to its wealth or potential wealth through taxes, loans, and credit. If currency warfare is successful, it will hurt both the military and the government. Paying for troops, supplies, and weapons will be harder, and the military may lose morale, which could lead to surrender or people leaving the army. On a political level, the stress on citizens caused by their money losing its buying power will put more pressure on the legitimacy of the warring state.

When cyber powers are added, they affect how currency wars are fought at the tactical level. Currencies are weak by nature, and they can be struck with a wide range of tools and strategies. Monetary methods include making fake money, making rival fiat (paper) currencies, using negative language to question the value or legitimacy of money, and changing the value of a currency by changing exchange rates. Traditional military power can also be used to go after currencies, as the air strikes against the Islamic State's cash storage sites have shown. Cyber skills offer a new way to wage currency war by giving the enemy new, fast, and mostly anonymous ways to attack their wealth. Other methods of currency warfare, like counterfeiting, used to need to be close by, but cyber skills have made that less important. This means that currencies can now be attacked from anywhere in the world.

This part goes on like this: Part I talks about how currencies are changing and how cyber skills (also called cyber power and cyber warfare) are being used more and more in modern wars. This is followed by an academic discussion of what money is and how it affects the security of a state at war, as well as an explanation of what currency warfare is and how it works. Part II is a study of three recent crises and one that is still going on in which cyber power has been used against a country's currency and financial institutions. The focus is on the strategic and operational levels of analysis to figure out how cyber weapons affect currency combat.

Emerging currency-cyber conflicts

In the past few decades, there has been a big change in how coins and money have been used in the past. Financial institutions, the free flow of capital, and business transactions have become more and more dependent on the internet and information networks for their day-to-day operations. This has brought huge benefits to people and increased economic activity across societies. But along with the perks of new technologies come new risks. The problem is that "with financial systems, the risk is that no one fully understands the weak spots and how actions can have ripple effects that lead to a crash." Paper money was made possible by the printing press, which made business easier. However, it was also easy to make fake paper money with the printing press. It shouldn't be a surprise that states are now catching up when it comes to using cyber power against the financial and monetary systems of their enemies that depend on networks.

If you look at the current research on cyberwarfare, you can see that cyber capabilities offer new ways to think about and understand old security concerns. Scholars of cyber war have asked important questions about the effects of the "proliferation of cyberwarfare capabilities on the nature and frequency of war" and shown that cyber-war operations can be used in a wide range of areas that are important to defense. Among the most important studies are ones about how cyberwar affects competition between big powers, nuclear deterrence, the war against ISIS, and how "network dependency" affects modern armies. The depth of these studies shows that cyberwar tactics can be used in a lot of different ways in both war and coercive diplomacy.

But students of money, cyberwar, and national security haven't looked into how cyberwarfare could affect currency warfare. When questions about money and currencies are looked into, they are generally grouped into a wide range of areas that can be hacked or used in cyberwarfare. Because of this, there aren't any unique strategic factors for how cyber power can affect and help currency warfare. This is scary because using cyber tools to attack financial institutions is becoming a common way to use force in both negotiation and war.

In response to Stuxnet, an American cyberattack on Iran's nuclear program, the Iranians attacked American banks like Bank of America with "some of the largest denial of service attacks ever seen." As a result, "websites were flooded with so many requests that they were overwhelmed," and "some banks" even went offline for a short time as they tried to figure out how to deal with the attacks. Richard Clarke, a well-known cyber and security expert, said, "I think the message from Tehran to the United States is: What if we did the wipe-out hit on American banks? We could do a lot of damage to the U.S. banking system." Also, it is no longer just a theory that a government's finances, including its currency, can and will be attacked by cyber power during armed wars. This is now a fact. Cyberwarfare has already been used to fight over money in three conflicts in the early 21st century: the 2008 Russo-Georgian War, the ongoing Russo-Ukrainian conflicts, and the American operation against ISIS. As global finance becomes more digital and automated and as the motivation to go after someone else's finances grows, it is very important to think strategically about how currency warfare and cyberwarfare will work together in the future.

Monetary Power

Why do countries fight over money, and why does it matter for how wars are fought? As will be shown, currency warfare is an old and unique type of war, but it's hard to study because it's hard to define what monetary power is and because it's not like other kinds of war. It's in between economics and other kinds of military force. Because of these two things, the study of currency fighting doesn't have a good place to live. To understand currency combat, you need to know what money is and how it works in relation to states and governments. It also needs to look at the background, strategy, and tactics of how traditional military and new forms of force, like cyber power, use money as a weapon and target it as part of military operations.

Seigniorage is the main gain that states get from making their own currency. Kenneth Rogoff says that seigniorage is "the government's total profit from printing money, including both the inflation tax and the monopoly rents earned by meeting higher real demand." Governments have known for a long time how important it is to be able to make acceptable ways to trade, and therefore wealth. There are two reasons for making money: The first is that it serves a purpose, which is to lower transaction costs and make the economy stronger. It also helps pay for government tasks like building roads, paying bureaucrats, and so on. The second goal is to make sure that people care more about the state and have stronger ties to it. Currencies connect the people directly to their leaders. Changes in the purchasing power of a currency will have both material and psychological effects on a government's ability to wage war and keep its legitimacy in the eyes of its people. This is because currencies can't be separated from the governments that make and use them. It is important for a government to be able to collect taxes and give and get credit in order to wage war.

Plain and simple, it's hard to fight a war, especially a long one, if you don't have enough money to pay for weapons, supplies, and troops. It is very important that there is a link between "financial and military power" and combat results.

Money is a key part of a country's ability to fight and win wars and to show power. Because of this, "states and their leaders are very careful about how their money is used." But being able to fight wars also rests on how much the people back the government. Because of the way governments and their people interact socially, there is always some thought given to what the people think and whether or not they agree with the wars being fought. As a result, "how people experience the financial costs of war affects how they feel about war and the set of rules that leaders have to follow when they lead a conflict." So, based on a country's financial system and wealth, governments have many ways to get money, such as taxation and borrowing, but they will choose the method that will cost the people the least. This, in turn, makes the leaders of warring states more vulnerable because it makes it harder for their people to get money, which could lead to a lot of anger and a loss of legitimacy for the warring government.

When talking about currency warfare, however, we must ask what exactly is being attacked and why scholars and politicians seem to use the terms currency, monetary, and financial power interchangeably. A.H. Quiggin once said, "Everyone except an economist knows what the word'money' means, and even economists can explain it in the course of a chapter or so." Even though this could be taken as a dig at economists, it's a good reminder that money, which seems like the simplest thing in the world, is actually a very complicated and malleable thing. Felix Martin says that, at its most basic level, "money is a system of credit accounts and their clearing, which is what currency represents." As part of this bigger system of accounting, currencies move money from one place to another and make it easy to trade goods and services across borders and between people. But in the end, the system of accounting depends on the infrastructure of banks and other financial institutions, the legitimacy of the government, and the trust of the people who give it worth. Because of this, currency warfare is its own type of war, even though it is related to economic warfare. Economic warfare is more about the physical effects of economic deprivation, such as "trade sanctions, embargoes, and blockades." In the end, currency warfare is about trying to change how people feel about their country and how they think about it.

So, the ability to pay for wars and the ability of a government to keep an effective system for making and taking money can be important for fighting long, successful wars and keeping its legitimacy. For states, the safety of their financial system and currency, which is the main unit of trade and store of value, is at the heart of their sovereignty and ability to work as an independent state. Currencies can be a very bad thing for any government.

Framework of a Currency Conflict

After looking at why states participate in currency warfare from a financial point of view, we need to figure out what it means in a broader sense. This part looks at the rules of currency warfare and how to think about it in a general way. By doing this, we can show how money is used and targeted for political and military reasons, not economic ones. Also, having a good currency-warfare typology makes it easier to find cases to study and figure out how offensive cyber-capabilities change the way currency-warfare is used in modern wars.

As part of a military operation, the author says that currency warfare is the use of money or military force against the monetary power of an enemy. Currency warfare starts with the idea that monetary instruments are being militarized. This means that money is being used to support a war effort and that monetary instruments and practices (like exchange-rate manipulation, counterfeiting, rhetoric, and fiat currencies) are being thought of as weapons that can be used alone or in combination with other forms of offensive power, such as military power. Currency warfare happens when there are armed battles and is used to help a government reach its political and military goals. So, currency warfare is not the same as currency wars. Economists use the term "currency wars" to describe how exchange rates are changed in relation to other currencies to gain trade benefits. The end goal of currency wars is to increase total wealth, while the goal of currency warfare is to destroy or significantly weaken the currencies of selected states. The purpose of currency fighting is set by its political and military goals, not by how much wealth it creates overall.

Currency warfare takes place on the currency battlefield, which is the place where direct force is used against the currencies or financial institutions of an opponent. It is where raw force and money power meet in the way wars are fought. The battlefield is everywhere, and its boundaries can be global or local, based on the strategy. At the international level, the battle is fought in the foreign-exchange markets. At the regional level, the battle is limited to the territory where the larger war between the government and the rebels is taking place. Depending on the size of the battlefield, decision makers will use different weapons and strategies to win, such as manipulating exchange rates, fiat currencies, harmful rhetoric, counterfeiting, traditional military power like precision-guided munitions against physical currencies, and cyber capabilities.

Currency wars are often fought in secret, by people who aren't supposed to be there, or in a way that makes it look like they didn't do it. Depending on the tools used, it can take a long time for the effects to be felt, like when counterfeiting, or they can happen quickly, like during the Suez Crisis of 1956 when foreign exchange markets were manipulated. It can be called "nonlethal," but like cyberwar, it makes it hard to tell who is fighting and who is not, making it a weapon that affects everyone and everything in society. It is a battle that is fought mostly in secret, but the results can be seen in its economic effects, such as possible hyperinflation and loss of buying power. If the battle is won, the enemy's ability to fight war and its sense of teamwork will be hurt. Currency warfare has only recently become such a visible and publicly acknowledged part of an ongoing military campaign. This is because of the war against the Islamic State.

Currency targeting is a policy that focuses on the development of strategy and the larger factors and conditions that affect the choice to use currency warfare as part of a larger coercive strategy to reach military and political goals during armed conflicts. At the level of currency targeting, the strategic, operational, and tactical parts of currency fighting are planned and chosen. At this level, currency targeting thinks of moneyed weapons as brute force and financial assets as military targets that can be destroyed. At this level, cyber power gives people in charge of making decisions new ways to fight a currency war.

Currency skirmishes prior to the Digital Revolution

War isn't the first time that money has been used as a goal. States have often gone after the currencies of their enemies to make it harder for them to pay for war. Also, we can see that currencies are attacked with the same kinds of technology that forces use, which shows that money is a physical thing. Now that we know what currency warfare is and how it works, it would be helpful to give a short, but not exhaustive, background of how currency warfare has been fought in the past. Doing so will show how states have used money as a weapon and military force in past wars. It will also provide a historical basis for figuring out how cyber powers fit into currency warfare.

Since ancient times, wars have always involved fighting over money. During the Peloponnesian War, the Spartans attacked Athenian silver mines on purpose to stop the production of silver, which was used to make Athenian coins. This changed the value of the Athenian currency. In Spain, when the Romans were fighting Carthage, the famous Roman General Scipio Africanus attacked Cartagena because he had heard that "most of the Carthaginians' money and war supplies were kept in this city." During the wars of the Italian Renaissance, Milan tried to get an edge over its enemy by making fake Venetian money. As part of his wars, it is said that Frederick the Great "flooded the country with counterfeit money." During the Seven Years War and the American Revolution, fake money was used as a tool. Even before the Declaration of Independence in July 1776, the British had started a plan to make the federal dollar and other new currencies worthless. Most of the value of the regional currencies was lost due to forgery, negative speech, and even manipulation of the exchange rate by taking specie out of circulation in North America. The phrase "not worth a continental" really meant something to both troops and civilians. This led to hyperinflation and a big drop in the value of the currency, which was similar to what happened in Weimar Germany in the 20th century. Without the money that the French gave, the war might have been lost. The British and Napoleon both made fake versions of each other's money.

During the First World War, the British made fake German and Turkish money, as well as money from their own countries, to use against their enemies. But during the Second World War, money was used as a tool like maybe never before. In 1916, Germany tried to change the value of the Russian ruble by selling its stockpiles of rubles on the "Stockholm market." Operation Bernhardt, which was run by Germany, faked the British pound so much that it almost caused the currency to fail. Its effects were felt for years after the war ended. During the war, the US thought about making fake German and Italian money, and the British overcame their fears to go after the German mark (the British may not have known how serious the Germans were about making fake money in the early years of the war). Japan used paper currencies in China as a way to weaken the Chinese government. In response, the United States and the United Kingdom bought silver in order to keep the Chinese currency and government from falling apart. Before he famously "returned," Douglas MacArthur gave the go-ahead for fake Japanese money to be made in the Philippines so that the local economy would collapse.

At the end of the Second World War, the United States fought its enemies in Korea, Vietnam, and Afghanistan by using fake money to steal their money. During the Suez Crisis in 1956, the US weakened the British pound sterling, which stopped military actions by Britain and France. This is one of the most well-known things the US has done. The Cold War did not put an end to currency wars. It seems that American officials ran a counterfeiting campaign against Iraq in the early 1990s, and now, as part of the war on terror, it is common to go after terrorists' money. As part of its war against the Islamic State, the U.S. is using air strikes to destroy the places where the group stores its money. From the point of view of currency warfare, what is new about combat in the twenty-first century is the use of cyber capabilities to attack the financial and monetary power of an enemy. Now, we will talk about this new part of the past of currency wars.

Shifts in the nature of Currency Warfare

Information warfare and cyber conflict are two different things, according to scholars. Information warfare is defined as "activities by a state or non-state actor to use the content or processing of information to his advantage in times of peace, crisis, or war, and to stop potential or actual enemies from using the same means against itself." Cyberwarfare is a natural outgrowth of information warfare. It makes the tools and methods used in information warfare easier to use in the real world. Cyberwarfare is the use of computer network attacks (CNA) in the form of digital weapons like viruses, worms, logic bombs, Trojan Horses, and denial of service (DOS) as part of a combined military campaign during armed conflicts to achieve strategic and operational goals in pursuit of a state's war goals.

Cyber warfare, which is the use of cyber weapons in armed battles, grew out of a focus on cyber espionage rather "than overt military action and cyber war." During the 1990s and early 2000s, however, information and cyber warfare started to be seen as the new weapon system that would change war in the same way that airplanes and atomic bombs had. People often talked "about cyber Pearl Harbors." This may have been because the internet age had made it easier to be surprised and more vulnerable. On the other hand, some people saw cyber warfare as a way to "exploit weaknesses in systems during conflicts, similar to how electronic warfare used to be done." People have called the Persian Gulf War the "first modern information war." At that time, there were operations called "computer intrusions" that were aimed at Iraq's radar and communications. The Iraq War was important because it showed that information systems needed to be used more and more in war. This was the start of what became known as the "Revolution in Military Affairs." In other words, "Bandwidth and connection would be important for war."

From the middle to the end of the 1990s, the world became more "connected." This was a step toward what became known as "globalization." The danger that "computer network attacks" pose to globalization was talked about more and more in terms of offensive capabilities rather than spying. It was "acknowledged that new weapons were needed," and in addition to traditional weapons, "viruses, worms, logic bombs, trapdoors, and Trojan horses" would be used to "disrupt, deny, degrade, or destroy information in computers and computer networks, or the computers and networks themselves."

But cyber warfare, as it came to be called, was a difficult thing for states to do. Compared to the cost of buying, keeping, and staffing conventional weapons systems, it wasn't too expensive to build a good cyber-warfare unit. So, even countries with few resources could manage to build a cyberwarfare system that could attack, defend, and strike back at cyberwarfare attacks. There was a real fear of setting a bad example and of getting back at vulnerable systems. This fear kept people from using computer weapons even when they were at war. This seems to be especially true when it comes to money. During the Kosovo war, there was talk about shutting down Serbia's banking system, probably as a way to hurt Slobodan Milosevic. Before the 2003 attack of Iraq, the U.S. treasury secretary "stopped the manipulation of Saddam Hussein's bank accounts." Given how quickly technology was changing and how cheaply it was becoming possible to seriously damage communications, world markets, and currency systems, it was only a matter of time before cyber warfare was used as a form of coercion. In fact, cyber warfare is now a standard part of non-traditional, asymmetric warfare against terrorist groups and in interstate battles like the one in Ukraine.

The Emerging Currency Battlefield

From the point of view of currency warfare, the use of cyber power, cyber operations, or information warfare is just the application of already-existing technology to the changes that have already turned money into an electronic configuration of "encrypted strings of digits" that are "coded into a series of zeros and ones." Because of these changes, it's easy to think of a way in which money and cyberwarfare are becoming more similar. There are some parallels between the two. Both are good ways to weaken a state from the inside, often quickly and with the promise of staying anonymous. Currency and cyberpower are interchangeable in the sense that they can be used in a variety of security-related situations, including on their own for coercive diplomacy or sabotage, and in ongoing armed battles. But cyber power gives currency fighting new ways to use tactics. It is not a replacement for strategy. Currency warfare in its digital form is also not a part of cyber warfare that isn't well-defined and replaces strategy with new technology. Also, cyberwarfare won't replace all other ways or tools that can be used in currency wars. Depending on how the enemy's money is stored, brute force, like destroying a bank or government vault, may be the best way to destroy a country's finances. Still to be seen is how successful a cyber attack on a country's finances can be, especially against a well-developed financial infrastructure and a global currency like the dollar, euro, ruble, or yuan. Also, like other weapons and methods of war that came before it, like air, tank, naval, chemical, and economic weapons, we must be careful about giving cyber warfare the promise of being the final way to fight a war. If history has taught us anything, it's that no single technique or weapon (except maybe nuclear weapons) has ever won a fight on its own.

In the following case studies, cyberwar was used as a tactic or way to attack the opponent's finances as part of a larger military action. In the next part, we'll talk about how cyberwar changed how currency wars were fought in real life.

Every new piece of technology that comes out gives the battlefield new strategic, operational, and tactical challenges and possibilities. So, each new weapon goes through a time of development and testing, during which lessons are learned and methods are improved. World War I was where the airplane and the tank were tested for the first time. The Spanish Civil War was a kind of test run for how to use these new tools of war as part of a tactical strategy. During their Blitzkrieg, or rapid war, the Germans almost got this right. They almost got a continent because of what they learned. In terms of history, the present time is one of testing and learning from experience about how to combine and use cyberwarfare capabilities. At least, this has been the main focus. Most of the time, the new currency-warfare battlefield in modern wars isn't getting as much attention as it should.

This part looks at the three armed conflicts in the early 21st century in which cyber capabilities were used to fight a currency war. In the following cases, two Russian ones (Georgia (2008) and Ukraine (2014-present)) and one American one (ISIS (2014-present)) show how cyberwarfare was used strategically and operationally against their opponents in similar ways. Russia's war goals are obviously different from those of the U.S. Russian war goals are expansionist because they want to get back what they think they lost. The US, on the other hand, is fighting a defensive war to stop an aggressive terrorist group from making a new Islamic Empire. Putting aside Russian and American war goals, however, it is clear in all three cases that the use of cyber-warfare techniques against the currencies and financial institutions of their enemies was part of a larger strategy of subversion. This is a plan to weaken the enemy from the inside by changing how its people and government see its legitimacy and strength. In the two examples from Russia, financial organizations were attacked as part of a Russian subversive strategy to either reintegrate former Soviet territory into Russia or stop pro-Western governments from moving toward the West.

At the operational level, cyber warfare was used in currency wars to stop the enemy from using important banking services and to attack the legitimacy of the government. Also, the cyberwar attacks were not done on their own. Instead, they were used as part of a larger military operation to reach certain war goals. In the United States' war against ISIS, currency warfare was done with a variety of tools, most notably air attacks and international cooperation. The goal was to stop ISIS from using international financial institutions, but cyberwarfare was eventually used as part of a larger plan to hurt the Islamic State's finances.

In the three cases we looked at, using cyber warfare made sense from a strategic and tactical point of view. The new thing about cyberwarfare is that it gives people a new way to weaken the power of currencies. Since currencies and global finance are becoming more and more digital and open to cyberattacks, it is not strange that cyberattacks are being used against finance. In this way, cyber capabilities are used to fight against an increasingly digital currency, just like the printing press was finally used to make fake paper money. In the future, these three cases will be the first places where offensive cyberwarfare can be tested as part of a combined-operations approach to war. During the Spanish Civil War, the Germans used the Condor Legion to test their blitzkrieg tactics and learn important lessons. In the same way, these three cases are likely to give us more information about how to use cyber and currency warfare in the future.

Even though the US is the first country to admit using cyber forces during a war, which is a first in military history, the Russian use of cyberwar in Georgia (2008) and Ukraine (2014-present) as part of its expansionist grand strategy is the first time cyber weapons have been used during a war. Experts agree that the cyberattacks on Georgia and Ukraine came from Russia with the approval and control of the government, even though the Russians have never said they did it. Russia is getting very good at its hybrid form of warfare, which includes using cyber skills to attack financial institutions and other important targets like power grids and government institutions. Now, we'll talk about the three times cyber skills were used to wage currency war.

Russo-Georgian War of 2008

The end of the Cold War led to the 2008 Russo-Georgian War and the ongoing 2014-present Russo-Ukrainian war. Angela Stent says, "Russia's main goal since 1992 has been to regain its status as a great power and be treated as an equal by the U.S." Russian hostility is mostly caused by its fear that the West will move into its "sphere of influence," which includes places like Eastern Europe and the Caucasus. Russia is also worried that these former Soviet and Russian provinces will strengthen their economic and security ties with the West. So, to get back what they thought they had lost in Eastern and Southeastern Europe, the Russians turned to hybrid warfare, which uses both traditional and nontraditional forces, such as cyber powers, as part of their military and coercive foreign policies. In 2008, Russia turned to Georgia, a small country in the Caucasus.

The Russo-Georgian War started when Georgia launched a "massive artillery attack" on Tskhinvali, the city of South Ossetia, one of Georgia's disputed provinces where Russian troops were stationed because of a deal from the early 1990s. The war started because Russia and Putin were worried about Georgian President Saakashvili's strong support for the "West" and his desire to join NATO and the European Union. NATO's possible growth into Georgia would be another way that the West would try to get closer to Russia, which Putin was determined not to let happen. In the end, Putin outwitted Saakashvili by getting him to start an attack that would be the "just cause" for Russia to invade Georgia. The

Bush administration said over and over again that it would not back Georgia's use of force to regain territory, but Georgia still attacked South Ossetia. No one listened to the warning.

The Russian army moved into Georgia on August 8, a day after Georgian weapons fired on Tskhinvali. The size and variety of the Russian forces involved show that Russia is ready for an attack, with a lot of armored, naval, and air forces being used. As the Russian military moved in, especially "through the 2.3-mile Roki tunnel connecting North and South Ossetia," Georgia was hit by "a massive, coordinated cyber-attack that shut down all the major government sites and financial institutions," making it harder for Georgia to defend itself. By using "private citizens" who "knew ahead of time what the Russian military was going to do and when they were going to do it," Russia was able to keep up the appearance that it wasn't involved in cyber warfare. The timing of the hacks, on the other hand, makes it clear that Russia was behind them. Fred Kaplan says that "at the exact moment the tanks and planes crossed the South Ossetian line, fifty-four Georgian websites related to the media, finance, government ministries, police, and armed forces were hacked and rerouted to Russian servers, which shut them down." Attacks on Georgia's financial institutions, like its National Bank, didn't change much about how the war turned out. This was due in large part to the fact that Georgia's infrastructure for the internet was not as well developed or as integrated into people's lives as it was in other countries. It should be mentioned that a cyberattack on Estonia's financial institutions a year earlier was much more successful. Estonia is a country where almost everyone does their banking online.

Even though Russia won because of its strong conventional military and not because of its cyber campaign, which was only a secondary factor, it is still possible to look at the more important strategic and operational reasons why cyber capabilities were used against financial targets on the battlefield. Russia's war goals were to get rid of the Saakashvili government and get a better hold on Abkhazia and South Ossetia. This would make the region safer and give Russia more control over how energy gets to and from the area. In order to reach these war goals, Russia used subversion to make it harder for the Georgian government to do its job by attacking its infrastructure, including its financial and banking systems.

At the operational level, the focus was on distributed denial of service attacks, especially against Georgia's banking institutions. These attacks could stop Georgia from paying for the war and could also stop Georgian support for the war, or at least weaken it. As was already said, attacks on Georgia's banking sector were limited because Georgia's Internet infrastructure was not fully connected to its government and people. So, using cyberwar against currency-financial power was a new way to fight currency wars, but it was still in line with the strategic and tactical goals of currency wars in the past.

Russo-Ukraine Conflict

As with the Russo-Georgian conflict, the ongoing Russo-Ukraine conflict has its roots in Russia's fears of Western encroachment into Eastern Europe, especially through Eastern Europe's closer ties with NATO and the European Union, and in Ukraine's historical relationship with Russia. From Putin's point of view, Ukraine has been a part of Russia for hundreds of years. If Ukraine went "West," it would be a big blow to Russian power and identity in the area. After Russia took over the Crimea in February 2014, the fighting between Ukraine and ethnic Russian, pro-Russian, ahd Russian military troops in Eastern Ukraine has turned into a never-ending war. Reports from the war zone say that Russia is using the fight as a kind of cyber-warfare testing ground. Andy Greenberg writes that Ukraine has been hit by a "digital blitzkrieg" that has been going on for three years. This is the longest cyber attack the world has ever seen. Russia's attack on Ukraine through cyberwarfare is similar to what it did to Georgia before. It is aimed at key institutions and sectors in Ukraine, such as "media, finance, transportation, the military, politics, and energy." Also, just like in Georgia, Russia has said it didn't do it, but cyber experts and Russian experts say that Russia is behind the coordinated and systematic strikes.

The use of cyber power by Russia or Russian-backed proxies has happened at the same time as Russia's use of special operations forces in the Crimea before it was annexed and the deployment and infiltration of Russian soldiers and weapons in the eastern part of Ukraine known as Donbass and the Donetsk region. This has led to a long-lasting civil war.

What is the purpose of cyber warfare in Ukraine, and what does Russia hope to gain by attacking Ukraine's banking institutions? Russia's war goals in Ukraine have been to keep Russian power in a part of the country that Putin thinks has always been part of Russia, to stop Ukraine from getting closer to the West on the economic and military fronts, and to bring Ukraine back into Russia as part of Putin's Novorossiya, or New Russia. So, when people in Kiev started to protest against Yanukovych, who was friendly with Russia, Putin decided to do something. First, he would try to save Yanukovych. Then, he would try to take back the Crimea for Russia. So, Russia would stop a new government in Kiev "that would quickly align itself with NATO and the European Union and become a Western dagger pointing at Russia's Heart." This could happen if Sevastopol, the historic home of the Russian Black Sea fleet, was used by NATO to expand its presence in the Black Sea. From Putin's point of view, this couldn't go on. He saw Ukraine as a threat to Russia, and because of his conspiracy theories about the West, he thought that Russia's nuclear forces should be put on watch in case the West attacked Russia on Ukraine's behalf.

To reach its war goals, Russia used a strategy of subversion to make fun of and undermine the sovereignty and legitimacy of the Ukrainian government on its land. From this point of view, using cyberwarfare against a wide range of Ukrainian institutions, including its banking sector, is in line with both cyberwarfare and currency warfare's operational goals. It is interesting to note that Putin was very worried that the International Monetary Fund could become Ukraine's only banker. This would tie Ukraine's authority to one of the West's most important global financial institutions.

From the point of view of currency warfare, the use of non-kinetic cyber skills against financial institutions shows how currency power is becoming more quick and vulnerable. Because cyberwar skills can be used in different ways, they can be used against any sector that depends on cyber networks to work. Targeting Ukraine's financial institutions would probably make the country's currency less valuable abroad. This would make it harder for the government to pay for its current war with Russia. Also, it would put more pressure on the civilian population to pay for the war and could make it impossible or very hard for Ukrainians to go about their daily lives, which could bring the country to a stop. The fact that this hasn't happened yet doesn't mean it won't happen. Russia has already gone after financial industries in the past. As it learns and gets better, we may see a more sustained effort against the currency and financial power of the opponent in the future.

The American War against ISIS

If the two Russian cases show how cyberattacks on financial and monetary power are becoming more and more integrated, then the American fight against the Islamic State has made currency fighting and the currency battlefield a major area of operations. ISIS's rapid growth in the Middle East, where it is trying to create an Islamic Caliphate nation-state, has made the area less stable, posed a threat to the U.S. and its partners' interests in the area, and led to the death of an American journalist. Because of these changes, President Obama stopped calling ISIS the "jayvee team" of terrorism and started a long-term military operation to destroy the regime.

Airstrikes were a big part of the American military campaign against ISIS because they were used to actually destroy the Islamic State's money. So, currency warfare has never been more visible or talked about so often and openly at the highest levels as part of a military operation to hurt the enemy. The Obama administration and its partners knew that the Islamic State needed money in order to become a sovereign state. The United States could hurt ISIS from the inside by destroying its money and currency. This could be done actually from the air, diplomatically by cutting ISIS off from international financial markets, and electronically by making it impossible for ISIS to get to its money. To weaken the currency of the Islamic State, the United States used a tactic called "subversion." At the operational level, the goals stayed true to what had been done in the past with currency warfare, which was to deny ISIS the money and legitimacy it needed to fight. ISIS's cash storage sites, where they kept a lot of hard currency, were regularly attacked and destroyed. Cyberfinancial operations helped with these attempts as well.

ISIS has used the internet for psychological warfare, to scare people, to recruit new members, to spread lies, and to raise money. It also tried to hide some of its money in digital currencies like bitcoin. So, Ash Carter, the Secretary of Defense, sent U.S. Cyber Command on its first mission during a war. Even though the details of the cyberwar are kept secret, there is proof that the US is using cyberwar to fight over currencies. In March 2015, the head of U.S. Cyber Command, Admiral Michael S. Rogers, was asked if ISIS could use the dark web "to raise money through bitcoin, a form of digital currency." The skipper didn't give any details, but he did say, "We're paying attention to ISIL's ability to make money and get resources." Admiral Rogers's comments were backed up by similar thoughts from Defense Secretary Carter at the time. Carter said that cyber capabilities had been used to "interrupt their ability to command their forces, interrupt their ability to plot, and undermine their finances, their ability to pay people."

Carter explained the role of Cyber Command at both the strategic and operational levels. He said that the strategy meant "interrupting their ability to command and control their forces, interrupting their ability to plot, including against us here and anywhere else, against our friends and allies around the world, interrupting their finances, interrupting their ability to dominate the population on territory where they have tried to establish this nasty ideology."

ISIS is vulnerable to cyber-based currency warfare because, like any modern nation-state, it uses computers to store personal information so that money can be distributed and the government can run. This is a vital function of sovereign states. Nance and Sampson say that ISIS needs a "treasury, a general accounting office, and a social security administration" because it "thought of itself as a nation." There is proof that ISIS members have used bitcoin to make money and that these sources have been the target of cyber operations, even if they were done by non-Americans.

We won't know exactly what U.S. Cyber Command was going after for a while, and even though cryptocurrencies are popular right now, we're not likely to see a full digitalization of currencies any time soon. What we will see, though, is a deeper use of electronic money (like ATMs), which makes money and the financial infrastructure that supports it almost the same thing. If you go after a bank, you are going after the people's money. So far, the war against ISIS has shown that states are able to use new forms of technology to fight changes in currencies and cyber banking/currency technology. This is from the point of view of currency warfare through cyberwar. This doesn't make other kinds of currency warfare methods useless, but cyberwarfare gives people a new way to fight that fits with how currencies and securities exchanges are changing because of new technology.

Conclusions

From the point of view of currency warfare, cyber warfare gives new ways to target monies during war. In three recent and ongoing wars, the ongoing war against ISIS (2014-present), the Russo-Ukrainian conflict (2014-present), and the Russo-Georgian War (2008), cyberwarfare has been used to weaken the monetary and financial power of the warring parties as part of a larger effort to force them to stop fighting. The argument here, which is backed by the three case studies, is that cyber power is a good addition to traditional currency warfare because it uses new technologies to deal with the changing digital nature of currencies, financial institutions, and exchanges. Using cyber skills to fight currency wars is a sign of how the digital world of money is changing and how technology is being used for military reasons to keep up with these changes. Cyberwarfare gives people the chance to attack a country's financial power from anywhere in the world. Cyber capabilities are having an effect on how currency fighting is set up at the tactical level. In the future, cyberwarfare tools will likely be used more and more to attack financial power as part of attacking military operations.

But the addition of cyberwarfare doesn't change the strategic and tactical reasons why money has always been a target during war. Even in the digital age, subversion is still the main reason why currency warfare is fought. This is not strange because the nature of war doesn't change; only the way it looks and how it is done changes. At the operational level, cyber warfare adds to and improves the ability to stop the enemy from getting money for war, but it hasn't changed the tactical goals or targets of the past. Even though policies that target currencies during armed conflicts don't seem to have much of an effect right now, except maybe in the war against ISIS, there is no doubt that future currency battlefields will be more and more digital, which will make it more important for cyber capabilities to target currencies. In the years to come, states will likely use cyberwar as part of their ongoing military operations against their enemies to do more currency warfare and make it more successful.

Chapter 8
Social Networking and Intelligence Gathering Strategies in the Middle East

Intelligence groups in many countries often use social media platforms to gather intelligence information. This is called SOCMINT, which stands for "Social Media Intelligence." The term was first used by Omand et al. in 2012. SOCMINT is the collection of publicly available data made by social media users for the purpose of sharing sensitive information between governments and people and bringing it to the attention of national intelligence services. Social media networks, especially Twitter and Facebook, have made it easier to organize protests in a number of countries in the Middle East, especially during the Arab Spring revolutions in Egypt and Tunisia in 2011.

This chapter gives an overview of how Social Media Platforms have been used to cause social unrest in a number of Middle Eastern countries since 2010. This is followed by a detailed look at how these platforms have been used in both Israel and the Palestinian Territories. The amount of information that can be found on these social networks for free grows by the hour. As part of their surveillance programs, intelligence organizations are only really interested in a small amount of this data. After looking at the kinds of data that intelligence agencies in the region receive, a model is proposed for filtering social network data by using socialbots. Using AI and other software, it is possible to design, make, and build socialbots that can look at the data output of enemy or terrorist groups. This chapter says that by combining socialbots and data mining, it is possible to make an effective software tool that would show a target audience and could even talk to the target and ask them for more information. Socialbots that were carefully made could spread propaganda for intelligence services.

At the moment, it is thought that 6000 tweets are sent every second. Every minute, 3.3 million posts are made on Facebook. Inside this huge amount of data are tweets and posts from worried citizens, rebels, and possible terrorists. Any pictures that were stuck on could show where they were in the world. Photos of cars could show the car's license plate, which could be used to get more information for data gathering. With these kinds of posts and tweets, it would be easy for a terrorist or other person with bad intentions to find and find out where a target is. Civilians could also post photos of military operations that showed the unit's symbol and the exact position. Information from social media can be a useful way for the military, intelligence organizations, and insurgents to gather tactical intelligence. Since 2009, anti-government groups in the Middle East have used social media sites in different ways.

SOCMINT is used by both national security intelligence services and organizations that are not part of the government. In 2011, the UN used SOCMINT in a big way to plan a campaign to help activists in Libya.

SOCMINT gatherers might be interested in different kinds of info from different social media sites. The Facebook page of a person can be a useful tool for spying on them. A user's posts, likes, shares, and a new feature called "Story," where they can post a picture or video that can be seen for up to 24 hours, can all be used to track them. On social networks like Facebook, connections between people can be looked at. Even when it's not clear that two people are friends, it can be implied by the pictures or comments they like. The friendships and likes given to posts on Facebook can be looked at as a network graph, and the effect of certain people over time can be studied because social network analysis can show hidden connections in a Facebook network.

Social Media Intelligence in the Middle East

Cheong and Lee (2011) say that terrorists don't use Twitter much, but rebels and activists are using social media platforms more and more to get information, spread propaganda, and find people who agree with their cause. By 2014, a lot of rebels in Iraq and Syria were using Twitter to spread propaganda, and foreign insurgents often retweeted comments that had already been sent out. Insurgents in Iraq and Syria also used Ask.fm, Facebook, Instagram, Whatsapp, Pal-Talk, kik, Viper, JustPaste.it, and Tumblr. Klausen (2015) says that encryption software is also used by insurgents.

Twitter was first built as an SMS platform that used the texting feature of GSM mobile phones. Twitter is free and easy to use, and tweets can now include pictures, links to other platforms, and text. It's easy to send tweets to everyone on an address list. Most social media sites need 3G or Wi-Fi to work, but Twitter can work on 2G GSM cell networks, which are less powerful.

Journalists often quote what they read on Twitter because the people who run the rebel Twitter accounts make it seem like they are real people. But top militants wrote these stories, even though they sound like they were written on the spot and with authority. When they get to the training camps, new recruits give up their cell phones, just like they do in many regular forces today. This means that they can't tweet.

It's also important to keep in mind that any study has to fit into a legitimate framework. The Israeli Defense Forces showed that closely watching someone's Facebook page is the same as de visu surveillance, which usually needs permission from a top police officer. When a user's security settings are tight, spying officers often use fake accounts to make friends with the person they are watching. Article 8 of the European Convention on Human Rights says that everyone has the right to a "private life." This goes against that right.

The social revolutions in Iran, Tunisia, Egypt, and other places showed that social media and networks can be used to help people get involved in politics. The shift from traditional media like TV, radio, and newspapers to digital media affects many parts of the intelligence community and gives intelligence organizations new technical, conceptual, and operational challenges. People who might be called "average" are now working as online journalists, broadcasting information in near real-time or even in real-time with Facebook "live" that anyone can see if they want to.

It's important to remember that social media platforms by themselves did not cause the Arab Spring social change. Instead, it was the people who, after decades of repression and economic problems, decided to protest against their governments.

Social media can be used to screen the posts and tweets of people who are being watched by the government. This lets the government see how many people are upset and how strongly they feel. A government can also do many things to stop its people from using social media. For example, it can directly interfere with service providers, shut them down, stop people from using certain apps, or do some kind of online filtering. Traditional media have a lot of power, and you shouldn't forget that. Citizen journalism can be used by standard news outlets if they find it interesting.

During the Arab Spring, the Egyptian police kept an eye on social networks, read emails, and watched Skype. Normal ways of getting to Twitter did not work. During the Arab Spring, Google made an app called "Speak2Tweet" that turned voice calls into tweets on Twitter. This made it easier for protestors to tweet.

There are many ways to look at the info that comes out of social media. Big Data analysis is the most obvious way to do this, but social network theory, like the Facebook Network Graph analysis described above, can also be used to understand how data is linked. The "swarming" idea of communication from social science can also be used to look at social media. Computational sociology and mood analysis are two other methods.

Gathering Data

With so much traffic on all social media sites, it can be hard for intelligence gathering agencies to know what is interesting and what is not. Omand et al. (2012) say that it's important to be able to separate "the wheat from the chaff" when looking at the data that comes out of social media. They say that there are selection and filtering tools that can be used, as well as methods that have been used in signals intelligence for more than 50 years. They also say that semantic searching through emails is possible, but they wonder how an analyst can make sense of these huge data sets.

Omand et al. (2012) offer a technique called "forest fire," in which links and nodes burn outward, creating more links and nodes from a random seed to make a sample, because social scientists haven't been interested in user activity or location-based techniques until now. Hashtag clouds, which are mostly used on Twitter and Instagram and have been copied by Facebook, have been used to make datasets, but this means that the data set is biased toward data that has a hashtag and a relevant hashtag. But many people tweet without using a hashtag, or they don't know which word is the most popular for a certain topic. People also think that a data set made by collecting a certain amount of Twitter data in a certain amount of time is biased and that the group is not representative.

Omand et al. (2012) also offer techniques that are like watering a garden. For example, the "firehose" technique gives access to all tweets, the "garden hose" gives access to 10% of tweets, and the "sprinkler" filters down to 1%. But no one knows how good the data is at any of these levels.

Machine learning could be used, where an algorithm is taught to find clusters and outliers in big sets of data. The use of "semantic analysis" seems like a good idea. In this method, an algorithm looks for certain qualities and properties in a piece of text and chooses if it matches an emotion or sentiment that has already been set. But it is very hard for a computer program to understand what people are thinking and feeling when they write. The way people misspell, use text language, slang, and emojis today makes the job even harder. Also, it is common for youth gangs to use words in a way that makes them sound like they mean the opposite of what they do.

A group of researchers looked at and coded more than 150,000 tweets from 59 rebels as part of a project to figure out what they meant. For every fifth tweet, the coders could not agree on which category it should go in. This raises the question, "If highly trained university researchers can't agree on how to code a tweet, how could a computer program?"

Sentiment analysis has already been used to predict how much money a movie will make at the box office and how Twitter users feel about different political parties. Omand et al. (2012) think it could be used to "gauge the mood of demonstrators" and the likelihood of violence breaking out over a certain topic. In a similar way, sentiment analysis should be able to measure the mood of dissent, how Twitter users feel about insurgency, and the likelihood that any one user would go from passively backing a "terrorist" cause to taking action.

Omand et al. (2012) say that the context is very important in this kind of research. No matter the semantics or linguistics, the meaning or connotation, all communication depends on the situation and society. For a study to make sense, you have to know a lot about the group in question.

Social media sites are used in different ways by different countries. Up until recently, Turkish people vented their frustrations on Facebook. However, after many people were jailed for making comments that were negative about President Erdogan, this has become less common, especially after the failed coup in Turkey in 2016.

Tweets can only be 140 characters long and can be typed on a computer or sent as a text message from a smartphone. They don't take into account the context of a normal conversation, and it's possible that the speaker's tone isn't known, the conversation's flow isn't looked at, and the data isn't in a natural setting. In signals intelligence, "scraping" a social media site, like Twitter or Facebook, is the same as making a filtered selection. Scraping is the process of getting raw text data from social media and other websites. It is also called site scraping, web harvesting, and web data extraction. When data is scraped, it is not clear if the data was part of a chat with a group or with a single friend unless more research is done. If a group is found, there are different ways to be a part of it, such as liking a page, following an account on Twitter, or participating in a protest.

Omand et al. (2012) say that there is a new field of sociology called "digital sociology" that studies the social and cultural effects of social media platforms.

When context isn't taken into account, the effects can be terrible. For example, in 2010, a man named Paul Chambers posted to his 650 followers that he was going to "blow airport sky high!! He was charged with breaking the American Communication Act of 2003, even though he said it was all a joke. The verdict was later thrown out. People's social media posts can sometimes keep them from getting into a country. In 2017, the U.S. Department of Homeland Security put out a notice in the Federal Register that they would collect and keep information from the social media accounts of people going through immigration, including asking for passwords.

Omand et al. (2012) say that any statistical analysis methods, like sentiment analysis, should involve analysts who are experts in the field and know the norms and behavior of the groups being studied, as well as the social media platforms being used and the specific online culture, language, and behavior. A program for gathering intelligence must first find out what the "norms" are before it can figure out what is different from the norm.

Sottlemyre and Sottlemyre (2012) explain how "crisis mapping" can be used to use Twitter data from interested parties to change how a military action turns out. Twitter users can use the work of citizen journalists or just interesting people who are willing to share information to collect data and make tactical maps. Crisis mapping brings together information from social media, like the geospatial information in a picture or a tweet, as well as information from citizens. All of this information can be added to a Google map.

Social media were used for the first time during a revolution in Greece in December 2008 and in Moldova in 2009. By early 2011, protesters and activists in Tunisia and Egypt were using social media to show how unfair their governments were. This was called the Arab Spring. A military operation can face a lot of problems and information leaks because of citizen journalism. Any general or operative may want to keep manoeuvres secret, but anyone can take a picture of a passing car and post it on social media. Whether it was done on purpose or not, a photo or video shared on social media can show what kind of markings are on a vehicle and where it is.

With the technology we have now, it's easy to look at the millions of public tweets on Twitter and the records of other social media sites like Facebook. Artificially intelligent bots can be set up to search through these huge databases, using keywords to lead data researchers to possible security breaches or whatever information they are looking for. Many intelligence organizations are already getting tactical intelligence from social media. The Arab Spring made the U.S. government and NATO collect statistics from social media, especially Twitter. This was also done during the Libyan Civil War in 2011.

Data on social media networking comes from many different places. As well as the information that is available to the public on Facebook and Twitter, there are also blogs and RSS feeds. Also included are comments on YouTube videos and picture hosting sites like Flickr. Also, there are many cases of organizations using social media to spread propaganda by making fake profiles with fake identities to hide people who are working in secret. Levesque (2012) says that the US Intelligence Agencies not only use fake identities on social media, but also hired outside contractors to make software that lets them handle up to 10 personas per user, for a total of 50 users. The created personas would have a full background, including a past, photos, and other things that add up to a full, accurate persona from a technical, cultural, and historical point of view. When the software is used, it gives each persona a random IP address, so a third party wouldn't be able to find out that all the personas are handled from the same computer on the same desk. Even the fact that the software would be used in both Kabul and Baghdad is written in the tender paper.

Of course, US Intelligence is not the only group that thinks of fake accounts. This is also done by many other groups, including criminal groups. From the University of Haifa, Professor Weimann (2011) says that 90% of planned terrorism on the Internet is done through social media. He also says that because the Internet has no borders, it is easy for them to get new users from anywhere in the world. The terrorist organizations don't just use Twitter. In ten years of study, Weimann has found that they use Facebook, chat rooms, YouTube, Myspace, and other social media sites as well. They reach out to people who might want to join by sending friend requests, sharing videos, and starting conversations in chat rooms. Some users don't check who they are making friends with, which makes it easy for terrorists to join many other groups. As part of its surveillance work, the Israel Defense Force also uses fake Facebook pages. The IDF keeps an eye on the Facebook posts of people who are interesting to them. If the Facebook user is good at protecting his or her privacy, the posts and friends might not be visible to the public. IDF agents will make fake Facebook accounts to get around this level of security. They will then trick the person into making friends with them on Facebook, which will give them access to all the information they want. Obviously, the fake accounts might not be very good and might not have any family photos, personal photos, or personal information on them. Also, the IDF will talk to Facebook about taking down certain posts. Before the post is taken down, a screenshot will be taken of it so that its presence can be kept track of and could be used in court in the future. Some people keep putting up things that have already been taken down. The Chief Superintendent, who is in charge of the Israel National Police Cybercrimes unit, says it's okay to use fake accounts and keep a close eye on people of interest. Insurgents, in turn, are keeping an eye on the IDF. Weimann (2011) says that Hezbollah is using Facebook to look for information about the Israeli Army.

Many military organizations try to limit how their soldiers use social media so that secret information doesn't get out. After all, people are the weakest link when it comes to keeping information safe. The British Army, the Canadian Army, the Turkish Army, the Greek Army, and the Republic of Cyprus Army do not allow their troops to use Facebook. However, both career soldiers and conscripts use social media, which can lead to important information about missions getting out. In a big change, the US Army went from completely banning social media to letting some people use it. The British army has told its soldiers that they can't use cell phones in active zones like Afghanistan and that they should never take pictures on their smartphones.

The impacts of Geospatial Tagging

The latest smartphones allow posts to be "tagged" or "checked in" so that people can see where the post or picture came from. This gives any terrorist group that looks at the post or picture clear information about the user's location. In addition to easy updates on Twitter or Facebook, tools like Swarm and Gowalla want users to share where they are so that friends in the same area can find them. A lot of dating sites have tools in their apps that are the same. These apps use the GPS on the user's phone to find out where the user is. They then post the user's location and give badges or points as rewards to get people to check in everywhere.

The processes and scope of the Israel Defense Forces (IDF) have been studied in depth. This has shown that the IDF "scrapes" a lot of information in an attempt to find terrorists in the Israeli state. The big change happened in 2017, when the IDF started using data from social media to learn about Hamas and what they were talking about in the Gaza Strip. In this case, social media was used to spread lies and to gather information. In 2008, during Operation Castlead, the IDF used YouTube, Twitter, and the blog of a specific IDF spokesman to spread propaganda. With a small team, they started spreading propaganda and talking directly with Hamas accounts in "tit-for-tat" conversations. In 2009, they started their own new media desk and have continued to spread information through specific writing on the IDF website and IDF blog as well as managing their presence on Facebook, Twitter, YouTube, Flickr, Instagram, and Tumblr through their new Interactive Media Branch. They make 200 to 300 blog posts and more than 10,000 tweets every month. More than 500,000 people like them on Facebook, and 250,000 people follow them on Twitter. During one campaign, they sent out 11 tweets per hour to encourage people to watch the campaign in real time. They put videos of examples of active warfare on YouTube. They even made an app that people could use to find safe places and bomb bunkers in case of a missile attack. All of this is done through Hebrew, Arabic, English, French, Spanish, and Russian.

Within four hours of the attack, footage of an insurgent's car driving through Gaza and then being destroyed by a drone was shared online. As well as spreading propaganda, the IDF does a lot of study into where Hezbollah members go.

In order to fight back against what the IDF is doing, the rebels also use social media to spread their message. Hamas started sharing pictures of dead and hurt children on Twitter with the hashtag #IDF. This is a problem for the IDF because it means that Hamas is always online and giving journalists information. Hamas often makes up stories using pictures from other places, like the war in Syria. They post fake news on Facebook to confuse IDF experts because they care more about getting people's attention and making them feel something than being true. Hamas has been busy in spreading their ideas about war by using the hashtag #GazaUnderAttack. Their hashtag got seven times more mentions on Twitter than the IDF's hashtag #IsraelUnderFire. The IDF still looks at information from social media to find out about possible rebels in Israel. Younger rebels, between the ages of 15 and 25, are more likely to use Facebook and Twitter. The IDF uses this information to build up profiles of the criminals by watching what these young people post on social media. They have made algorithms just for finding possible culprits.

Shin Bet security officers go to the homes of these young men and women and talk to them and their parents to let them know that they are being watched because of what they do on social media. The actions of Palestinian citizens are not the only things that are watched. Also being looked at are the social media accounts of Palestinian refugees in the Diaspora (private talk with Palestinian security forces at the Palestinian Embassy in Ankara, Turkey, May 2018).

The US Army says that troops shouldn't use social media because it could put them, their units, or their families in danger. Anything a soldier posts on a social media site could be used against him or her if a terrorist group gets a hold of him or her. Family pictures would be very helpful. A soldier can give away their habits, routes, and exact position by making inappropriate posts, which could lead to them being taken by a terrorist cell.

In 2007, a mortar attack on an aviation unit in Iraq damaged four AH-64 Apache helicopters. The people who are serving took pictures of this new fleet, which were then put on the Internet with a geotag. Because of this, the enemy was able to figure out where the planes were and attack them (Rodewig, 2010). Even though no one was hurt in this attack, it is easy to see how geotagging can put the lives of service members in danger, from revealing the exact locations of tools and people to revealing their and their coworkers' daily routines.

American service members aren't the only ones in the military who post things online that could be used against them. Even though it's against the rules, Turkish and Turkish Cypriot military forces often post on social media about where they and their troops are. Figure 1 shows a Foursquare post by Captain Zekiye from 2012. At the time, Foursquare was a very famous search and discovery app that let users "check in" to a place. In 2018, Major Zekiye is still letting people know where he is, but now he does it through the famous photo-sharing app Instagram, as shown in Figure 2.

AI-Powered Tactical Data Gathering

With the ever-growing levels of communication on social media platforms, various intelligence gathering agencies are using dedicated personnel to track and trace within the large bodies of data created by social media users. The Israeli Defence Force have a dedicated team, the National Police Cybercrimes Unit 443, to follow particular individuals on Facebook . While the IDF are successful in preventing attacks through their monitoring of personal Facebook accounts, they have also been condemned for their possible infringement of human rights as this data is personal .

But as the number of people using social media grows, it doesn't make sense or save money to hire people to keep track of Facebook, Twitter, and the growing number of social media sites. It makes sense that smart socialbots need to be made in order to keep an eye on the Twittersphere and Facebook pages of people of interest.

At this point, it's important to note that you can't just analyze SOCMINT in English. Treverton and Miles (2014) say that a lot of people in Syria use Arabic to talk to each other on social media. They also say that Hamas spreads misinformation through Twitter accounts like @QassanHebrew, which are often written in Hebrew.

Using a mathematical model, a computer program can search through the huge amounts of data on the Internet to find information. Web crawls that go through Twitter, Facebook, blogs, and RSS Feeds can be used to build large databases of useful information. Tools for handling natural language, like OpenCalais, can be used to find comments that are relevant to the information being sought. Secondary tools like NetMiner can be used to analyze the data and figure out how the network works, such as whether the data is unified, central, or spread out.

Open Source Intelligence (OSINT) is a way to find, pick, and get information from public sources like Twitter and Facebook. This information is then analyzed to make intelligence that can be used. Maltego, Creepy, Case File, FoxOne Scanner, Shodan, and Metagoofil are all free tools that you can use.

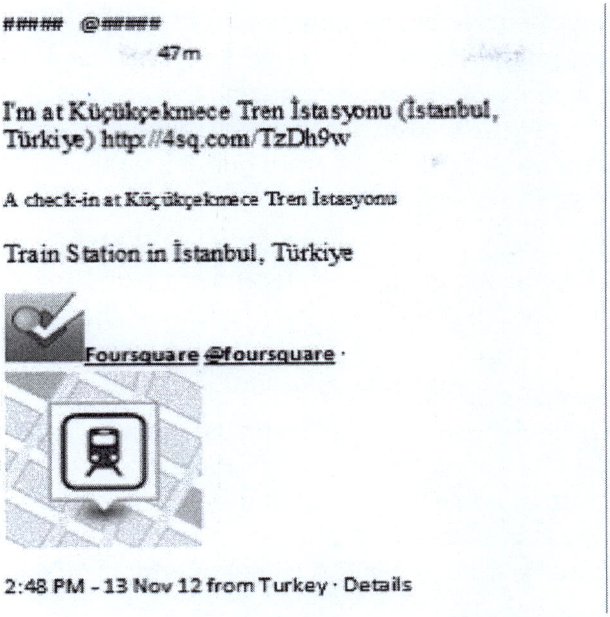

Figure 1. An inappropriate tweet by a Turkish Army Captain [Howells, 2012]

Figure 2. Another inappropriate tweet by Major Zekyce

Maltego is an open source intelligence and forensics application made by Paterva. It focuses on transforming data from open sources and displaying it in a graph style. It works best for data mining and link analysis. Its main goal is to show how people, groups, websites, domains, networks, internet infrastructure, and social media are connected in the real world. It is written in Java and can run on both Windows and Linux.

Kakavas made Creepy, which is a geolocation information aggregator. Creepy will gather information about a person's location from the social networks they use or from image hosting sites. Inside the application, the research is shown as a map that shows where all the information gathered comes from.

Insikt Intelligence, a company based in Barcelona that was founded in 2018, offers a solution called Invisio. They say that it uses natural language processing and social media monitoring to warn users about possible radicalization and when there is unusual behavior in a social media network. In a case study on their website, they talk about how they were able to find out where an extreme video on Twitter came from, but this is something that could be done quickly by hand.

Mahood (2015) says that the best way to use SOCMINT would be to look at patterns in social media today to make a model and then look for similar patterns in data from the future to predict what will happen.

Emerging Trends and Research

It makes sense to use artificial intelligence and other software tools to make socialbots right now. These socialbots would be made, built, and designed so that they could look at the data that enemy or terrorist groups send out. With more programming, these socialbots would be able to talk to their targets and spread propaganda for the spy agencies.

Software like @Botometer (2018) from Indiana University can tell if a Twitter account is likely to be a socialbot by looking at around 1200 features and matching them to features that machine learning models use. So, it is possible, to some extent, to label an account as a socialbot. Freitas et al.'s (2016) work, on the other hand, shows that socialbots can hide in the real world. Because of this, intelligence officers can use socialbots to help them do their jobs.

McCarthy (2011) made social robots with the help of computer science students at the University of Washington, Tacoma's Institute of Technology. The goal was for these social robots to run on their own for 5 days and get as many Twitter followers and comments as possible from the target audience.

In this trial, the socialbots did a great job. About 27% of the users chose to follow at least one of the socialbot sites. About 12% of the users tweeted about at least one of the socialbots. The socialbots blend parts of Artificial Intelligence, social networking, network security, technology, psychology, sociology, ethics, and politics. Most of the code for the socialbots was written in Python 2.6 and the Twitter API. Some even used a Python bot that was based on the old Eliza program.

Vergani and Bliuc (2018) are studying some of ISIS's writings by using Linguistic Inquiry and Word Count (LIWC) to look at texts in English from an ISIS online magazine called Dabiq. They are researching some of ISIS's output. The researchers looked at the first eleven issues of this online magazine. They chose LIWC because they think it works best when you need to understand the structure of the language, such as when you need to look closely at the "motives, emotions, and objects of interest" they found in the online text. The people who wrote Dabiq know that it is propaganda from ISIS, so they want to be careful and use the right way. The team looked closely at how the feelings were shown, how the writer felt about things like death or religion, and if any jargon was used. They were also interested in what the writers did as a group, how they showed their power, if they were part of ISIS, and what they had done individually. The software instantly opens the online journal's text files and figures out the percentages of each category that the researchers set up. Vergani and Bliuc's work from 2018 has given us some very interesting views into how ISIS works, how they change their ways to recruit people, and how they use language. Intelligence organizations need to do this kind of analysis in order to learn more about the groups they are looking into.

Conclusion

There are many good things about SOCMINT research. Using socialbots to collect data, which can then be analyzed, can help fill in gaps in standard intelligence gathering. Using socialbots in real time on social media sites like Twitter can help companies quickly figure out how a certain group of people feels. It would be possible to find insiders in the conversations on social networks. The conversations of these insiders could then be looked at more closely to see if they pose a threat to public safety. By analyzing the coming data as a network, it would be possible to find out where a certain feeling came from and who the most important people on the network are. Even though terrorists and insurgents still use social networks to spread their ideas, SOCMINT is a key part of finding the people behind the propaganda and possibly finding personal contacts between possible terror groups.

But one of the problems with SOCMINT is that it only uses data from social media networks, which may not be allowed in some places. In some countries, social media data from users is considered private, so police or other agencies would need to get a request from a local judge in order to access the data. Even though the information is available for free on the internet, collecting it can be seen as invasive, especially when agencies make fake social media accounts to get information. Getting this information in secret could be seen as a violation of human rights, so it needs to be thought about carefully before anything is done.

It is a new trend to use social media and online social networking to gather spy information. It is, however, a very dangerous change that these kinds of data are being used to watch for social unrest in other countries, spy on terrorist cells in different places, and make propaganda to spread to other places. Recent social events, especially in the Middle East, have led many intelligence agencies to use the data coming from social media for data mining and trend analysis.

This chapter wants to suggest that socialbots and data mining can be used together to make a very useful tool that can not only find a target community but also talk to a target. Also, using artificial intelligence, the language of the messages can be analyzed to find changes in strategy and figure out what kind of users are being attracted. Algorithms for analyzing social networks would find the members of any social network so that they could be looked into further. Socialbots could also get someone to say more about themselves. Socialbots could also be used to spread lies in interest groups on social networks. The software tools we have now only filter SOCMINT so that intelligence staff can do more research on it. Intelligence organizations could use a very powerful tool that combined socialbots, artificial intelligence, linguistic analysis, and social network analysis.

Because of this, it is important to do more study on socialbots and artificial intelligence with SOCMINT so that intelligence agencies can get the tools they need.

Chapter 9
Modern Practices in Blockchain Forensics

Blockchain forensics uses scientific methods to change data in order to create useful and helpful descriptions of the changed data. Blockchain forensics uses data from the blockchain to figure out how digital assets move. Investigators use complex tools for manipulating and displaying data to find out where stolen items have been. With these features, cybercriminals won't be able to hide their tracks by chain hopping, round-tripping, or any other way. Instead, they will just be able to make smoke screens that don't work. This chapter sets up a framework for investigating financial crimes on the blockchain. It starts with a brief explanation of blockchain forensics, the types of financial crimes that criminals commit using the blockchain, and how they can be stopped using OSINT's investigation process of data collection, data preservation, data processing, and data presentation. This chapter also talks about a community-based way to investigate financial crimes on the blockchain. The public and the victims themselves can share valuable information that law enforcement and security agencies can use to find and track criminals in the global fight against cybercrime.

Blockchain forensics and cryptocurrency forensics accounting both look at the flow of cryptocurrency assets on the blockchain and try to figure out what is going on. The information on the blockchain is public, but many wallet names and transactions need to be decoded, evaluated, and interpreted in each case to properly track the flow of funds and report on it.

A big part of the global economy is based on illegal business practices, especially in the digital financial world. It is against the law to get money from illegal business deals. The ends are all that count to the people who own these things. To clean these profits, a normal criminal would send them through several financial stops and different handlers until they got back to where they came from as legal and clean money. The average person who launders money wants to do it in a way that leaves no traces that could lead back to them. Because of this, cryptocurrency and their derivatives, like Decentralised Finance (DeFi) and Non-Fungible-Tokens (NFTs), have become safe places for stolen money.

On the blockchain, criminals use many different services and ways to send money to many different addresses or businesses. After that, the assets are sent to a target place or an exchange where they can be sold from a legal source. This makes it very hard to link money that has been laundered to illegal behavior. Now, the anonymity and decentralization of the blockchain, which are very new features, cause a lot of worry and fear about the technology, especially in the standard financial sector. Because of this, more and more rules are being made to guide and watch how cryptocurrency is used and to make sure that cryptocurrency organizations and service providers follow the rules strictly. For the purpose of classifying cryptocurrencies, these rules include registering exchanges and putting in place Know Your Customer (KYC) standards and Anti-Money Laundering (AML) complaint systems by cryptocurrency organizations.

Financial Impact of Blockchain Cyber Attacks

When cryptocurrency and the blockchain showed up on the financial market scene in 2009, it was the start of a new technology that would threaten the security of the traditional, centralized financial system. Some of the most interesting things about the technology were that it was anonymous and that its design and structure were not centralized. This meant that the global political leaders could not control it. But this wasn't a problem for the global financial body and its controlling political spine in the early days of the cryptocurrency and blockchain boom, when only a few strange-looking computer geeks used the technologies and they were worth much less than they are now.

"What could these tools do to the competition? How much harm could they do?"

In a way that was too dramatic, the world would later find out what a beautiful tree these crypto seeds could grow into in just ten years. According to CoinMarketCap, the value of the cryptocurrency market was a huge $1.03 trillion in November 2021. It had been 10 years since Laslo traded 10,000 bitcoins for two Papa John's pizzas. As of February 2022, NFTs are worth about $17 billion and DeFi is worth about $200 billion, so the coin market has grown.

Two short years ago, Binance was attacked quickly. At the time, it was the biggest cryptocurrency exchange, but it lost about 7,000 bitcoins, which were worth about $40.8 million at the time. This was one of the biggest cryptocurrency thefts ever. When authorities tracked where the stolen money from the Binance hack went, they found that about 5,000 bitcoins were moved and cleaned through a service called Chip Mixer.

A North Korean group stole $615 million from the famous play-to-earn game Axie Infinity in a hack that happened not too long ago. The US Treasury Department linked the theft of Ethereum coin from a software bridge used for the popular play-to-earn game Axie Infinity to the North Korean hacking group Lazarus. Even worse, the US government put the Ethereum addresses on the official OFAC sanctions list.

At the moment, billions of dollars change hands every day on the crypto market. Because of its speed and guarantee of anonymity, the industry invites money launderers, terrorists, hackers, drug traffickers, and other sellers of illegal goods to use the technology's ability to protect users' identities while letting them clean and put dirty money back into the financial system.

The global financial system needs to act quickly to recover these stolen funds, raise knowledge about cyber safety, and come up with new tools to deal with this new technology that cybercriminals are using more and more to hide and launder illegal assets around the world.

In the next part, we'll talk about how criminals hide how money moves on the blockchain and how some of the new tools and services offered by Bilic can be used to track them down and stop them.

Perpetrators disguising Transactions on the Blockchain

Decentralised Finance

Peer-to-peer financial protocols remove the need for a middleman in DeFi. This is in contrast to the way a centralized finance system works, which involves third-party intermediaries and leaves a lot of paper trails. With DeFi, anyone with a computer and an internet link can lend, borrow, bet on, and trade cryptocurrencies, just like in traditional finance. Also, unlike cryptocurrency exchanges, DeFi doesn't have strict rules for proving your name. So, when people use these sites, they can be sure that their identities are safe.

The fact that DeFi platforms hide their users' identities is an open door for people who try to move money. Recent news stories have shown that about half of the cryptocurrencies that were recently stolen were sent to DeFi sites. In another story from The Block, as of January 2022, about $192.82 billion was still locked up in DeFi. The fact that DeFi is not currently regulated is said to be one reason why it is being used more and more to clean and move illegal money.

DeFi is built on blockchain technology, which is a decentralized ledger. As a platform built on blockchain technology, transaction data can be viewed and tracked. So, people who launder money must use other methods to get rid of the digital traces of their activities on platforms. Some of the ways this is done are:

Peel Chain

Peel chain is used to move large amounts of cryptocurrencies into and out of DeFi platforms so that it can't be found by officials who look into transactions that are very bad. Peeling lets money launderers turn small deals into a lot of crypto assets. They can then send a lot of crypto assets to centralized or decentralized exchanges, where they can be changed into fiat currencies or other crypto assets. Money launderers make very long and complicated "peel chains" that make it hard and time-consuming to figure out where the money is going. For example, if someone wanted to move 100 ETH without being seen, they could do 200 separate deals of 0.5 ETH each. This might be a long process, but it looks like any other regular transaction to the sender, so it doesn't raise any red flags.

Chain Hopping

Chain hopping is another way that people who try to hide money do it. Users can move their access from one blockchain network to another using DeFi platforms like Change Finance, which is a multi-chain DeFi application that supports interoperability. Money launderers often move quickly from one chain or cryptocurrency to the next. This is done to confuse trackers and make their transaction history more complicated, making it almost impossible to follow the transactions to their final location.

Mixers (Tornado Cash)

The decentralized public ledger keeps track of all receipts and activities on the blockchain. This is because blockchain technology makes it impossible to link wallet addresses to specific people. So, transactions between wallets can be seen and tracked until too much data that isn't related is sorted, compared, and narrowed down to a few small factors that can be used to make better and more informed guesses. This is very good news for crypto security and a big deterrent for people who try to move money on the crypto market. Enter "mixers" for cryptocurrencies. Mixers are like digital shredders that destroy the records of transactions kept by the blockchain. This makes it hard to keep track of transactions. The Tornado Cash mixer is a very famous drink mixer.

It is said that hackers used the Ethereum DeFi application Tornado Cash to wash $100 million in stolen money. With mixers like Tornado Cash, cryptocurrencies are put into the application by the sending address, and the application limits the amount that can be put in. This could be in units of one, ten, or even hundreds. The most likely reason for this is that each wallet that puts money into the pool puts in the same amount, and when someone takes money out, it's hard to tell which wallet put in what and which wallet took out what.

The deposited funds are left for a short time so that they can mix with other funds in the system. This means that no transaction exists as a single transaction. Instead, a batch of transactions are layered, bunched, and mashed together to make a single transaction that can't be tied to a single wallet address. The money is then taken out of a different address, called the relayer, and sent to the address of the receiver, which is often different from the deposit address. This breaks the link between the payment address and the address of the person who got the money.

Also, it's important to know that most people who use the site use VPN services to hide their IP addresses. This is done so that the IP address used to deposit money doesn't match the IP address used to withdraw money. The fact that the Tornado Cash mixer can mash and mix transactions to hide the trails of cryptocurrency transfers to and from different wallets makes it a very useful tool for people who launder money. About 4006 ETH were stolen from crypto.com in January 2022. When the theft was looked into, it was found that the stolen ETH had been laundered through Tornado Cash and sent in groups of 100 to unknown wallets. In an interview with CoinDesk, Strom, the founder of Tornado Cash, said that Tornado version 2 would add a cryptographic note to the Ether transaction log to help figure out where the funds came from. Even though this might make it easier to track the movement of illegal funds through the platform, large cryptocurrency deals continue to use Tornado because of its ability to hide transaction information.

Money Laundering using NFT

Money launderers have always been interested in the physical art business because it has subjective prices, is scarce, is hard to predict, and is easy to manipulate. Without a doubt, all of these things, including secrecy, which is the icing on the cake, also play out in the NFT industry, which is why both honest and shady business people use the NFT industry. If you look closely at the NFT market, you can see that its prices have been going up for no reason and that large amounts of money are being moved around erratically to buy almost useless digital pieces. But so what? What James doesn't care about could be worth a lot to John, right? Well, isn't that the right way to use technology to change illegal money into money that can be spent legally?

Money launderers often use NFT sites to wash dirty money. One way they do this is through Wash Trading, which means putting an NFT up for sale and then buying it for yourself multiple times, which changes the value in a big way and raises the sale price.

Money launderers create accounts on NFT platforms, make or buy a piece of art on the platform, and "wash trade" it by using different accounts on the same platform to raise the price of the asset. When the price of the asset goes up a lot, they sell it to themselves and get their dirty, illegal money through the sale of an NFT. The dirty, illegal money is then taken out of the NFT and circulated in society.

In its study, Chainalysis found that 262 users sold an NFT to a self-funded address more than 25 times, making a profit of $8.5 million. Close research showed that some OpenSea transactions had very strange prices, and it was possible to track down accounts that had sent money to other wallet addresses and then used those addresses to buy NFTs from the foundation account. By doing these things, dirty and illegal money is put back into the system as clean money by going through a legal digital art platform.

Tracking Cyber Criminals on the Blockchain

Because cryptocurrencies are anonymous, it is hard, but not impossible, to find out who is behind a wallet handle. In fact, this is what makes NFTs and other coins appealing to people who want to do bad things.

But the accuracy of tracing and tracking cryptocurrency transactions and figuring out where they came from can be improved with the help of blockchain research tools and knowledge. The processes of attribution and tracking money flow make it possible to reduce the many variables and huge amount of data involved in a single transaction to a manageable level so that investigators can make the best choices they can with the information and data they have.

Most people think that if you trade in cryptocurrency, you can stay private. All you have to show is your wallet's public key or address. A street address is a string of 26 to 35 letters and numbers.

The truth is that crypto trade is done under a fake name. This means that you can't really hide who you are.

This brings us to the big question: Is it possible to track a Crypto Transaction? Yes, is the short answer. But it doesn't take 2 minutes. And you need to know how to do it.

If there is a hack or theft, a spy agency will need to find the wallet address of the hacker. Here, we'll talk more about these steps.

Deanonymization still has trouble with hash functions or strings that identify people or wallet addresses. One way to make sure that people are no longer anonymous on the blockchain is to make KYC (Know Your Customer) checks for NFT and DeFi platform users a must. This will make sure that wallet addresses can be tied to user information that can be checked outside of the blockchain. This will make tracing easier and more accurate.

Policy rules about using DeFi and NFTs have been tightened.

The goal of these rules would be to keep track of and stop the dangerous things that money launderers do. These rules about policy must be dynamic and changeable, but they must also get stricter over time.

Setting up the AML system needed to spot suspicious activities is a good idea. In August 2021, thieves stole cryptocurrency worth $610 million. About $33 million was put into the stable coin Tether. Ardoino, Tether's chief technology officer, found out about the behavior right away and moved quickly to stop it. This made it impossible for the hacker to get away with the money. Ardoino says that if the Tether network had wasted more time, the money might have been lost for good.

Recent recoveries of stolen cryptocurrencies show that cryptocurrencies are no longer a safe haven for thieves. The fact that Poly's stolen funds were found and returned shows, among other things, that blockchain agents and forensics are getting better at finding and returning stolen funds. For example, the colonial pipeline paid $2.3 million to hackers who broke into its computer network, and Kucoin was able to get $281 million worth of customer assets back. Both of these are examples of successful tracking that led to the return of stolen or dirty money.

Everyone knows that when people try to launder money, they send it to exchanges and DeFi sites. Especially those that don't have any KYC rules. Because of this, Lisa Monaco said that the best way to catch money launderers in the crypto area is to follow the money trail that the blockchain makes possible. The blockchain will record all transactions, no matter how complicatedly the money was moved to hide where it came from and where it was going.

Analysing and Investigating the Blockchain

To successfully follow the money, crypto investigators use complicated tools to look into where the money came from, where it went, and the digital traces left by the many layers of transactions.

Investigating the source of money is a way to find out where transactions come from, especially the location that starts the financial activity. As the transaction starts and continues, it leaves traces as it moves from one chain to the next, from one exchange to the next, or from one bank to the next.

Often, complex data mining methods like clustering, ownership analysis, and e-discovery are used to track the flow of crypto funds and analyze it:

1. Ownership analysis puts together a confluence of factors and evidence which uncovers the beneficiaries and identities behind wallet addresses under investigation.
2. Clustering algorithms, on the other hand, serve to sift, cross-reference, and identify wallet addresses that belong to the same wallet and owner. Clustering can identify thousands of addresses as belonging to a particular wallet. This helps to reduce the confusion caused by the peeling of funds and concerns the investigator with the end game in mind.
3. E-discovery helps to scrape crypto transaction and wallet data off the internet and personal devices and analytically weave the data into a giant digital roadmap which gives the investigator holistic insight. E-discovery often employs different tracing techniques to achieve its purpose.

Lastly, the goal of the destination of funds research is to find the wallets that get money after it has been washed through several layers of activities.

The creation and use of sophisticated software for tracking and analyzing is one of the most important things that has been done to improve crypto security. It is the most important thing that has been done so far, and it has turned the tide in favor of forensic experts. Bitquery, a company that makes analytical tools and software for research, is a good example.

Bilic: A Strategy for Blockchain Anti-Money Laundering (AML)

The Bilic framework is an all-inclusive set of tools, techniques, and ways to see data that gives analysts and prosecutors the power to find these stolen, laundered, or hacked funds. Our method aims to help government agencies, businesses, financial institutions, and regulators find and stop financial crimes that involve crypto assets. We do this by democratizing investigation through an open intelligence marketplace, which makes it easier for everyone to share information. The National Institute of Standards and Technology (NIST) approves of the way we do things.

Methodology

- **Data collection**: The data collection phase would use sophisticated software to scrape transaction data off the blockchain.

- **Data Processing**: The processing stage will convert the collected data into useful information used to track the origins, movements, and destinations of stolen funds.
- **Group Intelligence Gathering**: This phase involves the combination of different intelligence departments in gathering information. This helps to cross-reference information to ensure a confluence point where the different data meets to show that information gathering is credible and would promote informed decisionmaking.
- **Reporting**: The final phase involves presenting the findings of investigations for decision making.

Bilic: AML Features

Follow the Money (FTM) AML

FTM is our new blockchain research dashboard for exploring crypto-assets, seeing how they work, and keeping track of wallet transactions. The FTM works with more than 47 blockchain networks and has support for multichain graph network visualization. This means that experts can look at Ethereum and Bitcoin wallets on the same graph.

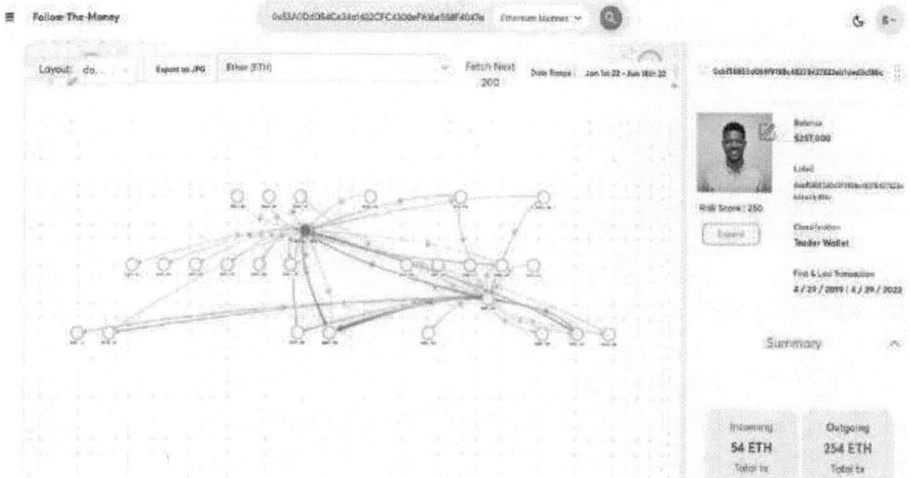

Figure 1. Showing the Follow the Money Wallet Investigation dashboard with a graph network of user transactions and wallet activities

The FTM screen shows the wallet's transaction history, including money sent and received, incoming and outgoing transfers, interactions with smart contracts, and activities that involve wallets that have been labeled. Investigators can use the FTM tool to look into transfers, find bad wallets that are involved in illegal ones, and follow the money. The FTM screen shows how much money comes into and goes out of the fund.

Users can make both public and private labels that can be used to mark suspicious wallets. This can be useful information for both future agents and people who use intelligence.

Intelligence Marketplace

The Intelligence Marketplace is an open intelligence tool that gives data creators money back when they look into illegal transactions and report on what they find. It also gives data users, like spy agencies and government organizations, secure, private access to information that can be used.

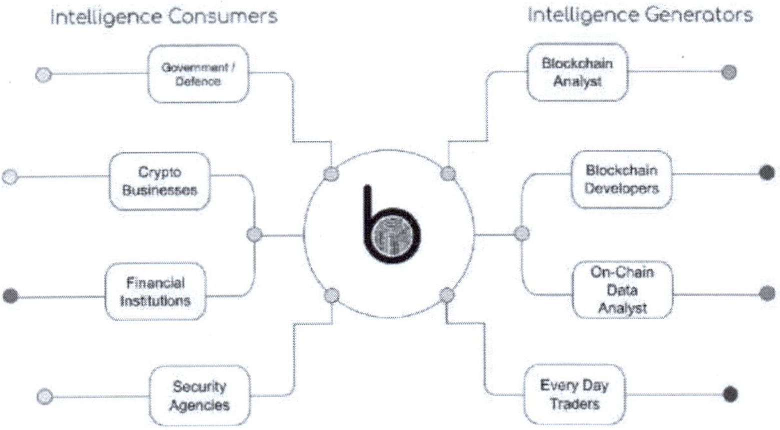

Figure 2. Showing the Follow the Money The intelligence marketplace information flow, with intelligence generators feeding and accessing data from the marketplace.

The marketplace is a one-stop shop for threat intelligence information. Users can report security problems like malware, hacks, scams, and theft. Our community of security pros looks at, tracks down, and verifies each incident report that is sent through the platform. After each report is checked to make sure it is true, the information is saved on the Intelligence Data Warehouse without putting the victims or reporters' privacy at risk.

Pattern Recognition Engine (PRE)

Pattern Recognition is the process of finding regularities and patterns in data by using computer programs. The PRE uses network analysis and machine learning algorithms to automatically find patterns and outliers in a user's behavior on the blockchain. Wallets that have been involved in fraud or money laundering, wallets that are linked to entities, wallets that are related to the well-known OFAC sanctioned list, etc., are examples of patterns and irregularities.

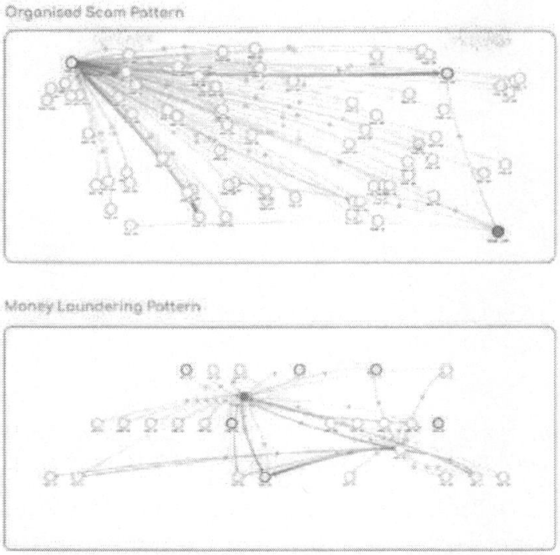

Figure 3. Showing 2 examples of pattern recognition from a wallet transaction network; the organised scam pattern above and the Money laundering Pattern below.

The engine allows the user to automatically detect a series of patterns to speed up investigations and factfinding. Such as:

- **Money laundering transactions patterns**: e.g., by tracking money back to another linked wallet or carousel type of patterns. As seen in Fig. 3;
- **KYC Pattern**: Patterns of regular interaction with KYC platform to allow investigators to easily deanonymise wallets;
- **Mixer Pattern**: Network patterns with links to mixers and tumblers;
- **Organised Scam Pattern**: A network pattern where funds are moved from one wallet to an operational wallet with a large number of smaller value transactions.

Intelligence Data Warehouse (IDW)

The IDW is our single source of truth. It is an organized and consolidated data warehouse that holds a lot of data from many different sources. Institutions can use the richness of this big data set to get useful intelligence insights that can help with investigations, being aware of threats, and making decisions. We've kept a record over time of labelled wallets, incoming and outgoing transactions, off-chain media data, the history of NFT transactions, and the relationship between wallets and any strange trends found in the PRE. Institutions and security analysts can use this information to their advantage. IDW can be thought of as the "single source of truth" for information about blockchain security.

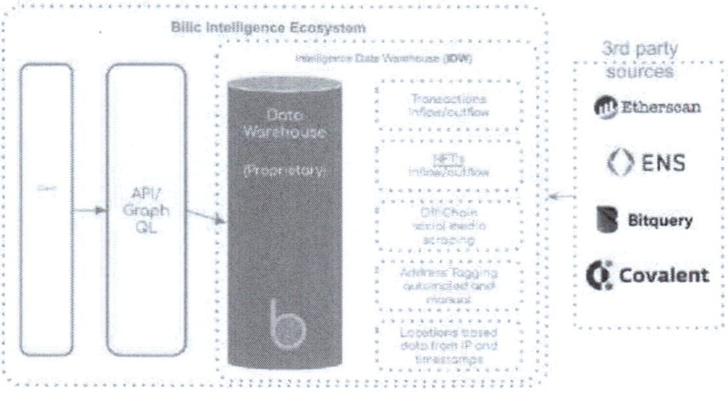

Figure 4. Showing the Intelligence Data Warehouse Architecture, with data types, storage method, providers and microprocessors clearly identified.

The data for the IDW comes from many different places to make a data warehouse that no one else can beat. The IDW is a key part of the Bilic intelligence ecosystem because it allows for significant high-level profiling, transaction segmentation, data scraping, and address tagging.

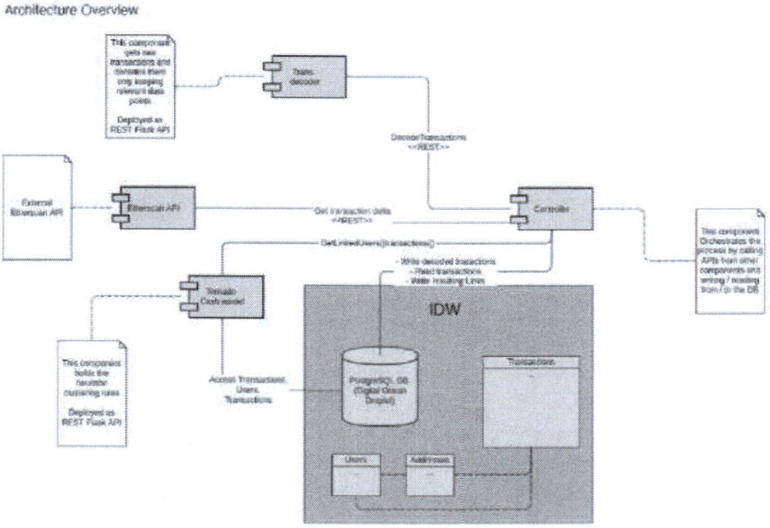

Figure 5. Showing the Intelligence Data Warehouse Architecture, with data types, storage method, providers and microprocessors clearly identified.

Verification

Verification is used by a new AML tool to check the risk factors of a wallet. As a digital shield, these verification methods can be used by financial institutions, companies, custodians, exchanges, security agencies, trading desks, and fintech users who use intelligence. This method keeps people from sending their digital assets to a fake wallet address in a way that can't be taken back. In the crypto industries, AML designs are now very popular. One example is the popular Know Your Customer practice, which some of the biggest exchanges have to do by law. With these AML designs, a business can get users' personal information, which links cryptocurrency wallets to real-world names. AML designs put a face to wallet addresses, making it easy to identify, track, and collect funds when their users commit frauds. This makes it harder for criminals to do bad things and makes it harder for criminals to do bad things. Users can simply query an endpoint or search for the bilic verify rating for a particular wallet to get a full breakdown of the wallet and a risk rating.

Conclusion

This chapter has shown that it is not true that cryptocurrency can't be tracked and is a safe place for thieves to hide. We've talked about how blockchain crimes affect businesses and how to find criminals who are trying to erase their digital footprints on the blockchain. We've also talked about and shown tools that can be used to track and trace these footprints and given a plan for how to look into blockchain-related crimes. The cryptocurrency space and the technologies that go with it, especially when it comes to security, are still new, which makes them very open to attacks. But hackers and money launderers no longer find it easy to put stolen money back into the market. There are getting to be more and more advanced ways to track and stop suspicious activities on the blockchain. Expert blockchain detectives and crypto forensic analysts are getting better at their jobs, but it's hard for them to do their jobs because criminals can use transaction mixers, round-tripping, and complex layering, among other things, to hide their tracks on the blockchain.

Chapter 10

Chinese views of Future Warfare and Implications for the United States

As of 2016, much of the public's attention has been on what China is doing in internet, just like in 2015 and 2014. People in the United States usually talk about Chinese information operations in terms of hacking into U.S. government databases like the Office of Personnel Management (OPM) and business databases. But it is very important to understand why and how China does what it does. You can't come up with policy responses to counter actions if you don't know what makes them happen in the first place.

How China sees information and future Warfare

The most important thing that comes out of Chinese writings about informationized warfare, information warfare, and information operations is that the Chinese government sees information as being tied to both the national interest and the survival of the party (or at least the CCP). It's important to remember that this doesn't just apply to how knowledge is used during war. The Chinese government isn't just worried about how information could be used in a military battle. Instead, the government sees information as a deciding factor in the ongoing competition between states as a whole.

This is because, as Chinese writings point out, knowledge is becoming more and more important in the economy and government of the 21st century. This is the Information Age, and the key to success is being able to get correct information quickly, send it to others, analyze it, and then use it quickly. These skills are the most important part of any plan to gain "information dominance," which is the ability to gather, send, analyze, and use information more quickly and correctly for one's own goals while preventing an opponent from doing the same.

At the same time, however, the free flow of information is a serious threat to CCP rule. Even though the Chinese Communist Party no longer stresses the idea that "from each according to their ability, to each according to their needs," it is still committed to its role as the "vanguard party" and, therefore, the only legitimate governmental authority in the PRC. It is also possible to see the fall of the Soviet Union as a result of not being able to keep the "vanguard party" role and, just as important, the loosening of controls over information. The other big Communist Party fell because of the policies of glasnost and perestroika, or opening and reform. Information is the currency of economic and military power, and it is also the source of political power.

This "conundrum" sets up the second most important point. As an authoritarian party that can learn from what happened to the Communist Party of the Soviet Union, the CCP cannot afford to let information move freely. This would give too many people a chance to question its rule. So, the Chinese government will try to control how information gets around.

In some ways, trying to keep this kind of control just means keeping rules that have been in place for a long time. The CCP has shown for a long time that it is willing to go to great lengths, like building a huge infrastructure to support suppression, to stop this flow. But the Information Age, with its many ties and links between different information networks, makes it impossible for the CCP to only control the flow of information within China. Instead, it needs to keep track of how information gets to China.

This attempt to control the flow of information to and from the country is a fundamental change in the way countries think about information as a resource. States have, of course, always tried to shape and change how they are seen. Limiting access to information from outside is also not a new thing. But the Chinese attempts are different in size and scope because of how they think the Information Age has changed things for the better. Controlling information now means putting limits on not only media and TV shows, but also how the Internet works around the world.

This fundamental change is also reflected in the way the PRC sees the international system, including how the international common areas are run. If the Chinese want to control and shape the flow of information into China, they will have to change the international structures that handle that flow. This doesn't mean that China is about to change the way things are. Chinese writings often say that the PRC is still in a time of "strategic opportunity," which China needs to take advantage of if it wants to get better and join the middle-developed powers. So, China needs to keep working on strategies of peaceful growth and interaction.

But as China has become steadily more powerful, it has questioned more and more the international frameworks that often limit its actions. Chinese writings say that these buildings were often made without the PRC's help. China is getting better, and the CCP wants to stay in power, so these restrictions from the outside are getting more and more annoying.

Still, it is more important than ever to challenge the current system because the PRC, and especially the CCP, sees itself as more and more in competition with the other big powers, especially the US. The United States is a big supporter of freedom on the Internet and, more generally, of the free flow of information. Also, many Chinese officials have said that it is American policies that urge China's neighbors to challenge Chinese control over its coastal waters or help the Dalai Lama and other sources of instability inside China.

This doesn't mean that the PRC thinks war or armed conflict is guaranteed. In fact, there is no reason to think that the PRC would openly attack its neighbors with weapons in the next ten years or so. There is no "Fulda Gap" possibility to think about like there was during the Cold War.

At the same time, the Chinese government knows that it can get what it wants by using different methods, such as "hybrid warfare." China has shown that it can use fishing boats and civilian ships for law enforcement to carry out its strategic goals. If Chinese battleships don't shoot at foreign ships, Chinese fishing boats are less likely to feel bad about physically getting in the way of foreign ships. The world's information networks, where it's much harder to say who did what, seem like the perfect place to fight the kind of gray conflict that is typical of hybrid warfare.

So, at the strategic level, the PRC will always try to shape how people inside and outside of the country see it through the information it sends out and projects. In the meantime, it will try to figure out and control how other countries see China and figure out what their strengths and flaws are. This is the same thing that every country does when it comes to gathering information about possible friends and enemies.

But where the PRC has started to do things differently from other states is in how much they want to control the information area in both peacetime and wartime. In particular, China's efforts to control information are somewhat limited by the international order in times of peace. However, if there is a war, these efforts are likely to be much bigger and more obvious.

This is shown by how the Chinese military has changed over the past few years. These changes are the result of nearly 25 years of thinking about the shape and needs of future war. With its focus on the role of information in all parts of future warfare, the Chinese idea of "local wars under informationized conditions" shows how this change is still happening. This idea comes from the lessons learned from watching the allied alliance in the first Gulf War in 1990–

1991, as well as the Balkan Wars of the 1990s and the American invasions of Afghanistan and Iraq. So, the PLA at first thought that future wars would be "local wars in modern, high-tech conditions." Later, however, they realized that not all high-tech was equally important.

With the conclusion that information technology is the most important part of high technology, which reflects the larger strategic shift from the Industrial Age to the Information Age, the PLA has developed a new doctrine to connect its idea of future wars to the kinds of forces it will use and the kinds of operations they will do. In this way, it looks like the PLA is once again improving its ideas.

From focusing on network warfare, electronic warfare, and psychological warfare at first, it now doesn't seem to be putting much emphasis on command-and-control warfare or information warfare. The implication seems to be that not all networks, electronic systems, or leaders are equally important. Instead, those in key decision-making roles and the people and systems that help them make choices should be higher-priority targets. It is important to note that this does not mean that the PLA will ignore other networks, systems, or people (like logistics or combat units) in its quest to win future informationized fights. Instead, it shows the goals for how to use resources and build skills.

This is clear from the work done over the past few years to get different kinds of new tools and improve joint training. Along with new fighters, warships, and self-propelled artillery, there are also new unmanned aerial vehicles, electronic warfare systems, and sensors. The huge reorganization that happened at the end of 2015 and the beginning of 2016 was a big step in this long-term plan to get the PLA ready "to fight and win future local wars in an informationized world."

How Chinese conclusions will shape Chinese Actions

Based on these Chinese findings, there are certain things that follow, which can be seen in the way the Chinese act.

China's acts must cover the whole picture and will do so. The PRC still thinks of itself as a country on the way up. Even though this is the second-largest GDP in the world, it must be shared among 1.3 billion people. As important, China is not always rich. It has a lot of untapped human and physical potential, but most of the country will stay poor until that potential is turned into real capacity and capability. In light of this, the Chinese are likely to take a more "whole-of-government" approach, if only to make the most of the resources they have. So, while the US has both a military and a civilian space program (with the civilian program being split into three large parts), China is not likely to follow a plan that requires a lot of redundancy and overlap.

This is going to be made worse by how important informationization is in general. Even though some of the top leaders' efforts have stalled at times, it is clear that Xi Jinping has made informationizing China a major policy goal. So long as the Chinese see their future as being inextricably linked to the Information Age, these efforts will have the backing of the highest levels of government, with efforts to cut down on silos and improve cooperation between different bureaucracies. This will lead to more teamwork not only within the military but also between the military and other national security agencies, as well as with a wider range of Chinese ministries and both public and private businesses.

Actions in China are based on Chinese goals and aren't likely to be changed much by outside pressure or bribes. If China's leaders think that information is important to their country's survival and that economic spying is a way to get that information, they won't be easy to stop. In the same way, if the Chinese government thinks that information flow is important to the survival of the system, Beijing will limit and direct information flow in ways that meet internal security needs. To reach this goal, the targets of Chinese actions will have to make Beijing pay very high costs, so that the wins aren't worth it for the PRC, if they want to change the way China acts.

The fact that China's leaders think they are already in a strategic battle with other countries makes it even harder to change their minds. The CCP thinks that the United States, Russia, India, and Japan, as well as non-state players like Uighur and Tibetan separatists, pose threats to China's security. In fact, it is important to realize that the Chinese government sees itself as already using global deterrence. This is a position it has held at least since the 1960s, when it thought that both the Soviet Union and the United States were threatening it.

The fact that the information area is both virtual and global, so it is not limited by any country's borders, adds to what the Chinese think about how big the threats are. So, for the Chinese government to control the flow and quality of information, they have to do things not just in China but all over the world. To do this, China must have access to foreign information sources and be able to influence foreign decision makers while keeping other countries from doing the same in China.

Because of this, the PRC is taking more and more steps outside of its own borders in an effort to take over areas that were once shared. This is true for both information space, like the Internet, and real space, like the seas and space. In fact, there are a lot of similarities between China's efforts to control and dominate information space and its efforts to control and dominate the South China Sea. In each case, the PRC wants to spread Chinese sovereignty, which includes its rules and administrative rights, into areas that were previously open.

In this way, China's actions are justified by a very different view of how domestic and foreign law work. In fact, Chinese ideas about legal fighting come from a very different view of the role of law in history and culture than those of the West. At heart, the Chinese believe in "rule-by-law," not "rule-of-law." In other words, the law is a tool for exercising power, but it doesn't stop people from using their power.

In the largest sense, Chinese society before 1911 saw the law as a tool, a way for the government to control the people but not a way for the people to control the government. The Confucian morality laid out a set of duties that were more important than the laws. In ancient China, the Legalist "school" put more stress on making legal codes than the Confucians did on making ethical codes. However, they also saw the law as a way to keep society and the state in control of the people. In China, there was never a strong tradition that said the law was just as important for the master as for the ruled.

During the early years of the PRC, the Marxist idea that "the law should serve as an ideological tool of politics" had an effect on how Chinese law was made. So, when the PRC was just starting out, the CCP saw the law in the same way as imperial China. The law was mostly a tool for running the country, but it didn't limit the party or Mao Zedong, the "Great Helmsman." In any case, the party ruled by decree instead of using the formal systems that were set up. During the Cultural Revolution, Mao himself got rid of both the judicial system and the court system. Since Mao's death, there have been some attempts to make a set of rules, but most of them have been about business and contracts. Also, the law is still a tool that mostly affects the people, not the party. In other words, the law exists to serve power, not to limit it.

This means that the Chinese government uses laws, treaties, and other legal tools to get what it wants, even if it goes against what people have always thought about the law or what the laws were meant to do. So, the Chinese don't think that trying to extend Chinese control over shared places is against international law. Instead, they see it as a form of political warfare. Those who try to stop them are also seen as trying to contain China and threaten CCP rule.

So, China's attempts to control the information realm aim not only to control the flow of information but also to discredit the idea that the information realm is a shared space that many different groups can use. The Chinese government has tried to make it harder for non-state actors to set the rules for the Internet. At the same time, it has tried to make it harder for dissidents, political leaders in Taiwan, Tibetan activists, and others who have tried to argue against China's stance to get their message out to both Chinese and international audiences. Information, whether it comes from inside or outside China, is seen by the

Chinese government as a danger to the country's very existence. Because of this, these efforts are seen as defensive measures to protect the regime.

China is expected to try to keep its information to itself. China's answer to the problem of information vulnerability is to make it harder for people to get knowledge. This isn't meant to be like North Korea's extreme form of isolation, but rather to make sure that information moves "with Chinese characteristics." In fact, Beijing wants to become informationally autonomous, meaning that it can get to information, make information, and send information all on its own. So, the PRC has made Chinese versions of information companies, is trying to build a chip industry to replace computer parts that it imports, and does other things to limit access to and from China of information.

This is an ironic way to say no to the fiscal policies of the last 40 years that have helped China grow and succeed. But just as the CCP accepts that the Great Firewall of China slows down the speed of the Chinese Internet, it also accepts that the wider restrictions on information flow have economic and innovative potential costs. This is a risky deal, though, because it looks like CCP leaders are trading long-term economic growth for short-term security and stopping immediate threats to their power. If the Chinese leaders are right that the future growth of "comprehensive national power" (CNP) is closely linked to the ability to use information, then their actions are likely to slow the growth of CNP in the long run.

Implications for American Policy Makers

Given what the Chinese have said about how knowledge affects their strategy and policy, American leaders need to realize how much they are already in competition with the PRC. This, in turn, has effects on a number of laws in the United States. In the same way, everyone interested in national security, not just decision makers, needs to be aware of the many things the PRC is doing and start to work against them.

The United States and China Are Competing

The most important thing to remember is that China's leaders see themselves in competition with the U.S. and with the rest of the world as a whole, and possibly in a state of war. It's important to remember that competing does not mean going to war. The PRC does not act like it is at war with the U.S. or its borders. But it sees its relationships with many of these countries, like the US and Japan, as fundamentally hostile. In the wake of the Tiananmen Square Massacre in 1989, restrictions were put on China's access to advanced technology. After that, more restrictions were put on the transfer of space and other technologies, and China was also limited in its ability to buy Western companies.

Several important people in the United States agree that China is one of the United States' biggest security rivals. The 1999 Cox Commission Report, the Office of the Director of National Intelligence's annual Worldwide Threat Assessment, and the DOD's annual report to Congress on China all show that China is becoming a bigger threat to American security in the western Pacific and around the world. This means that China needs to build up a wide range of new powers, both in its military and in the area of information warfare.

Ironically, many of the ideas behind these new skills seem to be similar to those in the United States. The way the Chinese talk about the need to control information is similar to how the Americans talk about the need to understand and use the information world, especially in Joint Pub 3-13 "Information Operations." When it comes to writings about military doctrine, it's clear that the two sides' uniformed forces have some things in common.

The United States and China Are Competing Orthogonally

Even though some of their written doctrines are similar, the Chinese and American approaches to information warfare are different. This shows the bigger, more fundamental gap between the two countries. In many ways, American leaders don't see how the U.S. and China are fighting with each other.

What's important is to know how much Chinese and American ideas about informationized warfare (not information warfare) come from very different places and start points. The two sides are not so much unequal, which means they take different approaches to the same problem, but orthogonal, which means they start from completely different places. For example, publications from the Joint Chiefs of Staff, like doctrinal statements about information operations or space operations, only apply to the U.S. military, which must follow the rules set by U.S. laws (such as the separation of military functions (Title 10) from intelligence functions (Title 50)). On the other hand, Chinese texts clearly include all national information sources, whether they are military, civilian, or not related to the government.

Part of this difference comes from the fact that Chinese and American leaders make decisions in very different historical situations than each other. As was already said, East and West have very different ideas about the role and nature of law and whether or not it limits power. In the same way, the United States, for example, thinks that information should flow freely. The Constitution and the rights it protects basically ensure that the government won't get in the way of the flow of information. This is done through freedom of the press, freedom of speech, and freedom of assembly, among other things. As important, the West's more liberal view of how the state and society work together has always seen a place for a strong civil society. This core idea is shown by the fact that the two things are seen as separate and different from each other.

On the other hand, the CCP has shown that it is not willing to allow free and open sharing of information. And the fact that party committees are everywhere means that China's civil society can only grow with the help and control of the party. This point of view isn't just a result of the CCP's policies; it comes from many different parts of Chinese society and history, such as the different ideas about the role of the law.

Because of this, the Chinese shouldn't be thought of as taking a "asymmetric" approach, since "asymmetric" means taking a different path from a similar starting point to reach basically the same goal. Beijing's starting point is very different because it was made by totally different things. It shouldn't come as a surprise that this completely different context leads to constraints and goals that are very different from our own—in other words, that they are orthogonal.

In this way, it's not true that the US and China always want to do things that are bad for each other. In fact, the two sides may sometimes agree on the goals, the means, or both. At other times, they will be trying to reach goals that have nothing to do with each other. But the interests of the two states will more and more often clash, even though they are motivated by different things.

Most importantly, the United States' desire to keep information flowing freely around the world, for philosophical, political, economic, and military reasons, will be a challenge to how China and the CCP see their own interests. As long as the CCP thinks that the survival of the government is the same as the survival of the country ("l'etat, c'est nous"), these efforts will be seen as threatening the party's hold on power, even if that is not why the U.S. is trying to help.

The Competition Is All-Encompassing

For the same reason, China's leaders think that the struggle with the US and the liberal Western order as a whole is all-encompassing. First of all, if the Chinese want to raise their CNP, the PRC needs to get better, not just in the defense or the economy, but in every way. This means making the business more advanced, getting better at science and technology, getting the government to work better together, and getting more diplomatic respect. All of these things involve information operations in some way, whether you are spying, gathering information, trying to get your way, or getting ready for armed operations. Because China is putting a lot of effort into improving its position during this "strategic opportunity," it is unlikely that its different information activities, such as economic and technological espionage or efforts to spread its influence around the world, will slow down.

Also, from Beijing's point of view, figuring out who controls the flow of information around the world and who has access to that information is not only important for national security but also for the survival of the government. The United States agrees with the idea that there are more than one group of people who have a right to say who should have access. This is shown by the fact that the United States backs ICANN and is open-minded about who can take part in setting the rules. The free flow of information doesn't change how stable the United States or its institutions are at their core.

For the people in charge in China, letting so many different groups have unrestricted access to the spread of information is a basic threat. Information can affect not only China's security in the future, but also how well the CCP can stay in power. First of all, if this split isn't stopped, there will be a lot more places where people can get information. Because of this, it would be almost impossible for the PRC to stop the flow. As important, the more different sources of information there are, the more likely it is that religious groups, separatists, and dissenters will be among them. That, in turn, would start to make these groups and what they say seem more respectable to Chinese people, making them a bigger threat to the CCP.

So, the PRC wants to limit entry to state-level players, if possible. So, it backs giving organizations like the United Nations International Telecommunications Union (ITU) more power over the Internet. If this worked, it would reduce the number of players and give Beijing the most power over each one. By using its economic power, China is more likely to be able to get other countries to stop giving groups Internet names and other things like that. (This is an example of uneven forces.) On the other hand, it will be harder to stop the spread of unfavorable information when the role of civil society organizations (like NGOs, the press, and faith groups) grows.

The Chinese forces will have the same kind of determination. On the one hand, the Chinese military will work harder to learn more about possible enemies like the US, Taiwan, Japan, Vietnam, India, and Russia. This will include not only technical knowledge about weapons systems, but also information about the organization and how things work, like who makes decisions and what procedures are used. All of this gives information about who to go after, when, and with what kinds of tools. It could be decided that it would be better to wait to attack a target until it has a single point of failure. For example, satellites could be attacked after undersea lines that carry much more bandwidth have been damaged. Or, it could be decided that it would be better to use trusted agents to change information instead of using hard-kill ways to destroy physical infrastructure. A lot of this will rest on how well information is gathered during times of peace.

At the same time, there will probably be more work to stop rivals from getting similar information about their Chinese partners. Intelligence gathering activities in the United States and other countries are likely to be big targets for physical, technical, and political interference. For example, the work China is doing to build islands in the South China Sea is likely to lead to the creation of an air defense identification zone. This zone will make it harder for American surveillance planes to fly over China's coasts. In the same way, being able to use different types of jamming and blinding against space systems will force enemies to think carefully about when (and if) they will use their satellites to watch the PRC. If there are gaps in coverage, Chinese armed forces will have more chances to do denial and deception operations that work better.

Given that the Chinese government is trying to combine civilian and military capabilities and assets, it is likely that more Chinese entities that aren't necessarily part of the military but have been given supporting tasks and roles will be involved in these efforts to gather and hide information. This will likely make it harder to figure out who did what than it was before. At the same time, the massive reorganization of the PLA is likely to make it harder to figure out who did what because it will disrupt past trends and, by extension, certain indicators.

The Competition Will Be Intensifying—and Militarizing

None of this means that China will stop trying to control vital information during times of peace. In fact, if China's economy slows down and this causes more trouble inside the country, the Chinese are likely to work harder to control the global information space. This will be done so that outsiders can't affect, make worse, or take advantage of the fighting at home as much as possible. At the same time, they will be even stricter on the Chinese information scene at home, for the same reason: to stop more general discontent and chaos.

Unfortunately, this is likely to mean that China will try even harder to keep foreign troops, especially American ones, out of the western Pacific coast. If Chinese officials think that the U.S. military encourages local states to reject Chinese claims of sovereignty, or if they think that the U.S. encourages such efforts outright, then limiting the U.S.'s freedom of action in the area will make that less appealing. Also, preventing American forces from establishing information dominance is a key way to discourage or force Washington to agree more with China's view of how the area should be run.

As different groups figure out what their responsibilities are, the PLA's reorganization is also likely to make it harder for the Chinese military to gather information. With a whole service (the PLASSF) focused on establishing information dominance through actions in the electromagnetic domain, network space, and outer space, that new organization will probably be just as busy as its previous parts (like the different GSD Third Department entities). In the same way, the newly formed permanent joint commands that are in charge of the different new war zones will also try to find out more about their areas of duty.

Policy options for the United States: Some Don'ts

The PRC will be a big problem for the United States, but it will be very different from the Soviet Union. The PRC is not necessarily trying to replace the United States. In fact, Chinese leaders say that all they want is for China to be a middle-developed country by 2049, when the PRC turns 100 years old. As important, because the Chinese threat is so different from what we want, it is likely to seem like it comes and goes. This is because what China wants is not only different from what we want, but it also often doesn't overlap with (or get in the way of) American interests.

This means that there will be just as many chances for China and the United States to work together as there will be for them to fight. The critical interests of the two states won't always be at odds with each other. This won't be a "zero-sum" situation. In fact, the Chinese should be praised if they choose to stick with the global trade system, which has been a big part of China's economic growth over the past 30 years.

Don't Make Concessions on the Principle of Free Information Flow

One of the most important areas where the two sides are unlikely to agree is on the question of who has the most information, including who gets to set the rules for how information is managed. The basic philosophical differences between the two systems and China's view that information is important to the survival of the regime are likely to create fundamental contradictions between the two states that will make it harder for them to get along. These contradictions will make it harder for the two countries to get what they want. Worse, because the CCP sees this as a matter of survival for the regime, it is likely to move strongly and leave little room for negotiations.

But for the same reasons, this is not an area where the U.S. can afford to give up a lot. The open flow of information is not only an important part of the American way of life and culture, but it is also important for the economy and national security. Just like the young American republic couldn't give up freedom of the seas to foreign rules because it would have killed the young American economy, the modern American economy and the global trading system it is a part of can't survive if the PRC keeps blocking the free flow of information. China can try to control how information moves around inside China. What happens behind the Great Firewall of China (GFWC) can stay behind the GFWC. But once Chinese actions affect other players, whether through cyber economic espionage, political and economic pressure to silence different parties, or efforts to rewrite the rules on Internet governance to extend sovereignty to shared informational spaces, it becomes a vital issue for the United States as well.

It is also important to remember that China is not the only important player, even though it is one of the most important. Unlike during the Cold War, when the world was mostly controlled by the relationship between the United States and the Soviet Union, American actions and choices in other parts of the world will have an effect on China. As with the factors that affect how the PLA thinks about the future of war, joint operations, and the rise of information-based warfare, it is likely that the Chinese will learn from other people's efforts to control information, including their use of computer networks. These efforts aren't just about American wars, though they probably are the most important ones. They also look at Russian and other countries' wartime events as well. In fact, the attacks on computer networks in Estonia, Georgia, and Ukraine are likely to have been used by the Chinese as a model for how to do similar attacks themselves, including how to hide who did them and use them for political gain.

If Russian operations in Syria, Ukraine, or the Caucasus are seen as successful, China will try to copy the things that made those operations successful in East Asia, the Indian Ocean, and Central Asia. On the other hand, if China sees that the Russians are failing, it is likely that China will also learn from that. So, the US needs to have a strong response to all attempts, not just those from the PRC, to control or limit the shared information spaces. Any and all of these plans will be strongly fought.

Because of all of these things, the United States needs to get used to the ideological and power-politics parts of the Sino-American struggle again. In the end, what Beijing wants is for the global information environment to become more fragmented and balkanized. This means that Beijing's rules, which will be supported by other authoritarian governments like Russia's, will be applied to more and more of the shared information spaces, making it harder for information to flow freely. The more open and inclusive American approach has economic benefits, but they must be paired with a focus on political issues, such as the dignity of the person (both as a source of information and a consumer of information).

Don't Underestimate the Difficulties of Keeping Information Secure

Even though the United States created the Internet, it does not have a stranglehold on making, sending, or using information. In fact, the United States is not a "superpower" when it comes to information. Instead, it is one of many "major powers" in this area. Even though it has a lot of information resources, such as IT companies, software developers, and Internet users, it does not control all of the information area the way the U.S. Navy still does in the seas.

The Internet is a great example of how hard it can be. The attacks on computer networks in Ukraine and Estonia are a warning that the information threats around the world are getting worse and more complicated. The truth is that making a secure global information space is probably not doable.

Many of the first people to work on the Internet have said that the system they made was never meant to be safe or to be used on such a large scale. This is made even worse by the way software weaknesses work. Even after vulnerabilities are found, they can't be fixed quickly.

> The sad reality is that the average zero day threat goes undetected for almost a year. Only once captured by anti-malware researchers and decompiled can this new vector of cyber attack be examined and the true nature of the cyber threat analyzed and evaluated. Then the company needs to write a fix or a "patch" for the security vulnerability, issue it, or distribute updated software. This could take weeks, or even months, just to issue the software upgrade.

> Then there is the patch problem. It takes around 21 days to upgrade and patch 50 per cent of corporate servers but it takes 62 days to patch 50 per cent of corporate desktop computers. Of course, some are never patched at all. Home computer users are even worse: it is estimated that over 40 per cent of the current computers attached to the Internet are at risk—simply because users never download and install current computer upgrades.

Hardware security has some of the same problems. Some people have suggested inspecting at least some of the chips and computers that come into the U.S. from China. However, this would be hard to do on a large scale (the U.S. imported $22 billion worth of semiconductors and other computer parts from China in 2014), and it's not clear what the inspections would be looking for. It's one thing to check a chip to see if it has a known virus or other malicious software. But, as the quote about software vulnerabilities says, it can take a year to find a zero-day exploit in a program. If malware was hidden on a chip on purpose, it would be even harder and take more time to find it. What happens between now and then?

Don't Ignore Inherent Chinese Advantages in Establishing Information Dominance

China's efforts to keep its information to itself add to its other strengths, especially in the military sense. Because of the way the world is, the PLA has some geographical benefits that the other side doesn't have. First of all, the PLA's main goal for the immediate future will still be to protect the PRC. Even though it is expanding its reach, it is likely to focus on the area within the first island chain during the first half of the 2020s. This chain goes from Japan in the north, through Okinawa, Taiwan, the Philippines, and the Straits of Malacca.

This, in turn, means that some people have more information than others. The PLA will have enough networks of sensors, communications, and other things that overlap in the area between the first island chain and the Chinese mainland to keep track of what's going on, even if there are coordinated strikes.

Also, a lot of these networks will be safer than others. The Chinese, for example, can use microwave, satellite, and other communication systems, as well as line-of-sight radio, which is hard to receive, and fiber-optic landlines, which are hard to tap. They can use their large fishing fleet and merchant fleet as extra eyes and radars to help their navy and coast guard keep track of what's going on in the maritime area. They can and do build new islands where they can put radars, sonar units, and airfields where planes and helicopters can take off.

American troops, on the other hand, that want to move to the area will have to bring their communications and sensors with them. China has a lot of sensors and ways to communicate, but the US relies a lot more on satellites to find and identify targets, coordinate forces, and figure out how bad a fight was. If China cut important undersea cables, which carry a large amount of the world's bandwidth, it would hurt American armed forces more than the PLA. This is also true in a broader sense. If the Chinese military is able to track and control the flow of information across different networks, it will be in a better position to create information dominance, because its internal networks are more robust, redundant, and secure.

This is important for both strategy and operations. If the PLA can control the flow of information, both the military and civilian leaders of China will be able to build a psychological advantage not only against the US but also against other states in the area. This, in turn, will help them use tactics that discourage and force people to do what they want, which is the main goal of their policies.

Don't Ignore Inherent Chinese Weaknesses in Establishing Information Dominance

But even though the PLA has some benefits in the fight for information dominance, the PRC as a whole has a lot of problems. Some are, ironically, because China doesn't follow the rules and doesn't care about how other countries act. It is thought that more than 200 million computers in China still use the old Windows XP software. It is thought that about three-quarters of Windows users in China are using illegal copies of that program. Since they haven't signed up, it's possible that many, if not most, of them will never get security updates. This means that many zero-day exploits that were stopped in other places could still be open in China and could be used.

China's problems aren't just in the area of information technology, either. The leaders in Beijing have to pay much more attention to both threats from inside and outside the country than those in Washington. The fact that the CCP is so focused on limiting the flow of information suggests that, from a national security point of view, the Chinese see domestic unrest as their biggest weakness. This is also shown by the fact that any social media message asking for action outside of party channels is quickly shut down, even if the action is supposed to help the CCP. If the slowdown in the economy that started in 2016 lasts for any length of time, this situation is likely to get worse. When the number of unemployed Chinese people goes up and their rising hopes aren't met, the Chinese people are likely to be more angry. More suppression and more restrictions on how information moves inside the country will only make it harder to keep control.

The possibility of unrest within the country is likely to drive up the need for more resources. Until 2014, when the Chinese stopped reporting statistics, the budget for internal security (which includes both national and provincial spending) grew faster than the budget for external security (which mostly pays for the PLA). In fact, official numbers showed that more money was spent on domestic security, which includes the People's Armed Police and the Ministry of Public Security, than on the military. Since then, only the numbers from the national government have been given. Even so, these numbers show that spending on internal security is still going up quickly. In 2015, China spent 7.2% more on public security, and in 2016, they spent an additional 5.3% more. Adding more censors to China's already large number of internal security troops would require more money to be spent on internal security.

This, in turn, could make one of China's biggest problems, which is that its organizations aren't working well together, worse. The past of the bureaucratic state in China goes back many thousands of years. Many Chinese writings suggest that bureaucratic interests should be overcome and information should flow freely. In fact, better information flow is seen as both a cause and an effect of lowering barriers between military services and branches and between government ministries. It is not clear if the internal and external security forces or the security and nonsecurity ministries are competing for resources. But if China's economy continues to slow down, the country's leaders will have to face the question of how to use resources, or "guns versus butter."

In fact, it is clear that part of the goal of the massive military reorganization is to break down barriers between the Chinese services, between the different departments that make up the Central Military Commission, and between the different commands in the former military regions, which are now war zone commands with permanent, standing joint headquarters. This shows that, at least in the armed military, there is a clear understanding of the need to get past these internal barriers to the flow of information.

This project is likely to take a long time, maybe even a decade, because technology and society around the world are always changing. In fact, the PLA is constantly changing, both in terms of doctrine and organization, and so are the many Chinese groups that have sprung up to deal with informationization. This shows that the Chinese government isn't necessarily stuck in its ways, but rather understands the need to change with the times. In the meantime, though, the PLA will be even more vulnerable as it makes changes to its organizations and ideology. This means that, if military concerns are the most important, the CCP leadership may move more carefully over the next ten years, depending more on pressure and threats and not using the military in a direct way.

Policy options for the United States: Some Do's

Because Washington and Beijing have completely different and opposite points of view, the PRC is not the best model for American leaders to follow. Restricting the flow of information to the general public, silencing civil society, and trying to limit the area where people can share information would only hurt the United States and other Western democracies. So, instead of trying to stop the flow of information, the United States needs an alternative model, which is also in line with the fact that the competition is orthogonal.

It could be argued that the United States should try to stop the PRC from being able to control information. This means, on the one hand, making sure that the United States will be able to collect, send, and use information successfully and on time, no matter what the Chinese do. At the same time, it is important to put at risk certain Chinese information systems, networks, and ways of making decisions so that the Chinese government can't reach its bigger political goals.

Here, it's important to remember that the focus is on political problems that could lead to a fight, like the South China Sea, the Senkaku Islands, and Taiwan. So, the United States shouldn't focus on information warfare. Instead, they should try to stop China from getting political success. Denying the Chinese the ability to control the flow of information only counts if it makes it harder for them to reach their political goals.

Do Give Greater Consideration to the Demands of Deterrence

Too often, people think that if the West has the same power to put Chinese systems at risk, that will be enough to stop them. For example, it is sometimes thought that if China builds a strong counterspace capability, the US needs to build a similar set of capabilities. Even more troublesome, it is sometimes thought that a power like this would stop China from doing something.

But deterrence only works when something important to the other side is at risk. First, you have to find out what the other side cares about. It's not clear that, for example, being able to stop Chinese satellite communications would have a big effect on Beijing, especially given the uneven geography and different political goals. This also raises the question of whether it is possible to put the whole set of systems and skills of the enemy at risk. It's possible that being able to threaten Chinese communication networks would stop the Chinese from acting. However, with so many of these systems already in place, it's not clear that this goal can be reached at a fair price.

In the case of the CCP, it seems clear that the Chinese value being able to gather information about the networks, decision-makers, and decision-making processes of their enemies, both in peacetime and in battle. If you could stop the Chinese from gathering information during times of peace, you could keep them from learning about the capabilities and methods of their enemies. This would likely put at risk the Chinese belief that they can create information dominance.

Because of how many offensive information tactics work, this would cause a lot of trouble. Like fixing zero-day exploits, putting information warfare into action on any given X-Day (the start of hostilities) needs a long list of steps to be taken days, weeks, months, or even years before X-Day. Not only is it important to collect a lot of data in peacetime, but for many types of information warfare (such as network and electronic warfare), weapons and capabilities must also be made and put in place a long time before they are needed. This makes information warfare less flexible and responsive than is often shown in popular entertainment. It also makes it possibly more dangerous, since it can be used against systems that have been thought to be safe for a long time. If China wasn't given information about key electronic systems, networks, and decision-making processes, or if these things were changed often, it would be more likely that weapons and methods wouldn't be ready in case of war. Worse, they might not match the skills that are actually used.

At the same time, it is clear that the CCP is worried about being able to keep things stable inside the country. This is a worry even when there is no war. If there is a war, these fears are likely to get worse. So, if America's Achilles' Heel is that it needs a large information network to be able to do expeditionary operations, China's Achilles' Heel is that its leaders are worried about internal resistance while they are fighting foreign enemies. If the U.S. wants to stop the PRC, it needs to be ready to use the PRC's fear of losing internal control against it.

So, for the CCP, losing the ability to keep an eye on the Chinese people and damage to the information networks that help censor traditional media, keep an eye on social media, and limit access to the outside world would be just as bad as the US not being able to detect missile launches or guide JDAMs. In fact, the loss of these systems could be even worse because, unlike their American peers, China's leaders see the People's Republic of China (PRC) as surrounded by enemies. Even if China won a fight with the U.S. over, say, Taiwan, it would not change the threat that could come from Russia, India, Uighur, or Tibetan rebels. A win over the United States that left internal and external security information systems crippled or even badly damaged could be seen as a Pyrrhic victory, since the available resources to keep up deterrence against remaining external threats and internal challenges would be severely weakened.

Do Promote Broader "Whole-of-Society" Participation

One part of the U.S.'s work should be to make our methods more open to everyone. It is important for American leaders to bridge both the gap between civilians and the military and the gap between the government and the business sector. The Chinese way is called "whole of government," and it is led by the CCP. That is enough in a system where the role of civil society and the business sector is kept to a minimum and tightly controlled.

The United States needs both a "whole-of-government" method and a "whole-of-society" approach. The military and civilian parts of the government are only a small part of the United States' overall information ability and potential. A lot of the most important information, like patents, formulas, and sometimes even military and spy information, is held by the private sector (for example, by government contractors). The state sector is affected by problems in the private sector and vice versa. But it's unlikely that a company could protect itself against a coordinated information attack backed by the government. Not only will we need to work together more if we want to protect information frontiers, but also if we want to use the vast pool of American and global knowledge.

Some steps are already being taken. For example, the Obama administration made it easier for businesses to play a bigger part in running space operations. Because of this, there are now a lot of new players, some of whom made their money in the IT field. SpaceX, which is run by Elon Musk, Blue Origin, which is run by Jeff Bezos, Virgin Galactic, which is run by Sir Richard Branson, and Bigelow Aerospace, which is run by Robert Bigelow, are just some of the best-known examples of efforts to go beyond the usual aerospace suppliers.

Just as important has been the rise of competitions like the Ansari X-Prize, which offer both money and recognition. Using measures like these to tap into a wider range of public interest is an example of a "bottom-up" approach that may be better at fostering innovation and finding answers than the "top-down" approach that Beijing wants to use. It is also a way of doing things that might be better from an American and Western point of view.

Do Promote Resiliency and Diversification

Approaches like these that try to stop active attacks would be helped by putting more emphasis on being able to keep information flowing, or what some might call "resiliency." By making it hard for the PRC to get information control, for example by continuing to work even when information denial and interference attempts are made, the US would show that attacks, even if they are successful, are not enough to win. If Chinese leaders can't reasonably expect to be able to control information for a decent amount of time, they also can't reasonably expect to win a fight.

This doesn't mean that antimalware, patches, and other security steps should be thrown out, but it does mean that they aren't enough. If you can't stop attacks, you need to plan for ways to make things better. The more information systems don't have backups or other options, the more valuable they are as a target set. On the other hand, the more diverse the information networks are and the fewer single points of failure there are, the more possible attackers will look for other target sets.

Unfortunately, governments tend to downplay the importance of resilience because it is often linked to duplication and, by extension, inefficiency. Aerospace has been full of these kinds of things to think about. Since GPS is so popular, for example, people don't pay as much attention to other ways to find their way. The decision to stop supporting the LORAN guidance system, which was a set of fixed radio beacons on the ground that helped people find their way for decades, was partly based on the idea that it was no longer needed in the age of GPS. In the same way, the Navy's decision in 2006 to stop teaching how to use a sextant (which was reversed in 2015) was based on the idea that it was no longer useful now that satellite navigation devices were available. In both cases, not much thought was given to what might happen if GPS systems broke down, were jammed, or became unusable in some other way.

Do Keep Calm and Carry On

Lastly, American security planners need to get a better idea of how much damage could be done by a full-scale information war. On the one hand, this would mean threats that do a lot more than just work on computer networks. It could involve attacks on space systems, shutting down infrastructure networks (like those for transportation, energy, and communications), and destroying important files and computer records. In turn, these things would cause second- and third-order effects. But such a big attack would also hurt the economies, facilities, and information networks of other countries. Chinese works warn that when kinetic antisatellite systems are used, the effects of debris on third parties must be taken into account. This doesn't mean that they won't be used, but it says that they shouldn't be used in a "shoot-out at the OK Space Corral." In the same way, shutting down and erasing the records of the American stock exchange would have global financial effects, which in turn would have international and political effects on the PRC.

Even if there is no way to protect all information systems and processes, there are still ways to lessen the damage done by attacks from enemies. If there's no way to make the Internet safe monetarily, taking steps to make sure that at least basic information services can continue to work or can be fixed in a short amount of time (days or weeks) would take away a lot of the pain while making it harder for people to do bad things. Putting the most important networks at the top of the list and taking steps to make them safer would help to enforce intellectual discipline. The size of the threat can't be eliminated, but it can be made easier to deal with by consulting more people, using more knowledge, and making systems that are more resilient.

Bibliography

Akhtar, N., Javed, H., & Sengar, G. (2013). Analysis of Facebook Social Network. In Proceedings of the 5th International Conference and Computational Intelligence and Communication Networks, Mathura (pp. 451454). doi:10.1109/CICN.2013.99

Allen, R. (2017). What happens online in 60 seconds. Smart Insights. Retrieved from https://www.smartinsights. com/internet-marketing-statistics/happens-online-60-seconds/

Altheide, D. (2017). Terrorism and the politics of fear. New York: Rowman & Littlefield.

Altheide, D. L. (2014). The Triumph of Fear: Connecting the Dots about Whistleblowers and Surveillance. International Journal of Cyber Warfare & Terrorism, 4(1), 1-7. doi:10.4018/ijcwt.2014010101

Amble, J. C. (2012). Combating terrorism in the new media environment. Studies in Conflict and Terrorism, 35(5), 339-353. doi:10.1080/105761 0X.2012.666819

Arthur, C. (2011a). Egypt blocks social media websites in attempted clampdown on unrest. The Guardian. Retrieved from https://www.theguardian.com

Arthur, C. (2011b). Google and Twitter launch service enabling Egyptians to tweet by phone. The Guardian. Retrieved from https://www.theguardian.com

Axie Infinity (2022). Retrieved June 29, 2022, from https://axieinfinity.com/

Batrinca, B., & Treleaven, P. C. (2015). Social media analytics: A survey of techniques, tools and platforms. AI & Society, 30(1), 89-116. doi:10.1007/ s00146-014-0549-4

Baudrillard, J. (2005). Violence of the virtual and integral reality. International Journal of Baudrillard Studies, 2(2), 1-16.

BBC News. (2012). US Army: Geotagged Facebook posts soldiers' lives at risk. Retrieved from http://www. bbc.co.uk

BBC News. (2018). Syria war: Turkey arrests hundreds for criticising Afrin offensive. Retrieved from http:// www.bbc.co.uk

Bellamy, A. J. (2007). Dirty hands and lesser evils in the war on terror. British Journal of Politics and International Relations, 9(3), 509-526. doi:10.1111/ j.1467-856x.2006.00255.x

Ben Ozer, T. (2018). What can social media tell us about the suspected terrorist, The Jerusalem Post. Retrieved from https://www.jpost.com

BilicA (2022). bilic | blockchain data forensics. Retrieved June 29, 2022, from https://www.bilic.io/

BilicB (2022). bilic | Can my transactions on the blockchain be tracked? - YouTube. Retrieved June 27, 2022, from bilic | Can my transactions on the blockchain be tracked ?

Binance (2022). Binance: Buy/Sell Bitcoin, Ether and Altcoins | Cryptocurrency .... Retrieved June 29, 2022, from https://www.binance.com/en

Botometer. (n.d.). Retrieved from https://botometer.iuni.iu.edu

Brown, D. (2021). Tracking stolen crypto is a booming business - The Washington Post. Retrieved June 27, 2022, from https://www.washingtonpost.com/ technology/2021/09/22/stolen-crypto/

Casaregola, V. (2016). Who screens security? Culture of surveialnce in films. In R.A. Cropf & T. Bagwell (Eds.). Ethical Issues and Citizen Rights in the Era of Digital Government Surveillance (pp. 57-77). Hershey, PA: IGI Global.

ChainalysisA (2022). Mixing, CoinJoins, Chain Hopping, and Privacy Coins - Chainalysis. Retrieved June 27, 2022, from https://go.chainalysis.com/ advanced-obfuscation-techniques-webinar.html

ChainalysisB (2022). NFT Money Laundering and Wash Trading - Chainalysis Blog. Retrieved June 27, 2022, from https://blog.chainalysis.com/reports/2022-crypto-crime-report-preview-nft-wash-trading-money-laundering/

Cheng, J. (2010). US military surrenders to social media, changes policy. Ars technica. Retrieved from http:// arstechnica.com/tech-policy/2010/03/us-militarys-social-media-policy-gets-a-makeover/

Cheong, M., & Lee, V. C. S. (2011). A microblogging-based approach to terrorism informatics: Exploration and chronicling civilian sentiment and response to terrorism events via Twitter. Information Systems Frontiers, 13(1), 45-59. doi:10.1007/s10796-010-9273-x

Chomsky, N. (2015). Culture of terrorism. New York: Haymarket Books.

CipherBlade (2022). Blockchain Forensics | CipherBlade. Retrieved June 27, 2022, from https://cipherblade.com/blockchain-forensics/

Cockcroft, L. (2009). Soldiers banned from Myspace and Facebook, The Telegraph. Retrieved from https:// www.telegraph.co.uk

Coinbase (2022). What is DeFi? - Coinbase. Retrieved June 27, 2022, from https:// www.coinbase.com/learn/crypto- basics/what-is-defi

CoinDesk (2022). Tornado Cash Co-Founder Says the Mixer Protocol Is Unstoppable. Retrieved June 27, 2022, from https://www.coindesk.com/ tech/2022/01/25/tornado-cash-co-founder-says-the-mixer-protocol-is-unstoppable/

CoinMarketCap (2022). Cryptocurrency Prices, Charts and Market .... Retrieved June 27, 2022, from https://coinmarketcap.com/

Consensys (2022). What Is Decentralized Finance (DeFi)? | Consensys, Retrieved June 30, 2022, from https://consensys.net/blockchain-use-cases/ decentralized-finance/

Crenshaw, C. (2021). Statement on DeFi Risks, Regulations, and Opportunities | US Securities and Exchange Commission. Retrieved June 30, 2022, from https://www.sec.gov/news/statement/crenshaw-defi-20211109

Cropf, R. A., & Bagwell, T. (Eds.). (2016). Ethical Issues and Citizen Rights in the Era of Digital Government Surveillance. Hershey, PA: IGI Global. doi:10.4018/978-1-4666-9905-2

Dearmer, A. (2022). Business Intelligence as A Service | Integrate.io. Retrieved June 30, 2022, from https://www.integrate.io/blog/business-intelligence-as-a-service/

Drumbl, M. A. (2004). Lesser evils in the war on terrorism. Case W. Res. J. Int'l L., 36, 335.

ECHR. (2002). European Convention on Human Rights, Council of Europe. Retrieved from https://www.echr. coe.int/Documents/Convention_ENG.pdf

Ellul, J. (1964). The technological society. New York: Vintage books.

Ethereum (2022). Non-fungible tokens (NFT) - Ethereum.org. Retrieved June 27, 2022, from https://ethereum.org/en/nft/ Hudson IntelligenceA (2022). Peel Chain | Cryptocurrency Investigation - Hudson Intelligence. Retrieved June 27, 2022, from https://www.fraudinvestigation.net/cryptocurrency/tracing/peel-chain

Federman, J. (2018). Israel: Social media monitoring nabs would-be attackers. AP News.

Fiske, R. (2016). The Borders of Corruption: living in the state of exemption. In R.A. Cropf & T. Bagwell (Eds.). Ethical Issues and Citizen Rights in the Era of Digital Government Surveillance. Hershey, PA: IGI Global. doi:10.4018/978-1-4666-9905-2.ch001

Fisogni, P. (2019). Cyber Terrorism and Self-Radicalization-Emergent Phenomena of Onlife Age: An Essay Through the General System Theory. International Journal of Cyber Warfare & Terrorism, 9(3), 21-35. doi:10.4018/IJCWT.2019070102

Fitsanakis, J., & Bolden, M. S. (2012). Social networking as a paradigm shift in tactical intelligence collection. In MCIS Yearbook 2012 (pp. 28-40). Mediterranean Council for Intelligence Studies.

Freitas, C., Benevenuto, F., & Veloso, A. (2016). An empirical study of socialbot infiltration strategies in the Twitter social network. Social Network Analysis and Mining, 6(23).

Gabbat, A. (2013). New York woman visited by police after researching pressure cookers online. The Guardian. Retrieved from https://www.theguardian.com/

Gitelman, L. (2006). Always already new: media, history and the data of culture. Cambridge: MIT Press.

Hodge, N. (2008). YouTube, Twitter: Weapons in Israel's info war. Wired. Retrieved from https://www.wired.com

Howells, K. (2012) Social Media Networking and Tactical Intelligence Collection. In Proceedings of the 7th FAE International Symposium, Cyprus.

Howells, K., & Ertugan, A. (2017). Applying Fuzzy Logic for Sentiment Analysis of Social Media Network Data in Marketing. Procedia Computer Science, 120, 653-689. doi:10.1016/j.procs.2017.11.293

Howie, L. (2012). Witnesses to terror: Understanding the meanings and consequences of terrorism. New York: Springer. doi:10.1057/9781137271761

Hudson IntelligenceB (2022). What is a Peel Chain? Hudson intelligence. Retrieved June 30, 2022, from https://www.fraudinvestigation.net/cryptocurrency/tracing/peel-chain

Human Rights Watch. (2018). Turkey: Crackdown on Social Media Posts, Detention, Prosecutions Over Criticisms of Turkish Army Actions in Syria. Retrieved from https://www.hrw.org

Ian Wong, J. (2018). Bitcoin Pizza Day 2018: Eight years ago, someone bought two .... Retrieved June 27, 2022, from https://qz.com/1285209/bitcoin-pizza-day-2018-eight-years-ago-someone-bought-two-pizzas-with-bitcoins-now- worth-82-million/

Ignatieff, M. (2013). The lesser evil: Political ethics in an age of terror. Princeton: Princeton University Press. doi:10.2307/j.ctt5hhp0h

Insikt Intelligence. (2018). Inviso-intelligence Platform. Retrieved from http://www.insiktintelligence.com/ our-solutions/inviso-intelligence-platform/

Jackson, R. (Ed.). (2016). Routledge handbook of critical terrorism studies. Abingdon: Routledge. doi:10.4324/9781315813462

Jeronimo, H., Garcia, J., & Mitcham, C. (2013). Introduction: Ellul return. In H. Jeronimo, L. Garcia, & C. Mitcham (Eds.), Jacques Ellul and the Technological Society in the 21st Century. Springer. doi:10.1007/978- 94-007-6658-7_1

Klausen, J. (2015). Tweeting the Jihad: Social Media Networks of Western Foreign Fighters in Syria and Iraq. Studies in Conflict and Terrorism, 38(1), 1-22. doi :10.1080/1057610X.2014.974948

Korstanje, M. E. (2016). The Rise of Thana Capitalism and Tourism. Abingdon: Routledge. doi:10.4324/9781315457482

Korstanje, M. E. (2018a). Tracing Spikes in Fear and Narcissism in Western Democracies since 9/11. Oxford: Peter Lang. doi:10.3726/b11863

Korstanje, M. E. (2018b). The Challenges of democracy in the War on terror: the liberal state before the advance of terrorism. Abingdon: Routledge.

Korstanje, M. E. (2019). The Society 4.0, Internet, Tourism and the War on Terror. In Digital Labour, Society and the Politics of Sensibilities (pp. 95-113). Cham: Palgrave Macmillan. doi:10.1007/978-3-030-12306-2_6

Kubovich, Y. (2016). The Facebook Squad: How Israel Police Tracks Activists on Social Media. Haaretz. Retrieved from https://www.haaretz.com

Levesque, J. (2012). Social Media "Tactical Intelligence Collection": Spying and propaganda using Facebook, Twitter. Global Research. Retrieved from https://www.globalresearch.ca

Liaropoulos, A. N. (2013). The Challenges of Social Media for the Intelligence Community. Journal of Mediterranean and Balkan Intelligence, 7(1), 5-14.

Linag; L.T. (2015). Battlefront New Media - Lessons For The SAF Based On A Study Of The Information Campaign During Operation Pillar Of Defence. Pointer: Journal of Singapore Armed Forces, 41(4), 55-68.

Lyon, D., & Bauman, Z. (2013). Liquid surveillance: A conversation. New York: John Wiley & Sons.

Mahadawi, A. (2018). Hand over my social media account to get a US visa? No thank you. The Guardian. Retrieved from https://www.theguardian.com

Mahoney, L. M., & Tang, T. (2016). Strategic Social Media: From Marketing to Social Change. Wiley Blackwell. doi:10.1002/9781119370680

Mahood, L. E. K. (2015). SOCMINT: Following And Liking Social Media Intelligence. JCSP 41. Canadian Forces College.

McCarthy, J. (2011). Socialbots 2: Artificial Intelligence, social intelligence and Twitter [blog]. Gumption. Retrieved from http://gumption.typepad.com/blog

Mitcham, C. (2013). How the technological society became more important in the United States than in France. In H. Jeronimo, L. Garcia, & C. Mitcham (Eds.), Jacques Ellul and the Technological Society in the 21st Century (pp. 17-34). Springer, doi:10.1007/978-94-007-6658-7_2

Moris, D. (2021). DeFi Is Like Nothing Regulators Have Seen Before. How Should They Tackle It? | CoinDesk. Retrieved June 30, 2022, from https://www.coindesk.com/policy/2021/10/19/defi-is-like-nothing-regulators-have-seen-before-how- should-they-tackle-it/

NASDAQ (2022). Marketplace Intelligence Technology Supplies time-sensitive insights and actionable information for a competitive edge | Nasdaq. Retrieved June 30, 2022, from https://www.nasdaq.com/solutions/ marketplace- intelligence-technology

NIST (2022). Cybersecurity Framework - NIST. Retrieved June 27, 2022, from https:// www.nist.gov/cyberframework NotaBene (2022). What is AML and how does it apply to Crypto (anti money laundering)? | NotaBene. Retrieved June 30,

Nixon, R. (2017, September 28). U.S. to Collect Social Media Data on All Immigrants Entering Country, New York Times.

Orme, J. (2019). Hackers loot £31 million in Bitcoin from Binance, wallet identified. Retrieved June 27, 2022, from https://www.techerati.com/news-hub/ hackers-loot-31-million-in-bitcoin-from-binance/

Ormond, S. D. (2012). Introducing Social Media Intelligence (SOCMINT). Intelligence and National Security, 27(6), 801-823. doi:10.1080/02684527. 2012.716965

OSINT (2022). OSINT Framework. Retrieved June 27, 2022, from https:// osintframework.com/

Palestinian Security Forces based in Ankara [Personal communication]. (2018, April 25).

Paterva. (2012). Maltego. Retrieved from http://www.paterva.com

Rawat, R. et al. (2022). Dark Web Pattern Recognition and Crime Analysis Using Machine Intelligence | IGI Global. Retrieved June 30, 2022, from https:// www.igi-global.com/book/dark-web-pattern-recognition-crime/286781

Republic of Cyprus Army Captain [Personal Communication]. (2012).

Reuters. (2012). How Internet detectives, and others, find out where you live. Retrieved from http://gadgets. ndtv.com

Reynolds, S. (2022). Crypto.com's Stolen Ether Being Mixed Through Tornado Cash. Retrieved June 27, 2022, from https://www.coindesk.com/ business/2022/01/18/cryptocoms-stolen-ether-being-laundered-via-tornado-cash/

Ritzer, G. (2013). The Technological Society: social theory, McDonalization and the presume. In H. Jeronimo, L. Garcia, & C. Mitcham (Eds.), Jacques Ellul and the Technological Society in the 21st Century (pp. 35-48). Springer,

Rodewig, C. (2012). Geotagging poses security risks. The Official Homepage of the United States Army. Retrieved from http://www.army.mil

Schwartau, W. (2010, February 2). Simply security: You cause data breaches. The SACompany. YouTube. Retrieved from http://www.youtube.com

Sharma, R. (2022). Decentralized Finance (DeFi) Definition | Investopia. Retrieved June 30, 2022, from https://www.investopedia.com/decentralized-finance-defi-5113835

Shirazi, F. (2013). Social media and the social movements in the Middle East and North Africa: A critical discourse analysis. Information Technology & People, 26(1), 28-49. doi:10.1108/09593841311307123

Singh, J. (2022). What are wash trading and money laundering in NFTs? Retrieved June 27, 2022, from https://cointelegraph.com/explained/what-are-wash-trading-and-money-laundering-in-nfts

Skoll, G. R. (2014). Stealing Consciousness: Using Cybernetics for Controlling Populations. International Journal of Cyber Warfare & Terrorism, 4(1), 27-35. doi:10.4018/ijcwt.2014010104

Skoll, G. R. (2016). Globalization of American fear culture: The empire in the twenty-first century. Basingstoke: Palgrave Macmillan. doi:10.1007/978-1-137-57034-5

Sottlemyre, S., & Sottlemyre, S. (2012). Crisis Mapping Intelligence Information During the Libyan Civil War: An Exploratory Case Study. Policy and Internet, 4(3-4), 24-39. doi:10.1002/poi3.9

Stampnitzky, L. (2013). Disciplining Terror: how experts invented terrorism. Cambridge: Cambridge University Press. doi:10.1017/CBO9781139208161

Sunstein, C. R. (2005). Laws of fear: Beyond the precautionary principle (Vol. 6). Cambridge: Cambridge University Press. doi:10.1017/CBO9780511790850

Tanash, R. S., Chen, Z., Marschall, M., & Wallach, D. S. (2017). The Decline of Social Media Censorship and the Rise of Self-Censorship after the 2016 Failed Turkish Coup. In Proceedings of the 7th USENIX Workshop on Free and Open Communications on the Internet. Alberta, Canada, August 14.

Taylor, R. W., Fritsch, E. J., & Liederbach, J. (2014). Digital crime and digital terrorism. London: Prentice Hall Press.

TechTarget (2022). What is de-anonymization (deanonymization)? Retrieved June 27, 2022, from https://www.techtarget.com/whatis/definition/de-anonymization-deanonymization

Tellidis, I. (2011). Orthodox, criticals and the missing context: Basque civil society's reaction (s) to terrorism. Critical Studies on Terrorism, 4(2), 181-197. doi:10.1080/17539153.2011.586204

ter Veen, J., Sarkani, S., & Mazzuchi, T. (2011). Effects of Systems Engineering on Command and Control Systems Utilizing Innovations in Social Networking. Lockheed Martin Corporation. Retrieved from http://www.dtic.mil/ndia/2011system/12957_terVeenThursday.pdf

The Block (2022). Value Locked - Ethereum and Binance Smart Chain - The Block. Retrieved June 27, 2022, from https://www.theblock.co/data/decentralized-finance/total-value-locked-tvl

The Economist. (2018). Israel is using social media to prevent terrorist attacks. Retrieved from https://www. economist.com

The Law Society (2022). Anti-money laundering | The Law Society. Retrieved June 27, 2022, from https://www.lawsociety.org.uk/topics/anti-money-laundering

TornadoCashA (2022). Retrieved June 29, 2022, from https://tornado.cash/

TornadoCashB (2022). Tornado cash. Non-custodial private transactions on Ethereum. Retrieved June 27, 2022, from https://github.com/tornadocash/tornado-core

Treverton, G. F., & Miles, R. (2014). Social Media and Intelligence. Centre for Asymmetric Threat Studies. Elainders Sverige, Sweden: Swedish National Defence College.

Twitter Usage Statistics. (2018). Internet Live stats. Retrieved from http://www.internetlivestats.com/twitter- statistics/van Niekerk, B., & Maharaj, M. (2013). Social Media and Information Conflict. International Journal of Communication, (7), 1162-1184.

U.S. Department of Treasury (2019). Treasury Sanctions North Korean State-Sponsored Malicious Cyber .... Retrieved June 27, 2022, from https://home.treasury.gov/news/press-releases/sm774

Veerasamy, N. (2020). Cyberterrorism-the spectre that is the convergence of the physical and virtual worlds. In Emerging Cyber Threats and Cognitive Vulnerabilities (pp. 27-52). New Jersey: Academic Press. doi:10.1016/ B978-0-12-816203-3.00002-2

Vergani, M., & Bliuc, A. (2018). The Language of New Terrorism: Differences in Psychological Dimensions of Communication in Dabiq and Inspire. Journal of Language and Social Psychology, 37(5), 523-540. doi:10.1177/0261927X17751011

Virilio, P. (2010). University of disaster. Cambridge: Polity Press.

Weimann, G. (2011). Al Qaeda has sent you a friend request: Terrorists using online social networking. Israeli Communication Association. Retrieved from http://95.211.138.23/wp-content/uploads/2012/08/2012-Terrorists- using-online-social-nerworking.pdf

Yang, M., & Nw, J. (2013). The collision of social media and social unrest: Why shutting down social media is the wrong response. HeinOnline. Retrieved from https://scholarlycommons.law.northwestern.edu/cgi/viewcontent.cgi?article=1208&context=njtip

Zizek, S. (2003). The puppet and the dwarf: The perverse core of Christianity. Cambridge: MIT Press. doi:10.7551/ mitpress/5706.001.0001

Zizek, S. (2008). Violence: Six sideways reflections. London: Verso.

Zizek, S. (2015). The Universal Exemption. London: Bloomsbury.

Index

G

H

I

K

L

M

N

O

P

R

S

T